Praise for *THE CRIME FIGHTER*

"Jack Maple's *The Crime Fighter* is one of the most important books I have ever read! It proves that skill, guts, determination, imagination, and hands-on leadership can substantially reduce crime. Of special interest to me, he shows how many of the leadership principles and tactics which have proven essential to Marine Corps victories on the battlefield are equally effective in combating crime. This is a must reading for those who care about the future safety and security of their fellow Americans."
—P. X. Kelley, 28th Commandant of the Marine Corps

"Cops and crooks—nobody knows them better than Jack Maple; and nobody has ever told their story quite like the 'Jackster.' He's been where the truth is stranger than fiction, and *The Crime Fighter* puts you right beside him."
—William J. Bratton, Former New York City Police Commissioner

"Jack Maple is this country's outstanding thinker about fighting crime in our cities. His ideas account for much of the success of the NYPD and he has shown that they can work in other cities, too. Anyone concerned with making our cities safer should read this very important, very practical, and very witty book."
—John F. Timoney, Police Commissioner, Philadelphia Police Department

"First, read this book to understand how Jack Maple saved a city that nobody believed could be saved. Then, read this book again for its wit, charm, and fun. After that, send it to your local police department and tell them to read it at least three times."
—Michael Daly, Columnist, *New York Daily News*

"Jack Maple is a combination of real-life Kojak and management wizard like Lee Iacocca. He fought crime with a gun in one hand and a computer in the other."
—Thomas A. Reppetto, President, Citizens Crime Commission

"*The Crime Fighter* is the first book I've read that combines smart criminology with great cop yarns."

—JERRY NACHMAN, Former Editor in Chief,
New York Post

"Jack Maple is the people's cop. He has spent his life making all our lives safer. It's all in this book. A great read and a manual for policing in the new millennium."

—TERRY GEORGE and JIM SHERIDAN, Writers/Directors,
In the Name of the Father, Some Mother's Son, The Boxer

"Maple will leave you cheering as he scores victories over hack police brass, cheap politicians, and most importantly for the rest of us, himself. Book him."

—DENNIS HAMILL, Columnist, *New York Daily News,*
Author of *Three Quarters* and *Throwing 7's*

THE CRIME FIGHTER

HOW YOU CAN MAKE YOUR COMMUNITY CRIME FREE

JACK MAPLE

WITH CHRIS MITCHELL

Broadway Books
New York

A hardcover edition of this book was originally published in 1999 by Doubleday. It is here reprinted by arrangement with Doubleday.

Designed by Julie Duquet

Library of Congress Cataloging-in-Publication Data
Maple, Jack.
The crime fighter: how you can make your community crime free / Jack Maple; with Chris Mitchell.
p. cm.
Originally published: New York : Doubleday, 1999.
Includes index.
1. New York (N.Y.) Police Dept.—Officials and employees—Biography.
2. Police—New York (State)—New York—Biography. 3. Crime prevention—New York (State)—New York. I. Mitchell, Chris, 1964– . II. Title.
HV7911.M343A3 2000
363.2′092—dc21
[B] 00-057166

ISBN 0-7679-0554-7

BVG 01

This book is dedicated
to all the victims of violent crime,
particularly those cops who died
for the greater good of all

CONTENTS

THE CRIME FIGHTER

ONE

PROLOGUE
It Ain't Over Till the Fat Man's Thin

The guy in the suit couldn't have seen what was coming. He was slumped against a wall at the top of a subway staircase at 47th and Broadway, his eyes closed, his tie and collar open, a cardboard party hat fixed with an elastic at the top of his forehead and a gold medallion of some kind draped outside his shirt.

The noise of the crowd that night could have lulled any drunken head into a stupor, and that's what looked like had happened here: This George McFly type wasn't hearing the party horns or the noisemakers anymore, the clap-clapping of hoofs on pavement as mounted patrolled the barriers, or even the icy splash of another champagne bottle or wine cooler shattering on the street. He had been swallowed whole by one of the world's most notorious celebrations and was about to be awakened, minutes before the big ball dropped, by a sudden sting at the back of his neck.

I started moving toward him—invisible, but with my eyes locked on another man. This one had been eyeing the drunk for several minutes, and he was suddenly surging toward his mark with one hand out and the other hidden underneath his coat. That hidden hand was the reason for alarm, but it kept quiet when the free hand shot out and grabbed the chain, so I waited until the chain's new owner turned and came a couple steps across the sidewalk before I threw my open fist at the spot where the hidden hand had been and hit the thief broadside with my right shoulder.

He was built more like a fullback than I'd expected, but I kept driving with my legs the way the high school coaches had taught me, and he fell to the curb under me just as my fingers concluded that only a layer or two of clothing separated them from a familiar casting of steel.

"Gun!" I yelled.

The shouts of the crowd now turned to screaming as the crook and I rolled around in horseshit and confetti underneath their churning feet. A second crook was already on top of me, and my own pistol was starting to slide up out my waistband into his grasp when Carol Sciannameo jumped onto the pile and pinned my gun against me.

The rest of my crew converged from all sides—Vertel Martin, Richie Doran, Julie Ewbanks, Billy Carter, Joe Quirke, Jeff Aiello, Liz Sheridan, Ronnie Pellechia; Jimmy Nuciforo dropped a party horn to pull another lookout down into the manure. In an instant, all three crooks lay prone in the gutter, and the storm of hoofs bearing in on us came from a world moving at a slower speed.

"Put away your guns," I told my guys. "Get out your badges and your colors."

The spit of the horses sprayed us as their bridles spun them backward in front of us, their riders trying to blink disbelief out of their eyes. We didn't look, I'm sure, like most of the cops they knew.

My gray sable hat had come off in the tussle, so as I got to my feet, I felt for the first time the night's cold breath on my almost barren scalp. There was straw stuck in the tangle of my three-inch beard and clinging to my black zip-front sweater, which wrapped a wreath of white *Playboy* bunny heads just above my waist. Among those who appreciated crookwear, that sweater was the bomb, and I had the matching *Playboy* bunny shoes to go with it. In our crew, only Officer Jerry Lyons had clearly outdressed me that night, and he had played the role of the drunk vic in the suit, the party hat, and the gold chain.

Our merry band vanished as quickly as we had materialized, leading the three prisoners downstairs through a locked gate into an empty subway station and then down to the district for processing.

The Mole People had made a good catch, but if we had paused a moment to take a last look around at the scene we'd left up on the street, we might have realized that our profession was being handed another humiliating defeat.

It was minutes before midnight, exactly fifteen years before the end of the "American Century," and Times Square, the scene of so many great victory parties across those hundred years, belonged to New York's crooks. Our team had cut short the night of one wolf pack, but there were scores more still snaking through the crowds in their sheepskin coats and Elmer Fudd hats, many of them wearing rings, medallions, and other trophies from crimes past, and some so bold that they couldn't be bothered to hide their foremost thought. "Snatch gold, snatch gold," they'd be hissing. When the ball fell at Times Square, it was like the starter's gun going off. How many pockets would be dug, how many bags snatched, how many windpipes throttled by a well-placed forearm before we all came back in a year to start the count all over again?

Over those next twelve months, the U.S. casualties of crime would come in faster than in any of the years when the news ticker at One Times Square was darkening the streets below with grim reports from the war in Vietnam. Nationwide, murders would leap 10 percent that year to 19,250. More than 500,000 robberies would be committed and almost 800,000 aggravated assaults. Seventy-eight cops would be killed in the line of duty.

And that was only 1986. Crime in America would get far worse before it ever got better.

If you were to return to the corner of 47th and Broadway in 1999, you might be stunned by the change in atmosphere. A gargantuan bas-relief of a Coke bottle still looms directly overhead, but that ad is now affixed to the Renaissance Hotel, one of a half-dozen family-friendly lodging places built at the "Crossroads of the World" in the years since. At one corner of the intersection, mitten-clad theatergoers push the Disney musical *Beauty and the Beast*—now in its sixth smash season!—to new box office records every night. At another, young tourists sip Starbucks coffee behind a plate-glass window while stock prices sprint past overhead on the towering headquarters of one of the world's largest financial services companies. Twenty paces away, a Planet Hollywood Hotel is rising out of the ground next to a billboard with a giant message paid for by John Lennon's widow. WAR IS OVER read its big black letters.

If people didn't know Yoko Ono better, they might think she was adding her dog-whistle soprano to a national chorus of voices claiming the transformation of Times Square as evidence of a sweeping national victory over crime.

The cops in New York deserve all the accolades they get, and more. In 1993, 1,946 men, women, and children were murdered in New York City; in 1998, the toll stopped at 629. That same year there were about 280,000 fewer victims of serious crimes in the city than there had been five years earlier. While the rest of the country experienced a 23 percent decline in murder over that period, New York's results were three times as good.

But America is like the 600-pound man who's lost 200 pounds. If you've only known him five years, he looks great. If you haven't seen him since 1961, you're amazed at what a fat slob he's become. Today, violent crime—murder, rape, robbery, and aggravated assault—is still being committed at a rate three and a half times higher than it was the year John F. Kennedy was sworn in. Nearly 10,000 more people are murdered in the United States each year than in 1961, and that's despite almost four decades of advances in emergency room medical care. New York City, meanwhile, can't afford to snicker. After five years of intense dieting, its violent crime rate is still double the bloated national figure.

Some of the citizens of this country, unfortunately, take the brunt of the violence. Among black males ages eighteen to twenty-four, the murder victimization rate is about 20 times the national rate, and about nine times that among white males in the same age group. If the sons of senators, congressmen, judges, criminologists, and journalists were dying at that rate, we wouldn't be celebrating any victories over crime just yet. We'd be talking about mandatory conscription for the war raging in our streets.

The truth is, we as a nation have only turned back the clock on violent crime to 1985, the year that ended for me with a roll in the horse manure with two crooks and a couple of loaded guns.

I know we can do better. If the cops of America are given a plan—and worthy leaders—they can make even 1961 look like the bad old days.

It's time to go for the win.

TWO

"A GAME OF BLUFF"
What's Wrong with Policing

I was forty-one in 1993 when I finally got a seat at the table. I had been a cop since about the time I was first allowed to walk into a bar unaccompanied by an adult, but in the very profession that had consumed most of my life, I had until that year been very much on the outside, my cheeks red from the cold and my nose pressed up against the window. In New York City, there were separate police forces for the streets, the subways, and public housing, but only one had manpower equal to the fifth-largest army in the world and a reputation equal to the New York Yankees. I was with one of the other two. In the eyes of the world, Transit was junior varsity. Transit was Naugahyde.

I already knew by 1993 a lot about what was right and what was wrong operationally with the Transit Police, but most of the NYPD problems I knew about firsthand walked around on two legs. They were the detectives who'd brag about the big cases they were working on while they were burning up the critical first few days of the investigation, sitting at a bar, bragging. They were the bareheaded patrol cops you'd see sleeping through the night in their radio cars as you drove along the FDR Highway south of Bellevue Hospital past one dead-end street after another. They were, worst of all, the conscientious objectors who sniffed, "We don't make collars," as if effecting an arrest was an activity reserved for lower life-forms. The NYPD, unfortunately, was not the only police force in the city cluttered up by such "pails"—which was the shorter, more polite term used by some of us to indicate what we thought they were full of.

The story is the same in any police department: Forty percent of the force hide behind their desks. Another 40 percent perform competently but without passion and without having much impact. Ten percent hate the job so much that they try to destroy everything positive that somebody else might try to accomplish.

The final 10 percent treat the job like a vocation; and those 10 percent do 90 percent of the work. During my years on patrol, I saw the same 20 Transit cops, the same 20 Housing cops, and the same 100 NYPD cops every day downtown at the courthouse. We were the only ones trying to arrest the bad guys.

But that's not a situation unique to policing. They say the same pattern holds true among the bad guys. With Norwegian rats, one in about twenty is a dominant male, who will, according to behavioral scientists, turn to crimes like rape and infanticide if he's given no other outlet for his dominance. Crooks have their own overachievers. Of the 10,000 boys born in 1945 who lived in Philadelphia from the ages of ten to eighteen, about a third were arrested at least once, but an elite 6 percent were responsible for fully two-thirds of the city's violent crime.

That's been the matchup for as long as anybody can remember: the cops' all-stars against the crooks' all-stars.

Unfortunately, only the crooks flourish in a hit-and-run battle. I always thought that if a police department could only double the share of its cops who were truly focused on catching crooks, the momentum might shift in the public's favor.

The conditions that most cops are asked to work under do very little to inspire wider devotion. The pay is miserable, for one thing. The Farfingtons of this world send their kids to Harvard, Princeton, and Yale to learn about the underlying social conditions that supposedly turn our nation's cities into infectious breeding grounds of crime, but the chief executive of the largest police department in the country can barely afford to send one child to state university. A first-grade detective in the NYPD, who has been recognized after years of service as belonging to an elite circle of criminal catchers, takes home less than a first-year analyst on Wall Street or a bricklayer who pays union dues.

Fifteen hundred years ago, when the Roman army was in deep decline, the great military adviser Vegetius laid much of the blame on deteriorating recruitment standards, noting that the ancients had drawn soldiers from "the flower of Roman youth" and that the army must once again attract the defenders of the Empire from families of good reputation. In policing, we had never taken many of our troops from the Farfingtons anyway, and the trend for many years has been a steady erosion in our entry requirements.

The ancient Roman soldiers, Vegetius also said, owed their superiority on the battlefield to discipline and rigorous training. In policing, we don't train recruits in crime-fighting at all. The manuals just say don't be late and follow the rules. When it comes time to subdue a prisoner resisting arrest, you have to rely on whatever tricks you'd picked up as a kid in the playground and then wait to see if you're going to be indicted for it. Academy instructors talk about how to fill out forms, and there is almost no training at all for officers who moved up the ranks to sergeant, lieutenant, captain and beyond. The U.S. armed forces will provide up to two years of training for a second lieutenant, and that second lieutenant may never have to fight a battle. In policing, where engagement with armed opponents occurs twenty-four hours a day, 365 days a year, a sergeant is lucky to receive a few weeks of specialized instruction.

The facilities, today just as when I was new to the job, say everything about where a cop stands in the world. Down in the subway, where the steam in the tunnels could cook a knish, the video surveillance cameras worked in an air-conditioned room, but we dressed in a locker room where the sweat was puddling on the floor by the time you buttoned up your uniform. Forget that the furniture was all busted and everything in sight was outdated; it wasn't even kept clean. The cops might blame an abstraction like City Hall, but the surroundings made it clear just what the bosses in their own department thought of them. The job sucks, the old-timers would say, and it was too easy to adopt the general consensus on that. In every department, the perception among the cops is that the citizens, the press, and the bosses are against them, so right out of the academy, most fall immediately into a siege mentality.

The cop who decides to be a crime fighter has a tough road. To begin with, an active cop creates problems for his bosses. A tour with no arrests is an easy tour for the boss, but every arrest that's made means added paperwork and added risk that some of the paperwork may be wrong. It means having to worry about a prisoner—his meals, his visits to the bathroom, and whether he gets smacked by the cop assigned to watch the cell or gets left alone and tries to hang himself in the cell. And because an arrest can take many hours to process, it means fielding questions from the captain about why the tour is running up overtime.

When the crime fighter takes a prisoner downtown for arraignment, there are no welcoming parades. The young prosecutors in the district attorney's office come from a different world than most cops—in Manhattan, they could have been a time-traveling delegation from Congress's Class of 2012—and they greet many arrests with suspicion. They'd be ten minutes out of law school and deciding the charge against the stickup man they were about to face at arraignment should be reduced to petit larceny, a misdemeanor, before the plea bargaining even began, but if the case were to go to trial a year or eighteen months later and the prosecutor didn't win, the cop could expect to catch hell for losing any details of the incident to the sea of similar encounters that filled the tours between.

More than in other cities, the wait until arraignment in New York was, when I was a cop, an exquisite torture. If an assistant D.A. hadn't drawn up the charges before Night Court's 1 A.M. adjournment, a cop could be sitting in an overheated courthouse for a day and a half; and even in the middle of the night, Internal Affairs' sleep deprivation squad would pop in from time to time to turn on the lights in the waiting area and make sure our eyes were open and we were sitting up straight on the molded plastic chairs.

Those were all problems a crime fighter could bet on. There was also an indeterminate risk associated with each arrest that the next would be the one that hung a civilian complaint around his neck for the next year or eighteen months. Even if the cop knew he'd done no wrong, that accusation would weigh on him every single day on the job and put all hopes for career advancement on hold.

Despite all the obstacles, a handful of idealists and innovators in every department hang tough. For what? It was hard to say. For a cop without a "hook," like an uncle in the borough commander's office, there was maybe an expectation that his climb through the ranks, while it would never be as rapid as that of the chief's nephew, would come about in the long run because the bosses would always need a few people around them who could actually carry the ball.

The day I joined Transit as an officer trainee—November 2, 1970—I didn't know enough to think that far ahead. I was about one week past my eighteenth birthday and only four months out of high school, where probably my greatest achievement had been playing football as a walk-on in my senior year. Brooklyn Tech is one of only four New York City public high schools that accept students solely on the basis of competitive exams, but even if I had wanted to, I couldn't have hung a framed diploma from that hallowed institution next to my uniform in my new locker. I hadn't earned one.

Growing up, I had never been one of the kids with the big box of crayons. In the Christmas pageants, I never played Joseph; I was the beast in the manger. In SRA, me and Philip "A." would be laboring over the reading exercises with the brown band on top when everybody else was on aqua. Sunday nights were the worst. Every week, I'd get the same sick feeling in my stomach at eight o'clock when Ed Sullivan came on. It meant the weekend was over, and everybody was going to have their book reports ready in the morning except me.

My father worked for the Post Office and my mother, after she'd raised seven kids, worked as a nurse's aide at a hospital a few miles from the block where I grew up in Richmond Hill, Queens. Like any other oldest son in any other Civil Service family, I was kicked out of bed every Saturday morning when I was about sixteen to take the tests for the Fire Department, the Post Office, the police, and Transit. The NYPD called once when I was still in high school and a second time when I was ready to join, but I was one of 100 recruits who read in the newspapers the weekend before we were to be sworn in that Mayor John Lindsay had put a freeze on hiring.

Transit wasn't affected by the freeze.

By twenty, I'd been on the job two years, was already married, had a mortgage on a house in Queens, and I wasn't even a full officer yet. That honor arrived at twenty-one.

From day one as a New York City Transit Police officer, I loved the crime-fighting part of the job. But like any kid, I had no idea how little I knew. Within a year, I had run up too close to a guy who was swinging a four-foot iron pipe as he chased another cop down a Brooklyn platform. I took a crack on the skull and was down on the ground about to catch another when I let off five rounds and blacked out. A third cop fired at the suspect too, and one of our bullets proved fatal. We never were told whose.

Fourteen months later, working in plainclothes in Manhattan, I bought some pot from a dealer near Bryant Park, and when I went to arrest him, he took my gun. Two shots were fired so close to my face that my cheek was burned by the muzzle flash, but as we were rolling around and I was about to give up, I found the trigger again and squeezed it. The barrel, luckily, was pointed at the dealer, and he fell off me wounded—though not wounded badly enough to stop beating me.

Not all of the hard lessons in those early years were life-and-death matters. Testifying at a pretrial hearing in Queens one day, I was asked by a defense attorney how I could remember if I had advised a defendant of each and every one of his Miranda rights. "I read them off an arrest sheet," I answered. "And how can you be sure all of them were on the arrest sheet?" the lawyer asked. I couldn't be sure, so the defendant's statement was quashed. But I went home, memorized the Miranda warnings, and recited them from memory to every other suspect I ever questioned.

I learned from those first two situations how to better protect myself, and from all three how to prevent them from happening again.

But being smarter and more cautious didn't mean I slowed down in chasing the bad guys.

In fact, because I had a habit of following crooks out of the subway and arresting them as they went to hit their victims on the street, I was soon under investigation by my own department.

By then, it was becoming clear there was something seriously out of whack with my profession.

A kind of contest arose between me and my bosses. The object: Who could torture whom the most? The ground rules: They didn't follow any, as far as I could tell. I, on the other hand, could counter only by doing the things a crime fighter is supposed to do. If I was going to bring on trouble, everything had to be by the book.

The fun really began on a Brooklyn subway platform under Transit Police headquarters. I had just finished working half a day at headquarters as my penance for having made a couple of robbery arrests off post in Times Square and was waiting for a train to take me back into Manhattan to join my partner. The platform was pretty much empty, except for a couple of Civil Service types who looked like they'd never been in a subway station in their lives. The other thing I noticed about them was even though they weren't standing together, they moved in cadence, the way the crooks on 42nd Street did whenever they locked onto a vic. This time, it was a good thing the hunters were about as dangerous as a couple of kids with squirt guns, because I was their target. They were emissaries of Internal Affairs.

When the train pulled in and opened its doors, they waited for me to board before entering the next car. I stepped out again, pretending to have changed my mind, and they followed. Now they were really having a hard time hiding their interest in me. Again, I got back on the train; again, they followed. Finally, just as the doors were about to close, I stepped off one last time. As the train pulled out of the station, I waited for the car carrying my two adversaries, then smiled and waved. It was cruel, I know, but even if my colleagues had never seen the inside of a subway station, at least they should have been familiar with the chase scene from *The French Connection.*

Hours later, my new friends were still shadowing me as I patrolled the platforms under Times Square, so I told my partner I wanted to take our meal up on the street. If Internal Affairs wanted to see how I could be making so many arrests off post, I was willing to put on a demonstration. Seven hours a day, I watched robbers and bag snatchers and pickpockets pass through the subway turnstiles on their way upstairs to where the money was, but every day at meal time, I was more than a cave cop: I was policeman to the world.

Forty-Second Street didn't take long to give my partner and me what we were looking for. Three little hoods were moving in to yoke a sailor, and as we were dashing across the street through yellow cabs and pimp mobiles to grab them, I couldn't help chuckling to myself about how reports of the arrests would be brought to the attention of the chief of patrol. "Two Internal Affairs officers were following me and they didn't assist in the collars," I eventually told him. "I think they should be arrested for nonfeasance."

It was a nice wisecrack, but a losing argument.

The battle, now, was escalating, so to keep my partners out of harm's way, I requested to be transferred out of plainclothes and back into uniform, which would allow me to work alone. At my new post out in Jamaica, Queens, the sergeant told me he planned to keep close watch on me. "I hope you carry an extra pair of cuffs, Sarge," I replied. "Because I'm going to be busy."

That first night I was put on a fixed post at an elevated station overlooking a large sporting goods store that happened to have been damaged by fire the night before. To keep the looters at bay, four NYPD cops in a couple patrol cars were stationed outside the doors, but they couldn't see the roof. I could, because I carried a spyglass for spotting pickpockets, so when I made out a figure crawling in and out of a hole up there, I ran downstairs and tried to give away the job to the cops in one of the radio cars. Unfortunately, they weren't carrying a twenty-foot ladder in their trunk and didn't know how they could get inside and grab this guy.

Just then, a fire truck approached—shiny, red; perfect. So what if I was afraid of heights? I flagged it down, climbed its ladder to the roof, and brought the burglar back down to be booked as a Transit arrest at the nearest NYPD precinct.

Two nights later was Thanksgiving, and I had been put on another dead post. This time a drunk who was roughing up his deaf-mute son passed through. The father had taken the kid out of a home for the night and had bought himself a bottle of whiskey with the $10 he'd been given to pay for a turkey dinner. After I locked him up, the lieutenant called me in. "I'm not in any trouble," I told him. "You got it mixed up. The guy who beat up his kid is in trouble."

They moved me again; I made another collar within the first hour. This time the victim was the son of a Transit who was coming to visit his father when he was jumped by some hump on the staircase. I heard no complaints about that arrest, but suddenly I was reassigned to the Bronx, meaning I was facing a three-hour daily subway commute from Howard Beach, Queens. This was the bosses' way of saying I should consider a new career, but I had other ideas. Two or three days a week, as my commute took me through Times Square, I'd arrest a drug dealer or some other local character who I knew had a warrant on him. "Listen," I'd tell the bosses, "when I see these crooks out there, I don't know if Internal Affairs is setting me up or not. I *have* to take action. I don't want to be arrested for dereliction of duty."

Finally, I raised the stakes again by filing a grievance about the overtime restrictions that got in the way of fighting crime. As I'd hoped, that got the attention of headquarters, and one day soon after the matter reached a formal conclusion, I was pulled aside when I was downtown at headquarters on other business after finishing a midnight tour. I was told the department's second-in-command, Deputy Chief Anthony V. Bouza, wished for me to pay him a visit. Of course, being a lucky guy, I had run into a pickpocket I had a warrant on while I was getting off the train under headquarters that morning. That meant a prisoner was waiting and my overtime clock running as I headed to Bouza's office.

Anthony V. Bouza had been a chief in the NYPD before moving over to Transit. He was highly thought of in certain circles of the profession, and he would later prove so popular as the top cop in Minneapolis that he seriously considered a run for governor of Minnesota.

Bouza looked like Bela Lugosi—tall, lanky, long-faced—and in 1977 he was still wearing suits with pencil-thin lapels while the rest of us were running around with airstrips on either side of our ties. He billed himself as "Socrates with a Gun," and he had been the guy who pulled the word "feral" out of a thesaurus, paired it with "youth," and created a phrase that's been a staple of law enforcement literature ever since.

He was "they"—one of the big bosses we always talked about in grand abstractions even as we took the liberty of collapsing the distance between us by using nicknames like "Bela." I was only twenty-five, and I had never been face-to-face with a "they" before.

"Sit down, Mr. Maple," Bouza said as I entered. "I've been waiting for a long time to meet you."

He had a computer printout in front of him that would have

showed many occurrences of the words "robbery" and "grand larceny." "I've been studying your arrest record," he said, glancing at the page. "You make excellent arrests."

For a moment, I dropped my guard: The principal actually liked me.

"Beyond that," he continued without dropping a beat, "you are the most immoral person I have ever met. By making these arrests, you are incurring overtime that is taking bread out of other people's mouths."

Now I was stunned. The breath had been knocked out of me, and I saw my Transit life flashing before my eyes—the cold nights when I was standing on a post with my feet freezing and my hands so numb I wasn't sure I'd be able to get my gun out of the holster if I needed it; the hot days when my thighs were rubbed raw from walking in the furnace-blast breath of the passing trains and the sweat making it feel like I'd pissed in my shoes. I thought about being shot at, and having my ass kicked on more than one occasion, and about never having accepted so much as a free coffee.

I also thought about other crime fighters I worked with—Stannish, Cassar, Boyd, Normile, Purcell, Zeckendorf—and about how much easier the pails had it because the pails didn't play straight the way we did. How many times did we get our balls busted by do-nothing bosses because we made their jobs more difficult? How many birthday parties and days with our families had we missed because we'd make a collar with twenty minutes left in the shift instead of looking the other way? Bouza wanted to blame me for the horrible arrest process? It was his job to fix it!

My face must have been betraying my emotions, because I noticed then that Anthony V. Bouza seemed to be enjoying himself a little too much. He looked like he'd toyed with scared, young cops before.

But who, really, was he to throw around his rank? To guys like him, landing at Transit was worse than getting sent to Siberia—it was under Siberia. If he wasn't a screwup in the world he came from, he wouldn't have even been sitting there in front of me.

That thought turned everything around. I was the one with the power, because I had played straight—me and the other crime fighters. I was the one with the clear conscience.

"Chief," I said, "can we speak for a moment just man to man?"

"Why certainly, Mr. Maple," he said.

"I mean not as a cop talking to a deputy chief, right?"

"Whatever you wish, Mr. Maple."

"You're sure?"

"Yes."

"Absolutely sure?"

He was still basking in his own sense of himself, and he held out his right hand, with the palm facing upward, in a gesture of charity. "Please, Mr. Maple," he said, "express yourself."

"Chief," I said in return, "you got some fucking balls saying what you did to me."

That was the beginning of a long speech—not as long as it would have been if I had a chance to do it again twenty minutes or twenty years later, but pretty long, given the short notice I'd been given.

It began with a review of the circumstances that had hastened the chief's departure from the NYPD: A year earlier he had been the Bronx borough commander during the Ali–Norton fight at Yankee Stadium when separate riots broke out among fans outside the stadium and among hundreds of off-duty cops who were protesting a contact delay. Aside from corruption, his inaction had contributed to one of the bigger scandals in the modern history of the department, and when the smoke had cleared, he had retired from the NYPD with a full pension before deciding there was nothing immoral about double-dipping for a second city paycheck by signing up as Transit's number two. Then again, the guy who hired Bouza, Chief Sandy Garelik, was doing exactly the same thing.

"Chief," I said, "you and I have a contract we go by. You make a contract with me that you'll pay me for the time it takes to process an arrest, and I make a contract with you that I will go to 42nd Street every day because that is my assignment. A lot of times, I'm afraid of those people on 42nd Street—I really am. But somehow, every day, I find the courage to face them. And I'll be damned if I'm going to start looking over my shoulder because of a guy down here wearing Ricky Nelson suits."

Chief Bouza must have thought that last remark was a compliment about his sartorial taste, because before I left his office, he told me that I seemed to be an excellent cop and that he would never bother me again.

(The chief might have had other motives for folding. When he was thrown out of the department two years later, he put in for a farewell check of $20,000, saying he had worked two hours of overtime every day for the last three years.)

Bouza came up with a second act in Minnesota, but my reputation within the department had been fixed. A few years later, the new chief of Transit told me I was an unguided missile.

"I'm not an unguided missile, sir," I answered. "I'm a missile. But I have a flight plan."

That chief, James B. Meehan, later signed off on the promotion list that made me, at twenty-eight, the youngest detective at Transit. I was lucky that Meehan's administration decided to overlook the troubles I'd caused the department in the past, but, believe me, there was no direct path from Transit detective to an upper floor at the headquarters of the NYPD. Smiled upon by one chief, out of favor with the next, I had another fourteen years in the tunnels to think about why "they" did things in my business the way they do.

In late 1993, I—suddenly—was a "they."

That December Mayor-elect Rudy Giuliani had chosen Bill Bratton, then the police chief in Boston, as New York's new commissioner.

Bratton was my guy. A few years earlier, he had come down from Boston to take command of the Transit Police and had quickly injected pride and a sense of mission into our afterthought organization. He also listened to new ideas, and when I staked out his coffee pot to get a ten-page proposal into his hands about how to knock down crime in the subways, not only did he read it, he made the ideas into reality, and along the way transformed me from a Transit lieutenant with a few pals in the press into a Transit lieutenant with a nice trumped-up title—special assistant to the commissioner. More important, I wound up with almost 100 cops under my command in a crime-fighting unit that had the authority and resources to go after just about every violent criminal who ever set foot on a subway platform. Felony crime went down 30 percent in Bratton's two years off-off-Broadway at Transit, and now, after a little backstage engineering by a few of us locals who appreciated the scope of his talents, he was returning to New York as a headliner at the Ziegfeld.

I was going to be there with him. Within a span of two or three months, I was graduating from glorified Transit lieutenant to the NYPD's deputy commissioner for crime control strategies. The promotion—a product of Bratton's daring—was the equivalent of an ensign in the Coast Guard waking up as a three-star admiral in the Navy, and I felt a little like when I was a kid sneaking into the box seats at Shea Stadium. At any moment, a meaty hand was liable to land on my shoulder, and I would be swiftly escorted to the nearest exit. Only this time, I was in the dugout filling up the manager's ear with strategies. And the ushers haven't shown up yet.

I'm pretty sure my reputation once again preceded me—though I'm not sure it had developed in a way anybody would have envied. To most NYPD cops, I was "Fatso," the commissioner's pal with the bow tie, homburg, and spectator shoes. Because Transit cops were considered a lower life-form, many of them might have even heard more about the hangouts I frequented than what I knew about fighting crime. More than ten years earlier, *New York* magazine had published a short feature about the wild ride I'd taken when I first made detective. The adventure had started purposively enough, with a five-week coffee-and-sardine diet that saved me ten inches on the waist line of three new designer suits I had purchased with the express intent of helping the crooks and the assistant district attorneys keep from lumping me in their category for "just another shithead cop." Momentum soon led to bold forays into the Oak Bar and the Palm Court at the Plaza Hotel, Peacock Alley at the Waldorf, the Rainbow Room at Rockefeller Center, and other foreign territories where most cops were afraid to venture—especially if they had to pay. Before it was over, I had mortgaged my home at the Money Store to borrow $28,000 (a sum greater than my annual salary), which I quickly converted into bottles of Dom Pérignon, Broadway shows, nights at the Waldorf, dinners at the River Cafe, and a few more $400 suits. When the money ran out, so did the babes. But at least I had memories.

Bratton had asked me to play chief headhunter during the transition period, so now I was interested in identifying other characters who were serious about fighting crime. Beginning with the fifty or so highest-ranking people in the department, I had in front of me a stack of individual personnel files right out of "Mission: Impossible." Page one had the photo, along with name, rank, current command, and past performance record. Attached was a detailed report the subject had written at our request about the operation of his or her command.

It was like combing through mug books, except we were looking for the heroes instead of the bad guys. The rejects were the ones whose reports brought to mind a remark made by Jacob Riis, the legendary chronicler of nineteenth-century New York, who covered the NYPD for the *Tribune* when the concept of gathering ambrotype likenesses of crooks into a "rogues' gallery" was a fresh and celebrated innovation that then Chief of Detectives Thomas J. Byrnes converted into an international bestseller. Riis had no argument with mug books, but he did take note of the department's skill at keeping the public in the dark about the true dimensions of crime and the police's success in combating it.

"Police work," Riis wrote, "is largely a game of bluff.

"The police do not like to tell the public of a robbery or a safe 'cracking,' " Riis elaborated. "They claim that it interferes with the ends of justice. What they really mean is that it brings ridicule or censure upon them to have the public know that they do not catch every thief, or even most of them."

A century later, the truth tellers within the department were still a small group, so midway into the transition period, I arranged to sit down with several of them a few different nights at a beat-up old yacht club forty-five minutes away from One Police Plaza in Sheepshead Bay, Brooklyn. Mike Scagnelli, a division commander in Brooklyn, had picked our unlikely hideout, and because he was also the head of the internal police organization that paid tribute to cops wounded in the line of duty, he knew as well as anybody which other commanders in the department were the real hard-chargers. We looked out from the Sheepshead Bay Yacht Club over the black water of the bay and began a thorough inspection of a police department that had a reputation as one of the greatest in the world. The more we poked at it, the wormier it looked. Operationally, she was a junker.

If we had spread it all out on a table, the department would seem to have all the tools. With 30,000 cops already on the job, 2,000 coming on courtesy of the outgoing mayor, and another 6,000 in Housing and Transit, which were to merge with the NYPD within the year, there was certainly no shortage of personnel. The Patrol Division had about two-thirds of the current total, and beyond the many thousands answering 911 calls in radio cars, the division was fielding various units meant for proactive tasks, including plainclothes Street Crime Units and a growing "community policing" subdivision. Narcotics, with about 1,500 people, had one unit that could conduct investigations of major druglords, another that could run buy-and-bust operations on the streets, and another that could sweep up scores of buyers at a time. The department's 4,000 detectives, working in the city's seventy-five precincts, in the Narcotics Division, and in various centralized investigative units, were merely the envy of the profession. For robberies, there were robbery squads; for fugitive apprehension, there were warrant squads; for gambling and prostitution, there was Vice.

The department also exhibited a fluency in the buzzwords and catchphrases of the moment—"outreach," "partnering," "collaboration," "empowerment." Precinct commanders knew all about toy drives and the national Night Out Against Crime. The idea behind that campaign was that police precincts or districts across the nation would compete to determine which ones put on the best pageants on one night of every year. It didn't seem to occur to any of the event organizers, however, that in policing, every night of the year is supposed to be a night out against crime.

Instead, when night fell, the NYPD went home. During almost any twenty-four hour period, shootings in the city peaked between 8 P.M. and 4 A.M., but the vaunted Narcotics Division went off-duty at 7 P.M. And I heard all the reasons why: The courts weren't equipped to process the arrests quickly enough at night, so the waiting would drive up overtime costs; the cops had to be able to identify suspects out on the street, but they don't see well enough in the dark; the last thing anybody wanted was for a cop to find himself in the middle of a gun battle in the wee hours of the morning. Oh, and somehow that all meant they couldn't work weekends either.

Narcotics wasn't barbecuing without company. The warrant squads, whose main job is to pull sleeping fugitives out of their beds, didn't hit any doors until at least 8 A.M., and they took weekends off too. The robbery squads were off weekends. Major Case was off weekends. The career criminal investigative squads were off weekends. The community policing officers, an army of baby cops who'd been more or less left on their own to solve all the problems in the city, were, to their credit, quick learners. Most all of them decided the best way to address crime and quality-of-life problems on their beats was to work from ten in the morning to six at night, but never on weekends.

Unfortunately, the bad guys work around the clock.

Part-time policing might have been a little bit more effective if the narcotics cops really were throwing barbecues with their confreres from the other divisions. Instead, they didn't even get together at the water cooler. The chief of detectives hardly ever spoke with the chief of patrol, the chief of patrol hadn't spoken to the chief of narcotics in more than a year, and the chief of department, who was the direct supervisor of all three, very rarely spoke to anybody but the first deputy commissioner.

The biggest lie in law enforcement is: "We work very closely together." And of course it's never a fainthearted lie. It's never just "We work closely together." It's always "We work very closely together—very closely."

Even most of the members of the Sheepshead Bay round table had been guilty of that one. A boroughwide narcotics commander might assure me his people worked very closely with homicide investigators to solve shootings and murders. But if I said, "Then tell me, what is the name of your counterpart in Homicide?," he would draw a blank. Drug trafficking was responsible for 30 to 50 percent of the city's murders, according to most everybody's back-of-the-envelope estimates, but narcotics and the detectives didn't get together to compare notes. They were both too territorial. The detectives wanted to wear their trenchcoats and pinky rings and "preserve the integrity of their investigations." Like Chief Byrnes 100 years earlier, they were all hoping to land book or movie deals. The narcotics cops, on the other hand, were always working on the biggest drug bust in the history of the city—never the second-biggest—and they were just dying for the day when they could throw a load of guns and white powder on a table and talk to the reporters about how many million billion kazillion dollars the shipment would have been worth if it had made it to the street. Secrecy was always of paramount importance. "We don't want anybody to know we're looking at them," they'd say. It would make me roll on the floor laughing. Wouldn't it be a wonderful thing, I thought, if we could make every crook in the entire city think we were hot on his trail?

As much as turf matters throughout law enforcement, the flip side is that nobody's ever satisfied to stay on post. If you send out a unit to clean up street trafficking in the East Village, they want to intercept shipments arriving off the coast of Brooklyn. If you put the same people in charge of harbor interdiction, they want to infiltrate a heroin ring in the Fujian Province of China. If you send them to China, they want to break an international money-laundering cabal based in Colombia. That's why if you ask the federal Drug Enforcement Agency who controls cocaine in Jamaica, Queens, or heroin in Washington Heights, they can't tell you. They're too busy chasing informants' tips out into some distant land that seems more important than the area they're supposed to be watching.

Patrol was always called the backbone of the department, which was an acknowledgment of their numbers, the hazards of their frontline position, and the burdens of giving the entire department a physical manifestation. But Patrol was powerless. When a patrol cop made an arrest and handed his prisoner over to the detective squad, he'd be lucky to hear "Nice work, kid." Detectives kept to their squad room on the second floor of every precinct and didn't much care what a street cop knew about the usual suspects on a corner where there'd been a shooting or two. If a patrol cop made a drug bust, he'd have to fill out an "Unusual Occurrence" report to explain how that could have happened.

The precinct commander, being a member of Patrol too, didn't get much more respect, even though he or she had to stand up in front of the community every month or so and hear about what a lousy job the cops were doing of clearing up this truancy hangout or that drug spot. I asked one commander what he would do if he walked in on his plainclothes cops watching television during their tour and all they did was look up and say, "Hey, Cap. How's it goin'?" He said he would throw the TV out the window. So I asked what if the same thing happened in the squad room. He said he wouldn't say a word, because he couldn't. But what would he like to be able to do? What should he be able to do? Throw the detectives' TV out the window and run over it with his car.

The detectives answered up their own chain of command to the chief of detectives, and nobody held them accountable for taking crooks off the street. As in every other detective bureau in America, all that mattered were "clearances," a term defining a resolution of each case that wouldn't meet most people's idea of a happy ending. A case is cleared whenever any one person is arrested for the crime, no matter how many pals the unlucky one might have had with him when he was knocking Mrs. McGinty down outside the check-cashing place and no matter how many other victims the rest of that crew took down in the weeks ahead. Many times, even the lack of one arrest was forgiven. "Exceptional" clearances were granted whenever the identity and location of a single suspect were known by investigators, but the suspect couldn't be brought in, either because he was dead, because he was being held in another jurisdiction and extradition had been denied, or because his victim was refusing to cooperate in pressing charges. More than a few detectives treated that last loophole as an invitation to sell every victim their layaway plan, which sent the victim home fully assured that he or she didn't have to worry about pressing charges immediately, but could sleep on it a few days and decide if it was really worth all the pain and lost workdays to see the case through to a trial and maybe even a conviction, only to learn later that the crook had made it back to the street in less than two weeks.

Since clearances counted, lives sometimes didn't. "Misdemeanor homicide" was a pervasive term in the Detective Bureau, used whenever a less-than-upstanding citizen was murdered and understood to mean that the investigation merited no more effort than a car theft. Shootings mattered even less. If a shooting victim didn't want to press charges, the detectives dropped the investigation altogether, even though the only difference between a murderer and most shooters is bad aim. Taking guns off the street didn't seem to interest the squads at all. During the previous year, patrol made almost 9,000 arrests for crimes in which a firearm was confiscated, but the entire Detective Bureau developed only four confidential informants to help identify gun sellers and took, as a result, fewer than fifty additional guns off the street. The crackerjack detective unit that was supposed to have been making all gun-trafficking cases citywide had been created less than two years earlier, but as is typical in policing, its mission had quickly fallen off the leadership's radar. The idea of using interrogations to identify and take out crack houses, chop shops, and fences had never even been on the radar.

At least the detectives had to share the same building with the precinct commander. Most narcotics operations moved in and out of the precincts without so much as a phone call, and when they arrived, they'd round up a bunch of buyers to pad their arrest records and leave the dealers where they were. Of course, the Housing police and the precincts weren't trusted to get involved in taking apart a drug crew, so if a citizen called 911 with a drug complaint, the cops would just pass by the location and turn around. Records of the public's complaints were only created for the calls made to special drug hot lines, but Narcotics didn't share the information from those calls with anybody, and 99 percent of the time they just filed the complaints away in a drawer somewhere for discovery by some future team of archaeologists. Even if Narcotics had been more interested in Patrol and Housing's reports, the Management Information Services Division downtown at One Police Plaza would be busy ensuring that all information gathered by the department was locked away in various closely guarded computer databases and shared by no one.

We had surrendered the city, I said to the Sheepshead Bay crew, and the citizens of New York were running up the white flags. Everywhere you went, you saw cars with little cardboard signs hanging from the rearview mirrors that said NO RADIO IN CAR. The next thing would be people putting signs in their windows saying NO TV IN HOUSE. When they had to go out to the store, they'd hang placards around their necks saying NO WALLET IN POCKET. Already, mothers were pushing five-drawer bureaus in front of their windows and telling their kids to sleep in the bathtub to stay clear of the crossfire.

Like every other police department in America, the NYPD never went for the win. We were like the Roman army under Fabius Maximus, who took command in 217 B.C. when Hannibal and his army were raping, robbing, and pillaging in the Italian countryside. Fabius decided he couldn't win a pitched battle with the brilliant Carthaginian, so he trailed the invading army at a safe distance, occasionally picking off a stray band of raiders, but generally just watching vineyards and villages burn and hoping time would wear the enemy down. Since policing began, its generals had been engaged in a grand-scale reenactment of the Fabian defense.

That December it snowed like the world was going to end. But long after dark every evening, when the meetings and interviews and head-butting were over, I'd head uptown to my favorite hangout, where the warm glow spilling to the sidewalk from its plate-glass windows could pull you in from three blocks away. I'd find a couple of hooks on a smoke-stained wall for my homburg and overcoat and settle in at one of the front tables for a long night of laughs, taunts, surprise table guests, and, when I was ready to listen, the newest installment in my informal, ongoing education.

Elaine's is a place where you can find yourself talking to a movie star one night, a politician the next, and a guy who runs one of the city's big dailies on the night after that. Or sometimes all three at once. Anybody who's really good at what they do seems to be attracted to the place, so for somebody like me, with my night school diploma, it was a path to an advanced degree in nocturnal studies.

Talking with Alec Baldwin once, my pal John Miller and I decided the speech Alec's character gave at the beginning of *Glengarry Glen Ross* was a perfect demonstration of how to generate high performance from a bunch of misfits. Their business was real estate sales, but the gist of the pep talk works just as well for a police commander: "You wanna talk about how hard it is to be a cop? Tell your troubles to your bowling buddies. You wanna tell me you can't catch this stickup guy or that crack dealer? If you can't catch them, you're not a cop. I can already see you sitting in a bar someday with a bunch of losers, telling them, 'Yeah, I tried being a cop once. Tough racket.' "

Baldwin's character had a motto: "Always be closing. A: Always. B: Be. C: Closing." In policing, I told him, it's "ABC^2: Always be catching crooks."

Miller, who'd introduced me to the place a few years earlier, is a guy anybody could learn from. Johnny was, and still is, the best reporter on TV. He was only fourteen when he did his first stand-up because he'd landed a job that allowed him to hang around a newsroom and he didn't blink when one of the bosses slipped up one night and said, "Send Miller out on that one." At fourteen he had the balls then to head out the door leading his own camera crew, and twenty-five years later he was still doing things like slipping into Afghanistan for "ABC World News Tonight" to get an exclusive interview with Osama Bin-Laden, a man the rest of the American press was calling the world's most dangerous terrorist.

When Miller and I started hanging out, he was already the prince of the city. He looked like John John, he dressed like Gotti, he thought like a squad commander, and he spoke like a Farfington. He could sit down with gangsters, models, and, of course, the cops, and he could make anybody he talked to think they were the only person in the world, especially the models. He was also a bit over the top—a little too much shine in the suit, a little too much gold in the watch, a little too much sparkle in the ring. Together, we belonged in a comic book.

"So how do you think we're gonna do?" he asked me one night at Elaine's soon after he'd talked his way into a $500,000-a-year salary cut and appointment to his dream job as DCPI—the NYPD's deputy commissioner for public information. We were a couple weeks away from being sworn in.

"Johnny," I said, "this is gonna be easy. They're not fighting crime. They don't work the right tours; they're not even talking to each other. It'll be like shooting fish in a barrel."

"Oh, that's an image they'll like," he said, "—the fat Transit lieutenant setting his crosshairs on the greatest police department in the world."

"OK, fucko, I'll give you a better image," I said. "You remember in the movie *Batman,* with Jack Nicholson as the Joker? He knows he's been written off as a force to be reckoned with, but then he turns to the camera for the first time with that big Cheshire Cat grin locked on his face. And what does he say, Johnny? What does he say?"

I answered myself. "You know," I said, "I met some of these chiefs at the Christmas tree lighting at Rockefeller Center, and I heard a few of their chuckles when Bratton told them I was going to be his crime guy. But inside, I'm smiling like Nicholson, and I'm thinking, 'Wait till they get a load of me.' "

As Jacob Riis said, "Police work is largely a game of bluff." Sure, I understood what was wrong with the NYPD, but I didn't yet know how to fix it.

The solution came to me at Elaine's several weeks later.

There is a lot to admire in Elaine Kaufman. She's intensely loyal to her friends, and neither money nor fame figure into those allegiances. In fact, she treated me like a movie star, even when I was a Transit lieutenant. Naysayers pan the food from her kitchen, but I think she serves the best linguini and white clam sauce in the city.

Beyond that, Elaine knows how to run a business. And that talent was the one I was interested in on this occasion.

Elaine, I knew, was on post at her restaurant probably 350 nights a year. If, however, she planned to be away for a night—to catch a play on Broadway or run uptown to 125th Street to hear Lonnie Youngblood at Showman's—she'd tell her staff she was going to be away a week and then surprise them by reappearing six nights early. If she intended to stay away a week, she'd say she was going to be out of town for one night only.

On this particular evening, she was, as is her habit, making frequent visits to her desk officer, who sits to one side of the bar, signing every check as it's paid and tallying up the receipts. She knew at all times, from checking his tape, exactly how well the night was going. If the receipts were down, she'd look for her waiters: Were they loitering near the coffee service area or were they out on the floor, anticipating and attending to the customers' every need? Chances are, she would also hit a few tables herself to keep the joint hopping.

How different business was in the NYPD, I thought. We didn't check our crime numbers hourly, daily, or even weekly. Headquarters gathered the numbers every six months, and then only because the department was required to report them to the FBI for inclusion in the national *Uniform Crime Reports*. I couldn't imagine that many of our precinct commanders checked the tape on their crime numbers every day. If the numbers were going the wrong way, would any of them be out on field inspections to determine what was going wrong?

The first couple weeks of the Bratton era had been organized chaos. Several chiefs were on their way out; new ones were ready to move in, and it was evident that if the bosses all fought the crooks as hard as they fought for corner offices, take-home vehicles, and reserved parking spaces, we could turn Fear City into Mayberry, R.F.D.

Many of them first had to overcome certain inhibitions, of course.

Some, I know, had long been conversant in the profanity-laced argot of the street cop, but none I had met were comfortable uttering the "C" word—whether or not a woman was in the room. I wanted to change that; I wanted to hear the word "crime" spoken at the top levels of the department every hour and every day.

Bratton had made a promising start. He had clearly communicated a revolutionary goal—to "win the war on crime." He had been seen everywhere by troops in the field. And he had filled key subordinate positions with skilled, audacious commanders.

Bratton was our George C. Marshall, the man of vision who shook the U.S. armed forces out of their sleep in 1941 and demonstrated an infallible instinct for identifying talent. Chief of Department John Timoney was our Eisenhower, as respected by the soldiers in the field as he was knowledgeable about the intricacies of managing a mammoth fighting organization. Chief of Patrol Louie Anemone was our Patton, a tireless motivator and brilliant field strategist who could move ground forces at warp speed. First Deputy Commissioner Dave Scott didn't have a World War II counterpart: He was Burt Lancaster in *Trapeze*. He wanted to help the young acrobats learn to fly, but he was also there to catch us if we fell.

We had also, by then, come up with sound strategies to address guns, drugs, domestic violence, youth crime, auto crime, quality-of-life problems, and police corruption, and we were beginning to roll the strategies out, one by one.

What worried me was that we had no process in place to ensure the strategies were carried out. We knew from history that the greatest ideas in the world are useless unless they are carried out.

By the time I started sipping my third glass of champagne on ice, the normal distractions had melted away. On the napkin in front of me, I started scratching out a few ideas about what any police department needs in order to operate as an undeterrable force against crime. Before long, I had reduced those ideas to four principles, which were to become our guideposts as we went about redefining the objectives, methods, and outcomes of the NYPD and, in turn, police organizations everywhere:

1. Accurate, timely intelligence
2. Rapid deployment
3. Effective tactics
4. Relentless follow-up and assessment

In the days and weeks that followed, I refined my definitions and misplaced the napkin, but I remained obsessed with the four principles. The NYPD wasn't ready to accomplish any of the four objectives the very next morning, but as we pushed toward meeting the ideals, the entire organization began to take on the personality and posture of a crime fighter.

The first principle—*accurate, timely intelligence that is clearly communicated to all*—meant we needed to gather crime numbers for every precinct daily, not once every six months, to spot problems early. We needed to map the crimes daily too, so we could identify hot spots, patterns, and trends and analyze their underlying causes.

The second principle—*rapid deployment that is concentrated, synchronized, and focused*—required that for the first time in history, the detectives, Narcotics, and the precinct commanders would talk to each other and combine their efforts to move swiftly against crime. We wanted the department's subordinate commanders to stop being territorial to their functions and become more territorial to actual territories.

Effective tactics are any tactics that reduce crime or improve the quality of life, so while we intended to encourage innovation, we also wanted to ensure that best practices were shared throughout the department and reinforced by our fundamental but comprehensive strategies.

Relentless follow-up and assessment may have been the most important principle of the four, because it gave birth to weekly meetings at which Louie Anemone and I and the rest of the department's executive corps debriefed precinct, narcotics, and squad commanders about crime maps for their areas and gauged their ongoing compliance with the four fundamental principles:

- Was the precinct or division's crime information timely and accurate?
- Was deployment rapid, synchronized, and focused?
- Were the tactics they used effective?
- Were the commanders relentless about follow-up and assessment? In other words, how were they verifying that the orders they gave to achieve the other three objectives were being carried out by the officers in the field?

Nobody ever got in trouble because crime numbers on their watch went up. I designed the process knowing that an organization as large as the NYPD never gets to Nirvana. Trouble arose only if the commanders didn't know why the numbers were up or didn't have a plan to address the problems.

The entire process, with the meetings as its centerpiece, soon came to be known as "Compstat" or "Comstat," a word invented as a slug name for the 386 computer in which we compiled and stored the first sets of crime numbers. The name was short for "computer statistics" or "comparative statistics"—nobody can be sure which. The important thing was not that we made use of a computer, but that the four steps reset the standards by which operations were assessed at every level of the organization, from the executive corps, to the borough commanders, to the precinct commanders, to the cops we sent out on the streets.

Our stay atop the NYPD was a little like a ride on the Cyclone at Coney Island—brief, terrifying at times, but ultimately exhilarating. From the morning of the first Comstat meeting to the weekend the commissioner stepped down and Timoney and I followed him out the door, we had just over two years. But during those two years, the pace at which murders were committed in the city declined by half, and the pace of felony crime dropped 39 percent. In numbers of victims, the reductions for murder and for overall serious crime were greater over 1994 and 1995 than over the next four years combined, and that was achieved with about 3,000 fewer cops and half the overtime budget. The difference in the pace of accomplishment can be credited to the inspirational leadership of Bill Bratton.

But that's not to say the NYPD was a better crime-fighting organization then. It's better now. We left behind an organization that had adopted a process for perpetual self-improvement that has since pushed city crime rates down to mid-1960s levels and has continued to serve as a model of the new thinking in policing for departments across the nation and around the world.

The New York story was no fluke. Everywhere else I've been, the same fundamental problems have to be addressed and the same fundamental solutions work a cure.

The four steps guide the way, but to understand why, first you have to consider the opponent, and how it is we catch them.

THREE

CROOKOLOGY 101
Stalking the Predatory Criminal

In Philadelphia, he would be a "dirtball." In New Orleans, a "jack-off." In Newark, a "shit'm." In L.A., just an "asshole."

To a New York City cop like me, James McClean was a "scum-bag."

McClean clearly took pride in the work he did. Unfortunately, the work he did was robbery, and over the course of a few months in late 1990 and early 1991, he and a small crew of his buddies probably raked in more money doing stickups than Jesse James did in a lifetime.

McClean had chosen a lucrative niche. Crews who did bank robberies netted only about $2,500 a job at the time, but by targeting token booths in the New York City subway system, McClean's gang regularly cleared three or four times that amount and never had to worry about video cameras or security guards.

As happens so often with crime, the victims of McClean's robberies probably found it hard to appreciate their assailant's enterprising spirit. Take Raymond Mills, a fifty-eight-year-old token clerk who walked out of his booth one night into unforgettable chaos. If McClean's crew played their parts as they were usually scripted, a gun was at Mills's head the moment he exited the booth, quickly followed by a command to lie facedown on the concrete. A second pair of shoes passing overhead might have been all Mills remembered of McClean if the clerk had just done what he was told. But something upset the robbers' plans—maybe Mills fought back, maybe he just made a sudden move. In any event, McClean's accomplice fired his gun, and only luck and the immediate attention of a team of surgeons kept Mills from dying a premature death.

Mills probably experienced the entire event as a sudden visitation of total disorder, but the crew's methods were anything but disorderly. Their work assignments, for example, were remarkably consistent: One man would stay with the getaway car; a second—usually a guy named Frank, or "Franco"—would stand lookout at the stairway leading up or down to the booth. McClean and a fourth man, who called himself Al Capone, would hit the booth.

McClean knew the system's work schedules, and his crew would wait in the dark outside a station until they saw a relief clerk drive up and head in to start the next shift or give the regular clerk a half hour for meal. McClean and Capone apparently took turns performing the critical tasks. The "drop," or gunman, would slide up next to the booth's door and wait for it to reopen. His partner would stay out of sight until both clerks had been ordered to the ground, then dash in carrying a laundry bag that he'd fill with cash and as many boxes of tokens as the pair could carry.

These guys would time themselves, and they tried to hold every stickup to no more than a minute. They also knew how much they could carry away, because they had trained for the real heists by running up and down subway stairs, hauling bags loaded with 100 pounds of rocks and bricks.

At this point, I could tell you his dedication made McClean something more than the usual "scumbag." But in the ways that affect the way the police should go about their work, he was, in fact, a fairly typical crook.

Why do I say that? Because crooks usually get caught because they've left themselves vulnerable in one way of four ways. Sometimes it's because they make reckless mistakes. Sometimes it's because they make smart decisions. Sometimes it's because a third party turns them in. And sometimes it's simply because they're crooks, and crooks are always trying to get over, even if it means taking down their pals.

Stupid mistakes have obvious consequences. But smart decisions can be just as much a threat to a crook's freedom. If a predatory criminal selects his victims intelligently, selects the setting for his crimes intelligently, and then tries to replicate his successes, he'll establish a pattern of behavior that will become predictable. In the case of McClean's crew, our stakeouts never snagged them, but they had established distinctive work habits, and that was a big part of their undoing.

That, and the fact that the members of the crew started cheating on each other.

It may have begun with Franco getting shortchanged on the split; before long he was being left out completely on some jobs. And not exactly being the brains of the outfit, he decided to get even with his pals by calling the city's crime hot line and giving up details on a holdup he'd been frozen out of. A small cash reward for the first tip apparently whetted his appetite, and before long he was phoning in useful details about jobs he too had participated in.

Capone was arrested first, when he ran into a uniformed cop while trying to go solo with his booth robbery career, but his mention of an accomplice named "Frank" soon led our detectives to an apartment building where those hot-line tips were coming from. Now enjoying Franco's full assistance, we caught up with McClean and tackled him late one night inside a Brooklyn bodega.

Franco's poor judgment gave our squad an opportunity to catch the crew that had nothing to do with their core mission of robbing the subway system. That's not uncommon. People who try to get over in big things usually try to get over in the little things too, creating opportunities the police can exploit if they're willing to look for them. In war, it is understood that an army should not attack the opponent where he's strongest but where he is weak, and crooks have a wealth of weaknesses. But the police need to have more than the criminals' weaknesses working for them. To enjoy consistent success, the cops need a way to take advantage of the things the scoundrels do pretty well.

In policing, we often talk about who within a department is "in the game," meaning which cops are really in the business of catching crooks. The game imagery is appropriate, because there has to be an element of sport to the work. But a more useful metaphor for intelligent policing is the hunt. Many of the people we're trying to catch, after all, are predators themselves. Robbers, rapists, and serial killers obviously fit into that category, but burglars, pickpockets, and even scam artists also use the logic of a predator in choosing their victims, their hunting grounds, and their hours of work. In short, they are all attracted by vulnerability. Wherever and whenever their victims are available and vulnerable, that's where they'll be.

The difference between their hunt and our "game" is we're obligated to follow rules of honorable engagement and they're not. That's what makes catching criminals so delicious.

Not all crooks play the game the way James McClean did. Other crooks are less professional, some are more deranged or more vicious; plenty are just knuckleheads. They may be stealing $10 at a time instead of $10,000. They may choose victims that are even harder to sympathize with than the New York City Transit Authority.

But rare is the crime that doesn't transform an otherwise mindless crook, at least momentarily, into a purposeful predator. A cop who's in the game understands that each choice the predator makes, each step of the criminal's method of operation, represents an opportunity. He will prowl the predators' hunting grounds. He'll trail potential victims—a little old lady counting the cash from her Social Security check, a drunk with a glittering Rolex watch who's stumbling out of a strip bar at midnight, a woman with an open handbag fighting her way down the crowded sidewalks of 34th Street—and wait for a purse snatcher to start following the same target. Sometimes he'll follow a group of robbers because he's learned to recognize the body language of a wolf pack getting ready to strike—their eyes targeting hands and pocketbooks, their head movements alerting each other to possible scores, the cadence of their steps synchronized, even if a few dozen paces separate them.

During the two decades I spent on and under the streets of New York, the predatory criminal was my principal opponent, and he taught me a few things about crooks of all kinds. Though there are some miscreants out there who operate according to somewhat different principles—most notably drug crews, whose violence usually springs from their desire to preserve profits, protect turf, and enforce discipline—the predator illuminates better than any other type of criminal the nature of the work the police are in and the thinking we need to adopt in order to win at our game.

You would think that young cops coming out of the police academies across the world would have earned a good number of their credits studying the ways to identify and catch the predatory criminal. Instead, recruits are taught how to take reports, a skills set passed on at the precincts by training officers who are usually young and inexperienced themselves. They, in turn, are supervised by inexperienced and undertrained sergeants. In essence, we have kids who know very little training kids who know even less training kids who know nothing. And then we send our most underprepared students out to face the most experienced criminals day in and day out, many times alone.

Fledgling predatory criminals are also trained by kids, but they start when they're twelve or younger, often with on-the-job training in such fields as pickpocketing, shoplifting, and boosting cars. As sophomores, they become experts in robbery and burglary, then they graduate into narcotics management positions or take up shootings and sometimes murder. Many are both victims and assailants in sexual assaults, domestic violence, and child abuse. Many have superior strength, and, because they're young, feel they are invincible.

To prepare cops to face those opponents, every academy should make "The Art of Catching Crooks" a central part of the curriculum. It would be a series of courses, each taught by a real commander instead of some clerk who was assigned to the academy because he was afraid of the streets. Drawing on the instructors' real-life experiences in patrol, these courses would focus on crime-fighting tactics and strategies that address narcotics, robbery, and burglary crews; shootings and murders; sexual assaults and domestic violence; car-theft rings, fugitive apprehension, fear reduction, and quality-of-life enforcement. Then, following graduation, the new officers would not be permanently assigned to patrol until they had each completed a two-year cycle that would expose them to the tactics and strategies of a narcotics division, a detective bureau, and a fugitive apprehension unit.

That would be the ideal, and it would require a substantial investment of time and money. For now, though, it's worth beginning the job.

THE WATERING HOLES

My own early lessons in crookology came by way of Times Square and the New York City subway system—places fixed in the public imagination as two of the main carnival grounds for one of crime's greatest quarter-century runs.

Walking around midtown Manhattan today, I get a little nostalgic for the old days. I don't miss the casbah-like atmosphere of that time—or lost landmarks like the little alley on West 34th Street that all the robbers, pickpockets, and drug dealers used as an escape route—but I do miss the simplicity of the work back then. As a young cop, I didn't have to think about policing in terms of budgets, work rules and political ramifications. It was just the bad guys and us. There's nothing like that feeling.

Sometimes it's still that simple. About a year and a half after I retired my deputy commissioner's badge, I was meeting John Miller for lunch at the Carnegie Deli on West 55th Street when I came upon a character who was bullying pedestrians into handing over their pocket money, then dropping it on the ground and making them pick it up again. For a brief, shining moment, I was a cop again, and the bleats and buzz of the streets went quiet as I grabbed the guy by the shirt and made him a promise about how long I was going to have him locked up if he ever showed his face on that block again. At forty-five, I was a little fatter and a little slower than I was as a patrol cop, but thank God I was a better actor. The bully backed down, and I was able to slip right back into my new life as a high-priced clerk and phone the local precinct to get a real cop after the guy.

His was a caveman crime, but fundamentally it was no different from the McClean booth robberies. In each case, the predator had a clear objective (money, or in the bully's case, money and the thrill of intimidating other people). In each case, the predator chose victims who were in positions of relative vulnerability. In each case, the time and location of the crime offered a high probability that the rewards would be worth the predator's time, effort, and risk. And in each case, the predator locked into a pattern, as if he believed crime was a calling requiring the reliability of a monk.

With certain crimes, the similarities to the action you see on television nature shows almost can't be ignored.

Predators of the criminal world hunt the old, the young, the weak, and the disabled, though the strong too can become their victims if the predators hold a lopsided advantage in numbers or see an offering too good to pass up.

They hunt alone, with a partner, or sometimes in packs—by location, season, and time of day. They may run their victims down, lie in wait and pounce, or circle their targets while making an assessment. Some may even lay careful plans before making their attack, which is usually swift, ferocious, and efficient.

Sometimes the predators kill for simple material gains, but they will also kill each other over turf, prey, or a mate. Unlike the predators of the animal kingdom, however, the predatory criminal will attack, and sometimes kill, for pleasure, for trophies, or even to relieve boredom.

On the nature shows, the watering hole is the scene of many attacks. The lions, hungry for dinner, will head for the watering hole at dusk and surprise the zebras refreshing themselves there. Maybe the lions are just as surprised when they find their dinner there, but they act as if they understand the habits of their prey and consciously put themselves in position to capitalize. If you're a cop trying to bag a crook, you're just like a hunter trying to bag a lion, so you better be down at the watering hole too.

Times Square was one big watering hole, a place a subway cop could always turn to for a live robbery when things were slow downstairs. Down in the hole, the work could be numbing—hour after hour of climbing stairs and roaming platforms, knowing that even though 100 percent of the robbery crews rode trains to get to 42nd Street, or "the Deuce," 90 percent of the robberies happened up on the street.

To make the work interesting in the trains, I would try to spot people carrying guns. That, I figured, might save a few lives. So I taught myself how to spot a concealed weapon. I'd stand in front of a full-length mirror and study the way a gun looked under a jacket, over the shoulder, inside the waistband—anywhere on the body it could be hidden. On the job, I'd stop two or three people a day who were carrying concealed weapons. Many of the guns were licensed; some were not.

The drill went like this: With my nonshooting hand, I make my first move by grabbing the handle of his gun. He freezes and usually obeys an order to put his hands on his head. If he doesn't, my hold on his gun and waistband put him off-balance, so I can spin him around and get cuffs on him anyway.

One guy I arrested with a gun taught me a humbling lesson when he was sitting a few feet away from me on a bench in the holding area. He had his hands cuffed behind him, and he was squirming. When I went to look why, I discovered he had a second gun on the small of his back and he had almost worked it free. From that day on, I included a new step in every gun arrest: After getting the cuffs on, always look for the second gun.

Lions, tigers, and bears are born with their own weapons, but humans who want that kind of physical advantage usually have to go out and buy it, creating another opportunity for the cops. A few steps west of a subway entrance on Eighth Avenue there was a novelty store famous for its role in making pornography into Time Square's bread-and-butter industry. In 1966, its owner introduced peep shows to New York City consumers, and the mountains of quarters he carted out every day soon inspired just about every other business owner in the area to learn the ins and outs of his newest venture, and of course they all mopped up. This pioneer of pay-per-view porn also did a brisk business in knives, gun holsters, handcuffs, throwing stars, blackjacks, bludgeons, switchblades, and phony police badges from a section of the store that served as a kind of scumbag sporting goods department, so a few of us came to the conclusion that we might be able to collar some stickup men if we kept our eyes on his customers.

One cold December night I set up outside the novelty store and soon spotted a few guys inside trying on holsters. I told my partner I was sure they had a gun or two somewhere, and soon enough, out they came, like kids coming out of a toy store, pulling out their new purchases before they were halfway down the block. It brought back fond memories of the "Detective Special," a snub-nosed .38 with a shoulder strap that my dad had given me back in the days before Mattel reconsidered the wisdom of supplying children with plastic bullets that actually whizzed across the living room. Around the corner at 43rd Street, the suspects opened their car and we grabbed them.

Inside the car were several guns and a stash of wallets still holding their owners' IDs. Turned out our holster-shoppers were wannabes and associates of the nearly defunct Black Liberation Army who'd been sticking up bars and social clubs throughout Brooklyn.

The arrests and the confessions we coaxed out of these guys put me and my partner over the top to get our detectives' gold shields. And the experience taught me two things: one, that even the real hard guys will rat on each other, and two, that one way cops can make a dent in violent crime is to sit on any location likely to attract predatory criminals. Years later, incidentally, that novelty store was one of a couple I shut down for selling illegal weapons, despite protests by one of the managers that he had been faithful in paying off the local precinct. (I guess he'd never heard of the Transit Police.)

Times Square was a smorgasbord for every miscreant, thief, robber, and trickster of the day. Consider its assets: the Port Authority Bus Terminal, the budget entrance to New York City from New Jersey and points west, poured runaways, thrillseekers, out-of-town hicks, and defenseless wage earners onto Eighth Avenue at 40th Street. The choice victims were everywhere—flush with cash, loaded up on booze or drugs, and more than willing to take foolish chances with their money or their safety. The prostitutes, who stood about four deep on the sidewalk, were like their own little criminal ecosystem. Some, of course, suffered beatings and worse at the hands of violent pimps and psychotic johns. But there were others who teamed up with pickpocket and robbery crews to empty the wallets of their weaker customers.

Some of the crooks were comical. Gregory Gadson was the worst pickpocket in the world. The kid had these big swollen hands and he was so awkward he almost never finished digging a pocket before the victim was staring him straight in the eyes. The only thing Gregory had going for him was his twin brother, Glenn. The Gadsons both worked the same blocks, so unless the cops caught one "live," he always had an alibi.

In the early '90s, one group of crooks discovered that the junk-food joints lining the streets were as good at lining up victims as the neighborhood's sex and drug trades. These characters would squirt a gob of ketchup on a tourist's shirt and grab his bag while he was looking down. Another one of their tricks was to throw a dollar on the floor and ask if you'd dropped some money. I once had to chase two of these humps back and forth through a crowded Popeye's after the cop I was eating with had her pocketbook snatched off the back of her chair. Of course, to save myself from well-deserved ridicule, I told everybody we were running a decoy.

Times Square also had con men working every conceivable angle. At places like Las Vegas Nights, a guy would walk in, buy himself a drink for about $5, then start to get friendly with one of the nude dancers. Her cocktails inevitably cost $75 apiece, and when the mark refused to pay the tab, the bouncers would simply rob him and throw him out in the street. As for drug trafficking, I'm sure some people purchased serious narcotics in Times Square at one time or another, but oregano and baking soda sold just as well as pot and cocaine, and plenty of customers were willing to pay for the less-heralded high of "spitback"—an orange juice-like concoction that the methadone users manufactured by spitting out their daily ration from the clinics.

Scams work on the principle that victims have a little bit of crook in them too, that there's a little larceny in everybody's heart, so Times Square was thick with easy marks. Even visitors who had no interest in cheap sex or quick highs were easily fooled into believing they could profit from the lawlessness of this thieves' bazaar. A guy with a $5 phony gold chain would walk up to an out-of-towner, show the mark a $500 price tag from Macy's, and tell him the piece could be his for $50. "Real gold doesn't tarnish in a flame," he'd say, then he'd hold the necklace over a lighter. People bought the stuff because they figured they were getting stolen merchandise at a discount. But I'd tell these guys that there's another way to test for gold. I called it the "throw test," and when they'd ask me to demonstrate, I'd heave the chain across 42nd Street and tell them you can't throw real gold that far. I didn't have a comparable routine for the empty television sets some of these humps were always hawking, but I have to confess I discovered once that if you tap one of these TVs firmly against a nearby fire hydrant, it will turn into broken glass, shards of plastic, and a pile of red bricks. The guys who worked these scams were borrowing a page from the Mafia, who make a load of money by marking up the prices on cheap jogging suits and telling their customers they "fell off a truck somewhere."

The three-card monte games were probably the most visible scams on the streets. The best monte players worked with a partner, often dressed in a Brooks Brothers suit, who would enter the game reluctantly, draw a crowd, and walk away a big winner. The real victim would be somebody in the audience who'd either concluded he had stumbled upon the world's only honest monte game or that he, like the Brooks Brothers guy, had picked up on the card turner's clumsy attempt at cheating. For a few plays, he'd watch the card with the creased corner and double or even quadruple his money. But suddenly the creased card would change color. The vic always walked away at least a few bills poorer.

The monte games thrived on Times Square until the Bratton era, when we finally got serious about locking up the hustlers on gambling charges. The games were enough of a problem in themselves: They created a visual blight on the streets and sent a lot of tourists home from the city with humbling losses and sour memories.

But the bleeding didn't end there. Every game created a natural environment for pickpockets, who preyed on the spectators pressing in to watch the action and even on passersby slowed by the sidewalk bottlenecks. A little pileup was all the thieves needed to jostle a target, dig his pockets, and walk away with an extra wallet. In fact, the pickpockets found crowded sidewalks so irresistible that sometimes we'd put up police barricades just to squeeze pedestrian traffic and lure the crooks in for arrests by sending a decoy through with an unlatched Louis Vuitton or Gucci bag. In other words, we created a watering hole where we could maintain control over the action, or, if you like, an artificial reef where we could watch the predators swoop in on the bait fish.

Some predators, like the pedophile who cruises playgrounds and schoolyards or a Ted Bundy who targets his prey in college towns, choose watering holes that aren't natural hotbeds of crime, but the typical watering hole attracts predators of all kinds. In official police language, a watering hole is called "a chronic condition," meaning the prevailing characteristics of the location encourage a high rate of crime. A check-cashing business that serves a lot of senior citizens can create a chronic condition. So can an auto junkyard that buys stolen airbags. Rush hour crowds in the 34th Street and 42nd Street subway stations are a chronic condition that arrives every day as predictably as the tide.

When cops run into a chronic condition, they have two courses of action from which to choose: They can pick off the predators attracted by the prevailing conditions or they can try to change the prevailing conditions. When a watering hole pops up because of the proximity of enterprises like the monte games that themselves cause people harm, there really is no choice. Those operations have to be shut down. It may hurt the arrest records of a few cops who use the chronic locations as their own fishing holes, but it's the only reasonable thing to do for the sake of crime's victims.

Keep that thought in mind, because every drug trafficking spot in every city in America is a watering hole, and law enforcement has so far been less than serious about shutting them all down. Most of the time, the cops arrest the buyers instead of the dealers.

We've all heard plenty said about the war on drugs, but never have so many done so little about so much.

THE VICS

One spring day a young guy I know named Danny dressed the part of a victim, as he often did, when he went to work. This time the act called for a Hasidic man, and with his thick, black beard, a dark suit and a wide-brimmed black fedora, Danny looked authentic enough to fool most other subway riders.

But Danny was a little worried that the people he most needed to fool might have eyes for finer details, so before leaving home, he cut some strings from his mother's mop and tied those into his clothing as an approximation of the tassels that dangle from a traditional Jewish prayer shawl. When a colleague handed him a large black attaché loaded with phony jewelry, his costume was complete.

Danny was a Transit cop in a unit that appreciated the finer points of victimology. Before a person becomes a victim, he or she is, in the eyes of the predator, merely an opportunity. Cops who catch criminals understand that victims, because they are the bait fish, unwittingly choose the time and location of many crimes. All that matters to the crook is where and when the opportunity for crime arises, and the same is true if the criminal's target is not a person but a house, a business, or a car.

For several months in 1992, the Transit Police and a couple of Lower Manhattan precincts had been fielding phone calls from jewelry manufacturers who reported that their sales representatives were being robbed as they headed back uptown to 47th Street after making their daily rounds among the lower-priced retailers on Canal Street.

"Well, how much jewelry was taken?" the detectives would ask.

"Half a million dollars' worth."

"How was your salesman carrying it?"

"In an attaché case."

"Do you know what the crooks looked like?"

"He said there were about five or six young black men. He didn't really get a good look at them."

"And why was he riding alone on a New York City subway train with half a million dollars in jewelry sitting on his lap?"

"He's a senior citizen. He gets half-fare on the tokens."

It was no mystery why many cops had written off a lot of these cases as insurance fraud. Lloyds of London must have been taking a bath on all the claims pouring in from the jewelry manufacturers.

Billy Carter, a detective from one of my old squads, Central Robbery, and a guy I'd handpicked to work with me on my decoy unit several years earlier, was the first to notice a hint of truth in the complaints. Going over the old reports, he'd picked up on an odd wrinkle in the pattern: The robberies always occurred at the end of a workday, but never on a Friday. When he discovered that the Hasidic salesmen quit early on Fridays to be home for the Sabbath before sunset, he decided the robbery spree had to be real.

Carter soon learned that the subway wasn't an entirely nutty choice of transportation for a salesman carrying up to $500,000 in jewels. Riding the subway was a variation on a trick used by every shopowner in the world who carries his cash receipts to the bank in a paper bag, hoping nobody will suspect its contents are valuable. Also, the way the jewelry guys figured it, they were easy targets anyway. If they used a cab or private car, the crooks could put a nail in the toe of a shoe, kick one of the tires before the car left 47th Street, then do a holdup midway downtown when the driver pulled over to fix the flat. The salesmen for the different manufacturers did try to reduce the risks by riding the trains downtown together, but when they hit Canal Street, they had to make their rounds on their own. Given the choices, a half-fare subway ride on a busy train line did sound better than sitting in Midtown traffic every day.

However they chose to travel, the salesmen were bound to attract predators. But as I said, victims are often the ones who are calling the dance. Without them, the crooks would be adrift.

So when Danny the cop stepped out of an unmarked Transit Police van late that Friday afternoon, he was playing to an extremely attentive audience. Crossing the street, he strolled right in front of a crew of six very frustrated thieves who hadn't yet figured out why there were no other bearded men on the street at that hour who were carrying attachés full of jewelry.

The merchants were surprised to see Danny too, and not just because of the time of day. They didn't know what to make of this stranger trying to pass off "slum" jewelry as the real thing, but the crooks looking in from the sidewalk couldn't hear the conversation. They saw only a familiar glitter and 100 little price tags dangling on strings.

With the crew in pursuit, Danny slung the strap of the attaché over his shoulder and headed for the subway, about to find out how dangerous the life of a victim can be. The uptown train pulled in almost immediately, leaving two undercover cops stranded in the line for the token booth. Danny had to make a quick decision: If he let the train go, he risked blowing his cover, and most cops would rather take a confrontation on the train than on a platform near an open track bed. There were six crooks and only one other undercover already on the platform. Danny boarded the train.

As the cars rattled uptown, a member of the crew walked up, showed a box cutter cupped in his palm, and leaned over to whisper in Danny's ear, "Give me the bag." Danny just ignored the request, winning a retreat that allowed him to draw out his 9mm semiautomatic and hide it behind the attaché. Sensing a bluff, the guy with the blade stepped forward again and slashed the shoulder strap before Danny came up with his weapon. The robber had miscalculated: He'd brought a razor to a gunfight, and even though Danny emerged from the train at 34th Street with his black suit cut to ribbons, he and his backup had made the pinch on the Canal Street robbery ring.

People often wonder what they can do to prevent becoming the victims of crime. Some people, through no fault of their own, can't escape being targeted. The Hasidim could have done a better job of "target hardening" by staying together at all times or traveling with personal bodyguards, but they couldn't change their distinctive appearance and could do little to adjust their commuting patterns. They were natural prey for the predators, who, as I said, target the young, the old, the weak, and the disabled. And sometimes you don't even have to be particularly weak to become a target. The criminals will go after the things they want if a weapon or a clear advantage in numbers makes them confident of their chances.

We have to recognize that we are all potential victims and we should do all we can to make ourselves less inviting targets for the crooks. I myself was the victim of back-to-back burglaries when I first moved into Manhattan. I had anticrime gates on one window but not on the other, so guess which way the burglars came in? I was lucky in a way, though, because I had just lost a lot of weight and they stole my thin suits instead of my old fat ones. If my weight had been heading in the other direction, I would have looked like a salami when I went out to work the next day.

Sometimes victims don't look hard enough at what it was that made them a lure to the criminals. Take the victims of the subway system's lush workers. Lush workers are kind of like catfish—bottom feeders on the predator food chain. They don't go after victims who are merely weak, they go after victims who are unconscious. What they hunt for is the drunk who has passed out on a train or platform. The cautious ones carry no weapons and will sit next to their victim and patiently tug at the lining of the drunk's pocket until the wallet or billfold spills out. The others simply slash the pocket open with a razor.

You could guess when the lush workers like to operate: Their peak hours begin just before midnight and end about an hour after the bars close. You'd be wrong, though, if you guessed their favorite feeding grounds coincide with the heaviest concentrations of bars. Instead, they usually camp out at the ends of the lines or at stations where long waits for transfers are common. Those are the places where their victims are most likely to be dead asleep.

For about a year in the late '70s, I worked steady midnights in plainclothes and got to know a number of lush workers: Nate Nappa, Six-Finger Gibson, Teddy Leonard—who dressed in fine suits and a nice light-brown fedora whenever he was working. They were old guys, mostly. Some of them had birth dates from before the turn of the century.

The rule of the little game we had with the lush workers was we had to get them right: We had to catch these guys actually taking property from a victim, not just patting his pockets, which is a lesser crime. It was a challenge, because there aren't many places to hide in an empty subway station, and many of the lush workers knew all the cops on the midnight tour by sight.

One night a young bartender at a Midtown dive started drinking a little bit near the end of his shift. This was something of a habit for him, so when he arrived at a familiar wooden bench along the platform at the Lexington Avenue station, he couldn't resist putting up his feet and dozing. By the time I spotted him, he was already being circled by a lush worker named Harlow Haywood and one of Harlow's pals. Unfortunately, Harlow also spotted me.

Knowing that lush workers take their sweet time casing an opportunity—especially on an open platform—I decided to board the train when it came in and get off at the next stop. Up on 53rd Street, I flagged down a cab and directed the driver right back where I'd come from, raced down the long escalator, and then to the outside edge of the platform, where a line of pillars kept me hidden as I closed in on the bench. When I sprung out into the open, the bartender was still snoozing, but Harlow and his pal had just made their move. They wound up getting one-and-a-half to three years for waiting so long to put their hands in the guy's pockets.

Maybe that experience changed the bartender's life, but I doubt it. He showed up to testify in court wearing a pair of pants whose pocket had been stitched up after a run-in with another lush worker. He was a vic, plain and simple. He could quit riding the subways, take a job at a different bar in a different part of the city, but as long as he traveled alone in the middle of the night in a state of impaired consciousness, he was going to continue to lose his money. He was a zebra; if a lion didn't find him, a crocodile would.

THE MOMENT OF TRUTH

In just about every persons crime, there is a moment when the predator locks onto his target and the rest of the world dissolves. If you've ever watched a cat hunting, it's that moment when the eyes set on a point, the head goes down, the shoulders up, and the animal's muscles roll into a low, slow creep. In the middle of the century, some Harvard scientist discovered that if you put a caged mouse in front of a household cat, a sharp noise from the other side of the room doesn't even register in the cat's brain. It's not that the brain ignores the information sent to it by the eardrum; the electronic impulse sent by the eardrum is blocked before it even races up the nerve. For a few short moments, the victim is the predator's whole world.

Most people would be lucky never to see that fixed look in the eyes of another human being, but for a cop it's the signal to spring. I can't remember how many times I've trailed predators on the streets, waiting for that moment, knowing it'd give me several heartbeats at most to close the ground between us. At the same time, the chase would trip the cat switch in my own head, so that nothing but my target and his intended victim would seem to matter as I fought through a crowd or cut across four lanes of 42nd Street traffic. In a strong-arm robbery, I had to have a hand on his collar at the same instant he threw his arm across the victim's throat. A moment sooner and I'd have no grounds for an arrest. A moment later and the victim was going to get hurt. I've always thought that the Secret Service ought to have its agents spend some time with a pickpocket or robbery squad so they'd learn to recognize that look. It's the same look whether the crook is about to snatch a bag, take down a drunk with a sleeper hold, or point a pistol at the President, but if you've never seen it, you wouldn't know what you were looking for.

Robbery was a very popular sport in New York City for the better part of thirty years. In 1980, when robberies peaked, there were almost 300 reported on the average day. The cops knocked the pace down in the middle of the decade, but lax enforcement let it rise again to about 275 a day in 1990. Maybe the crooks weren't ready to post another record-breaking year, but they were still putting up Babe Ruth-like numbers and, thanks to the explosion of crack, were probably spreading more fear than ever.

The crime that captured the spirit of those years was the wolf-pack robbery. The elements of the crime were simple: A crew of four, five, six—sometimes as many as thirty or forty teenagers—would roam the streets of Manhattan, hunting for a likely victim. Occasionally, a crew had a knife, a box cutter, or even a gun, but most preferred to take down a victim with a sleeper hold and sheer numbers. Fear was their ally, but they could have gotten the job done without it. The victims, if the sleeper hadn't left them unconscious, would be lost in a storm of punches, kicks, and grabbing hands and rarely could remember a face.

I used to walk past the George M. Cohan statue in Times Square and wonder if these were the characters old Georgie Boy was hoping to run into when he wrote the words on the inscription: TELL ALL THE GANG ON 42ND STREET THAT I WILL SOON BE THERE. A lot of the crews who shaped up in the penny arcade under Eighth Avenue or at any of several little parks or traffic islands had an anthem of their own they liked to chant: "Manhattan make it, Brooklyn take it."

The viciousness of some of the attacks I can't explain. It was like watching bluefish in a feeding frenzy—bluefish will keep attacking the bait fish until they're so far past full that they actually puke into the water.

Sometimes the decision to commit a robbery seemed almost to sneak up on the individual members in the wolf packs. They'd set out from "Crooklyn," the Bronx or Queens with some vague urge to "get paid," a craving they might just as easily satisfy by "boosting," or shoplifting, some of the latest gear from Guess or Calvin Klein. But if the mood struck, they'd start wandering the streets in search of potential "herbs," or victims. On one afternoon, they might find nobody they liked. On another, the crew would fall in behind a good prospect until one of them took it upon himself to shout, "Set it off!" My theory is the crews themselves came about almost by accident, that teenagers from the outer-borough neighborhoods started traveling into Manhattan in large numbers to keep from being harassed by crews from other neighborhoods. Often, there was no real leader, and about the only two kids with clearly assigned roles were the one who liked to throw the "yoke," or chokehold, and the smallest one, who would assess the victim's potential for resistance. Invariably, he was known as "Shorty."

As mindless as the wolf-pack robberies sometimes seemed, they came with fixed protocols that every kid in the city seemed to understand. If there was any chance your crew was going to do a robbery, you brought along a "throwaway"—a shirt or jacket that could be pulled on before the crime and tossed aside after it.

Shorty's assignment also followed certain guidelines. He'd approach the victim with some small excuse for conversation, which really was a way to get an up-close reading on whether the target was a good choice, or, in the worst-case scenario, a cop. The most common line was, "Yo—you know what time it is?" Well, the joke was on the vic—it was time to "get paid." But first the prospective victim was likely to reveal two things: what kind of watch he was wearing and whether he was afraid. Sometimes Shorty would open the conversation with an amusing insult or two, making the most of a rare opportunity in his life to act like a tough guy.

The wolf packs' tricks were fairly effective in minimizing their risk of arrest. By a strict headcount, the cops probably had these crooks far outnumbered, but the crooks were winning because we were acting as if the opposite was true. If a cop was lucky enough to make an arrest on a wolf-pack robbery, he'd normally get the one kid for just the single robbery. For the crooks, arrests like those represented acceptable losses. We didn't start to slow the robberies until we realized we would always be outnumbered at the moment of truth unless we learned to work as a team.

In 1985, I was put in command of a new plainclothes unit created for the purpose of running decoys in the trains, meaning my cops were supposed to dress like vics so we could collar anybody who came after them. I had my pick of personnel, so I chose twelve people who were real smart but had no lives, because those are the people who make the best cops. I had Billy Carter in that unit, as well as Jimmy Nuciforo, Vertel Martin, Wayne Richardson, and eight other wonderful character actors. They were Jack's original Broken Toys, and I tried to teach them that it was okay to have a little fun.

I was interested in going after the wolf packs, so we worked mostly from about ten at night until five in the morning. I also banned the traditional ploy of the decoy cop—playing a lone drunk with a dollar hanging out of his pocket. I wanted only the real predators, so we baited our decoys with imitation Rolex watches and gold chains. Any kid out for a lark might be tempted by an unguarded $1 bill, but it takes a different type to snap a chain right off a man's neck.

Before long, we also abandoned the standard of working in four-member teams. Four cops on a subway car weren't enough to guard all the exits, weren't enough to prevent a standoff and weren't enough to allow us any flexibility when it appeared that the crooks had us made. We could get more done and do it more safely if we all worked together; the trick was figuring out ways to hide eight to ten cops on the last car of a subway train.

The last car was always the wildest. On every train, the motorman is stationed in the first car and the conductor in the middle, so any rider interested in smoking pot, drinking wine coolers, or bobbing to Curtis Blow and Doug E. Fresh headed for the back of the train. There the only worries were the occasional appearances of a uniformed officer or of a pair of plainclothes cops who usually looked the part. Joints were palmed and the music went quiet whenever the train made station stops.

With our numbers, we could afford to sacrifice a couple members of our team to the crooks' suspicions. Two members of the team would each wear the "uniform" of the plainclothes cop: windbreaker or Army jacket, sneakers, and a pair of jeans with a pale circle on the rear pocket where handcuffs had worn the denim thin. Billy Carter, blasting a boom box and smoking a joint made of Lipton tea leaves, would start to ridicule them. "Yo—check out Inspector and Mrs. Gadget over here. Gadget, you and the missus ever seen this part of Brooklyn before?" The targets would get ruffled, try a lame comeback, then step off the train at the next stop with the whole car laughing at them. Either that, or they'd arrest Carter for disorderly conduct and take him off the train with them. Now the predators felt free to turn their attention to the vic, who'd be slouched over on another seat in the car. He'd be easy to pick out: Sometimes we'd go so far as to stick a conventioneer's name tag on his lapel—HI! MY NAME IS VIC. Or HI! MY NAME IS HERB. The crooks were always more attentive to the jewelry he was wearing, so we made sure they'd find a 14K or 18K inscribed on the back of the vic's medallion when they checked for authenticity before the snatch.

We had a revolving cast of characters—the blind man, the drunken lawyer, the pizzeria worker, the foreign tourists. But the best were the ones that played against stereotypes of what cops might be willing to do. I'd be a belligerent gay man, sniping with another passenger about some perceived slight. We had mixed-race couples fighting off insults before dozing off in a drunken embrace. I even convinced Billy Courtney, the prettiest guy in the unit, to borrow one of his mother's bras so he could play a hairy-armed transvestite heading home with a nearsighted drunk—anything that helped a predator put aside concerns that one of us might be a cop. Sometimes they just asked us, "Are you guys cops?" and accepted our answer as if a police officer was bound by oath to tell no lies. Other times, we'd jump and yell, "Macy's Security!" Many times, we'd just answer, "Yeah, we're cops," and roar laughing. But a couple of the humps we collared had no excuse for buying our act: In their pockets, they were carrying full-color photos of us that had appeared along with a cover story in *New York* magazine.

Years of uncreative policing must have taught the crooks to overestimate how much they could get away with, because despite our notoriety, our unit enjoyed a front-row view of the predatory instinct at work. One thing we soon figured out was that, at least on the trains, the moment of truth wasn't the best moment to grab a predator. As long as the decoy wasn't in jeopardy, we'd wait until the crook had sat back down and his adrenaline rush had slowed before one of our backups put a hand on him. More often than not, the other predators in the car wouldn't see this initial arrest because their eyes were still locked on the vic.

"Sit back and enjoy the show," we'd tell Crook No. 1.

And the robbing would go on and on.

THE SCAVENGERS

Unlike the predators in the nature shows, the predatory criminal often has more work to do after completing a successful hunt. He's like a lion who can't eat antelope meat until he's dragged it to the chef at his favorite Italian joint: He needs a fence to turn his stolen goods into cash.

For the cops, that extra transaction presents another huge opportunity.

When I was a young cop working Anti-Crime, I used to walk down 47th Street in Manhattan's Diamond District and watch hawkers out on the sidewalk try to steer jewelry thieves into their stores. At the time, the crooks all wore those green snorkel coats with the periscope-style, furry-edged hoods, and they were pouring in from all over the city, carrying broken chains and looking for the best price per pennyweight of gold. (That coat, by the way, should be in the Smithsonian next to Fonzie's leather jacket. Before the eight-ball jacket, the Georgetown jacket, the shearling coat, Triple Phat Goose and North Face took turns as the only coat worth stealing, that cheap vinyl snorkel jacket gave birth to the very notion of modern crookwear.)

Anyway, I figured the jewelers were generating more havoc than any one mugger, so I grabbed one of the chain snatchers out on 47th Street and sat him down for a debriefing. Not only did he give up that he'd done his crimes in the subway, he agreed to work with an undercover and wear a wire so we could send him back into the store and lock up the jeweler who was buying from him. The jewelers always knew where the merchandise was coming from. "You gotta grab the chains with the diamonds," they'd tell the thieves.

The Transit Police eventually began using the same tactic on a routine basis, and within a couple of years, there were noticeably fewer jewelry stores, pawn shops, and bodegas throughout the city that were advertising their predisposition to crime with little signs in the window that said WE BUY GOLD.

Likewise, car theft and car break-ins can be slowed by arresting the crooks who are smuggling stolen parts into the chop shops and by sending them back with a wire and an undercover. Bag snatchings or robberies can be knocked down if the cops go after the rings that specialize in fencing stolen credit cards.

Because people who fence stolen goods usually have some interest in maintaining legitimate businesses, they're probably more inclined than the predators to quit their criminal activities when the cost of continuing them appears too high. Their interest in crime is fairly pure: They want the extra profits. They buy short and sell long. One of the jewelry manufacturers who'd been victimized by the Canal Street robberies seemed to think that absolved the fence of any responsibility. When he was told that the robbery crews were selling all the stolen gems to a jeweler in Queens, he just shrugged. "That's a good businessman," he told Billy Carter. "He's buying the stuff at 10 percent of the value."

In fact, the robbers probably would have taken a few more days off if the crews hadn't found a fence. Billy Carter eventually locked up about twelve guys for those robberies, and along the way he learned that the idea of hitting on the Hasidic salesmen had been passed along from father to son and from older brother to younger brother. The discovery of a fence basically revived the old family tradition.

Ten cents on the dollar may seem like a raw deal, but that was enough to allow members of the crew to plunk down cash for late-model Lexuses they bought from some guy on Hillside Avenue in Queens. Carter tried to tell me that all the rest of the crews' riches was frittered away on clothes, sneakers, and dinners at Red Lobster with their girlfriends. But I knew that a crook is only human, that they can't resist keeping trophies to commemorate their conquests. As young detectives, my partner Jack Cassidy and I once stopped a string of robberies in the subway men's rooms when we collared a guy named Clifford Malone, who thought it was fun to beat his victims unconscious. When we brought him in, he was still wearing the bloody wedding ring he'd taken from his last victim.

If woman's jewelry is involved, the temptation to keep a memento is even greater. A man doesn't bring home a bagful of diamonds and gold without thinking about how appreciative his babe might be if he presented her with a trinket or two from his pile. The same drama is played out at Tiffany's or Cartier every day when the fifty-five-year-old business executive dips into his fortune to buy favor with his young goom. Carter resisted, but I told him he ought to pay a visit to the girlfriends.

Sure enough, one of the crew's girlfriends had about six diamond rings on her fingers and tennis bracelets up to her elbow. Because the manufacturers all stamp their insignia on the inside of the bracelets, we were able to link each one to a particular robbery. As they say at the end of *King Kong,* "Twasn't the machine guns or the airplanes, 'twas beauty killed the beast."

Another kid in the crew had showered gifts on his godmother. When Carter paid her a visit, she answered the door wearing a nightgown and another three diamonds, then asked why he'd bother locking her up for "slum." When he told her each ring was worth about $30,000, she gasped. "And I'm walking around in 'em?" she said. "If I had known they were worth all that I would've bought some furniture and a case of liquor."

She too could have used a fence.

METHODS VERSUS MADNESS

For everything that can be said about the crooks' rational side, there've got to be a few wires loose in the human brain that would explain some of their crankier moments. For every Rondell Wilkins, a kid who transformed himself by hard work and determination into the king of the turnstile breaker-inners, there's the Mankiewicz gang, who lived like vampires in windowless black rooms, only to come out at night in Halloween masks to rob token booths by sticking a spear through the token slot and smashing the bulletproof glass with picks and axes.

Rondell, I had to admire. He understood better than the police department the value of realistic training. One day he took a bag of tools to the quiet end of a quiet subway station in the Bronx and experimented until he figured out the quickest way to spill every token out of a turnstile. With his sharpened screwdriver and his feel for the ebb and flow of every station, he was soon averaging $8,000 a week after fencing the tokens, and a little while before he made his first million, he bought himself some baby gator shoes and a four-finger ring that spelled out TRANSIT in gold letters. His mistake was, he shared his secret with too many other crooks, and finally, when the cost of token thievery reached $2 million a year, the Transit Authority was moved to introduce a more impregnable turnstile. I picked Rondell up on a want—I mean, literally, picked him up. We found him at home in a crack stupor, and I carried him out the door by the back of his belt.

Mankiewicz, I was just as happy not to meet, though I sat on stakeouts for him many times. No predator of the animal kingdom would ever get off like that on generating violence and terror. "Mankie," as we called him, wound up getting shot during one of the stakeouts, and we quickly rounded up the whole crew.

There are plenty of other flashing lights indicating madness plays a big role in many crimes. Every year countless people are murdered by somebody who thinks he or she has been "dissed." A few years ago in New York, a woman torched her boyfriend on the family room sofa because of some offhand compliment he paid to a TV game show hostess. A few years earlier, a drug king tested out his new AK-47 on a passing driver just because the driver's pickup had inadvertently cut the gangster off at an intersection. Most anybody can understand how a small slight can throw a person into a rage, but only a very small percentage of people actually become murderous.

A cop has to respond to the madness with relentless, rational effort. If the academies ever get realistic and begin schooling the average cop thoroughly in "The Art of Catching Crooks," the cop will appreciate how important it is to further his or her education by getting to know as much as possible about the predatory criminals on his or her watch—including their identities, habits, methods, hangouts, and hunting grounds. When issuing a summons or making a stop, the cop should, of course, always run a check to see if the subject is wanted on any outstanding warrants. But whether or not the subject is wanted, the cop should later look up the subject's entire criminal history just to become familiar with it.

Ideally, the cop should also regularly review the photos of all residents of his or her beat who are on parole or probation and all people arrested in the precinct for violent crimes. He or she should get to know the restrictions on individual parolees and probationers, such as the locations they can't go to and the people they can't associate with. Knowing these restrictions can be useful at a later date if the officer wants to stop a parolee or probationer on a violation for the purpose of questioning him about a crime or searching him for a weapon.

I'm afraid, however, there may always be some things the cops will never know about the criminal mind.

It seems, for example, that though there may be no such thing as a "born" criminal, there are a variety of hereditary, environmental, and accidental factors that may contribute to an individual's predisposition to criminal or violent behavior, from low serotonin levels in the brain to high testosterone levels in the bloodstream to repeated exposure to physical or sexual abuse. If our understanding of these factors was more definitive, we'd have a chance to direct resources toward preventing more kids in each generation from turning to crime. For the police, the advantages would be dramatic, even if the number of people predisposed to crime declined by only 5 or 10 percent.

Unfortunately, after centuries of the nature-versus-nurture debate and despite impressive recent advances in brain-imaging technologies, the scientific community isn't very close to a conclusive answer about the sources of criminality. Instead, they're hunkered down in several camps who've each broken off a little piece of the question—and of the funding available for studying it—and are devoting much of their energy to defending their turf and dismissing the claims of all the other camps.

What I'd like to do is bring all the neurologists, anthropologists, sociologists, and psychologists together in one room and ask them to select a large criminal population and initiate a long-term, comprehensive study that would fill a file on each crook with PET scans, CT scans, and MRI scans, with charts tracking the ebb and flow of his or her adrenaline, testosterone, and seratonin levels, and with personal histories related to head injuries, animal torture, left-handedness, itchy feet, and physical or sexual abuse.

But before the study commenced, I would first ask the neurologists, anthropologists, sociologists, and psychologists to run the same battery of tests on themselves.

Maybe then we'd understand why human beings are so territorial that they won't work together—even on a matter of vital public interest—unless somebody forces them to do it.

FOUR

TRENCHCOAT WARFARE

Reeducating the World's Greatest Detectives

In the predawn darkness of a cold morning in early 1994, three cars pulled up in front of a modest, glazed-brick building in the most dangerous section of Brooklyn. Inside that building was a sign:

WELCOME TO THE 75TH PRECINCT—HOME OF THE WORLD'S GREATEST DETECTIVES.

Sonny Archer, Eddie Norris, and Jimmy Nuciforo didn't bother to go in and check out the competition. I had sent them to the Seven-Five on a mission, and they knew they couldn't show their faces again at headquarters until they had collared at least 30 of the roughly 300 thugs living in the precinct who were wanted for violent crimes.

Norris, my protégé at the time, was the ranking officer of the three. He'd served as commander of a detective squad in Manhattan and chief investigator at City Hall's Department of Investigation, and I'd known him since I was a uniform sergeant at Times Square and he was a young city cop working 42nd Street. Eventually, he would inherit my deputy commissioner post, and together with Louie Anemone drive the department to crime levels far lower than were achieved during my two-year tenure.

Nuciforo had been with me since I was a plainclothes sergeant. During my whole career, I've given two rings away. Norris got my deputy commissioner ring in 1997; Nuciforo got my detective ring a decade earlier, each for the same reason.

The student had surpassed the teacher; "Grasshopper" had snatched the pebble from my hand.

Of the three, Sonny Archer was the most humble about the talent he had, but he was the kind of detective who made other members of the squad say, "Slow down, you're making us look bad." Besides that, he was the best tracker I've ever known, and what I needed most out in the Seven-Five at that moment was a tracker.

I wasn't interested in showing up anybody in the Seven-Five squad. In fact, of all the squads in the city that displayed signs claiming to be the "world's greatest," few if any others cracked as many cases as the detectives in East New York. But with our first winter at headquarters soon melting into spring, it was time that every squad in the city understood that even the department's very best were forgetting some fundamentals. For the department as a whole to become a powerful crime-fighting organization, it needed the detectives to operate at all times with two thoughts in mind:

1. Every case is a big case.
2. The initial arrest is not enough.

Downtown, the numbers I had been pulling out of the chiefs and the data keepers were telling me that throughout the city, the detective squads weren't earning superlatives in all aspects of their game. Their record on fugitive apprehension was just one example. In the previous two years alone, at least 12,000 people who had been positively identified as the perpetrators of violent crimes in New York City hadn't been arrested for those crimes. These crimes weren't page-one material, so the suspects, instead of being hunted down and thrown in the poky, had suffered no further inconvenience than that their names were entered onto index cards and filed in drawers marked WANTED. In the 5.6 square miles of the Seven-Five, which had logged a record 125 homicides in 1993, having 300 of these characters running around free was like declaring open season on more killings.

Sending in my three musketeers, or Maple-ettes, as they were called by their more polite detractors, was one way I knew we could show the world's greatest detectives that even though they weren't quite as good as they thought they were, they had no idea how magnificent they could be.

For years, of course, the whole New York Police Department had lived off the good name won for it by the stars in the detective division who handled the big press cases and who truly are the best in the world.

The amount of press attention on a case is directly correlated to its chances of being solved. Press cases everywhere get a lot of police attention. Large task forces are created, photos and pictures are made, leads are followed up on; every forensic test imaginable is done. The press attention itself, meanwhile, helps bring in additional evidence and witnesses and ensures there'll be no quit in the investigation. As a result, high-profile cases everywhere enjoy a very high "solve rate." What distinguished the NYPD was that its stars could solve any ten big cases simultaneously at any given time.

Unfortunately, there were 1,946 murders, 5,933 shootings, and 86,000 robberies in New York in 1993, and the NYPD detectives, with another 4,000 people wearing the gold or silver badge, didn't have a very strong bench.

In our first several weeks at the NYPD, I liked to ask police buffs how many arrests they thought the average New York City detective made in a year. "Seventy-five to a hundred," some would guess. "Maybe a hundred and twenty." In reality, the average NYPD detective made fewer than half a dozen arrests in 1993. Aside from the stars, the myth was doing most of the work.

Celebrated cases capture the public's interest, spread fear, and polish up the detective bureau's reputation, but the average citizen has a much greater chance of being murdered, shot, stabbed, robbed, or raped by a noncelebrity criminal. Unfortunately, in most cities, the everyday murders, robberies, rapes, assaults, burglaries, thefts, and auto thefts are often assigned to poorly led second-stringers who simply go through the motions of their investigations—if they even know what the motions are. Not surprisingly, these detectives are often unsuccessful, but even worse, they are often uncaring about the consequences of their failures.

Nationwide, arrests are made in only one in every four robberies and one in every seven burglaries or auto thefts. People even get away with murder half the time, so it's almost surprising that more of us don't become crooks.

Part of the myth of the detectives' expertise has its roots in the actual demands of the job. Reading a crime scene, for example, is an art that may require a detective with no more than three weeks of specialized training to exhibit a solid understanding of anatomy, ballistics, botany, blood splatters and other body fluids, chemistry, computer science, criminal law, fingerprints, forensic anthropology, manmade and natural fibers, physics, photography, telecommunication technologies, toxicology, and even, in a couple of serial-killing investigations, the signs of the zodiac.

In larger departments like the NYPD, a special crime scene unit takes the photographs and gathers materials that will be taken back to a lab for analysis, but the detective who catches the case has to know enough to run the whole show. A smart detective knows the technicians can't be trusted to take particular photos or samples they haven't been specifically instructed to take, the fingerprint division can't be trusted to find fingerprint matches even when they have them, and the bosses, especially the bigshots, can't be trusted to keep from traipsing through the victim's blood or kicking a spent bullet shell down a sewer.

With all the attention a crime scene demands, detectives in the latter half of the twentieth century may have convinced themselves that science and forensic evidence solved all crimes. Until the spell was broken by defense tactics in the O. J. Simpson murder trial and subsequent revelations about the Pinocchios employed at the FBI's esteemed national crime lab, there was a widespread belief throughout law enforcement that nothing else could touch scientific evidence for its power to win convictions in jury trials. Whether or not that was the cause, detective bureaus everywhere became complacent about some fundamental tools and tactics of the trade that detectives had been using to solve crimes long before any fingerprint ever brought a killer to justice.

In every police department I've seen, the complacency bred failures in several fundamental aspects of the detectives' work:

- They didn't work each case systematically.
- They didn't pay enough attention to pattern crimes.
- They didn't get enough out of interrogations and interviews (which meant they also weren't following up on the new leads that should come out of those conversations).
- And—in the Seven-Five and everywhere else—they didn't track down all suspects who'd been successfully identified.

It would be foolish for any police force to throw away the advantages of having a reliable, professional lab, but if the tasks above were all performed well, every crime lab in the country could be closed and crime would still go down, because attention to the other fundamentals transforms the detectives from a bureau that chases criminals one by one into a team that is spreading a net the criminals can't escape.

Norris, Nuciforo, and Archer would be demonstrating how one corner of that net ought to be tied down.

But we had many other repairs to make in that net before we could honestly say that the detectives of the NYPD had learned to treat every one of their cases as if it were a press case.

The neglect of fundamentals began with the NYPD detectives where you might think most cases end—in the interrogation room. The detectives weren't interviewing many prisoners, they weren't getting many statements, and even when they did get statements, they settled for far less information than they should have.

In early '94, Chief of Patrol Louie Anemone, Chief of Detectives Joe Borelli, and I began demanding that all prisoners be debriefed, and we soon tied that order to a number of objectives we expected the detectives and other cops to pursue during each and every interview.

Looking back, my only regret is that we used the word "debrief" at all. Astronauts and foreign emissaries are "debriefed"; the police shouldn't be afraid to say what they do with people who are arrested for crimes is an "interrogation."

So for every interrogation, here's what we wanted the detectives to come away with:

- an inculpatory statement about the crime in question
- inculpatory statements about any other crimes the suspect may have committed in the past
- the identities and whereabouts of his or her accomplices
- physical evidence—like bloody clothes, stolen property, drugs, or weapons—that might strengthen the case against the suspect
- information about other crimes or about other contraband—like drugs, guns, and stolen property—that the suspect only knows about. Did he know the shooter in last weekend's drive-by? Could he name a spot where they could go at that very moment and buy an illegal gun? What about crack houses? Chop shops? Fences for stolen TVs?

The reasoning behind that final objective was as old as policing itself: The bad guys know who the other bad guys are and what they're up to. They hang around in the same places, they boast to each other about their exploits, and they're almost always in the market for new accomplices and new opportunities.

Initially, the squad commanders tried to tell us that juvenile criminals might be easy enough to crack but the hardened criminals didn't talk. When attention turned to their debriefing of juveniles, they said those interviews never came to anything because there always had to be a parent or guardian present. The squad commanders couldn't have it both ways. Having taken hundreds of statements myself and having watched the young detectives I trained learn the trade and then win thousands more, I knew that 99 percent of the crooks would fold quicker than the Iraqi Republican Army if our detectives were trained and motivated. Even cops who are caught up in corruption scandals sing like canaries in the interrogation rooms, and they're supposed to know better.

The way I see it, there is no acceptable failure rate in the interrogation room. Everybody talks. If a suspect doesn't talk, it's the fault of the detective doing the interview. Everybody has some button inside. Everybody can be convinced that talking is beneficial. Most people have a need to tell somebody at least something of the truth, whether it's because they're sorry or they want to brag about their outlaw adventures, and those who don't tell the truth at least give the detectives a false statement that can help the case when it's proven false.

Either we had scores of squad commanders who didn't have the background to know when their detectives were putting them on or we had almost 4,000 detectives who didn't know when the criminals were putting them on. I suspect it was a lot of both.

The detectives might have fooled me too if all the people I'd locked up during my career hadn't taught me better. A kid named David Gunn admitted to me he'd used a gun. James Innocent told me he wasn't. A cop shooter wrote me a statement when I made him believe we had trace evidence tying him to the gun. A guy who'd raped a woman on the L line in Brooklyn confessed after I'd prayed with him. A security guard who'd crippled a police officer in a hit-and-run accident turned himself in after I'd paid him a visit at his job and fooled him into thinking the case against him couldn't be shot down even with the Smith & Wesson he had strapped to his hip.

To make the point that it's always possible to get statements, all I ever had to say around the NYPD were three words: "Central Park Jogger." In one of the city's most notorious crimes of the past quarter-century, a young woman jogging in the park early one April morning was raped, beaten, and left to die by a gang of teenagers who had apparently spent the entire night terrorizing random victims. Within forty-eight hours, five young men had confessed on videotape, each with one or two parents looking on, to participating in the attack. Though there was no physical evidence or eyewitnesses who could place them at the scene of the crime, four of the teenagers were convicted and the fifth pleaded guilty on a reduced charge.

To prove my point with a bunch of nondetectives, I once accepted a barroom challenge to take on somebody who'd won even more confessions than me. I started in by challenging him about his background. "I know what kind of kid you were," I said. "You had the big box of crayons, right? Your mother sent you to school with money in your socks, so you'd still have enough left to buy lunch after the bullies were through with you." Within about ten minutes, I had him on the record for several serious juvenile offenses, including a few arson fires. When he realized what he had said, Father Jerry was one embarrassed priest.

How does a detective learn to do that? Police departments do provide instruction in the techniques of interrogation, but like any art, it requires practice. Young detectives learn by doing, by observing, and by being observed. Screwing up a few interrogations is part of the learning process, and it helps the young detective if one of the experienced interrogators he's listening to and observing is a boss who's still in the game. Because many departments don't have enough of those kinds of bosses around, they hire interrogation experts who'll just come in and tell old war stories (like I'm doing now). There's nothing wrong with hiring the experts, but the department should insist that they perform a few real interrogations while the trainees watch from behind a one-way mirror. Then the guru should sit in while the trainees do their own "live" interviews. If the experts refuse to accept those conditions of their employment, they're fakers. Don't hire them.

Experienced interrogators should be spot-checked in a similar manner to root out habits that are counterproductive or that may cause problems when the case goes to trial. In many of the cities I've worked since leaving the NYPD, detectives would read each prisoner his Miranda warnings in a crowded holding cell and then ask the prisoner if he wanted to go into another room and talk. That's a fatal mistake. And the prisoner is usually smart enough to know that if everybody in that cell sees him agree to talk, he's the one most likely to wind up dead. A good detective establishes a one-on-one rapport with a suspect before ever bringing up the Miranda warnings and then the first question related to the case.

Another advantage of having a boss engaged in the interrogation process is that the boss can act as a closer in winning the subjects' cooperation. Crooks, like everybody else, have egos, and they like to feel they've made their deal with the top guy. Car salesmen play the same trick every time they tell a customer, "Let me talk to the boss to see what else we can do for you."

Ego also makes a crook open to the suggestion that he's the perfect guy to go undercover so the cops can take down his pals. Transit and Queens detectives once took out a violent robbery crew by telling one of the hoods they'd foot the bill for a "hooky jam" if he'd host the party and bring back Polaroids and video footage of all his outlaw pals. The crooks not only accepted their buddy's invitation, they posed for him with their machine guns.

Ego, finally, is probably the main reason that the worst thing a detective can do in an interrogation room is try to out-tough the subject the way everybody loves to see it done on NYPD Blue. Forget that smacking somebody around is illegal and just plain wrong, it's also the quickest way to ruin the chances of getting a statement of any kind. Look at it this way: Most of the people the cops arrest are built like Rocky Balboa and are about ten times tougher than we are. To take a beating is nothing to them. Violence or the threat of it only causes them to shut down—or worse, laugh. Either way, it's a horror show.

During the interrogations I did, I wanted the suspect to feel like there were no walls between him and me, that nothing he'd done is so horrible that I couldn't empathize. I've laughed, joked, and, as in the case with the subway rapist, prayed with suspects to get statements. The most serious crimes are usually the hardest for people to admit. A killer might not admit to murder, for example, but he'll admit to firing bullets in the direction of the victim—maybe claiming the gun went off by accident or that he was acting in self-defense. A rapist might be too ashamed to accept full responsibility, but he may be willing to blame his crime on a sickness if he's assured that many other men fight off similar violent impulses every day. Detectives should let the suspect admit less than the worst about himself, then go for the complete confession.

Many times, the cops can also play on the crook's urge to always be getting over. If they've grabbed somebody on a robbery, the patter might go like this:

"Look, we don't really care about this one—we all know you did this one. But how many other robberies have you done? Twenty? Thirty? Because if you've done thirty, you're going to be in thirty times more trouble than you are now."

"No, no, man. This was the only one—the only one."

That's his first inculpatory statement.

"Then why did your buddy say you were there at least two other times?"

"I was there, but I didn't do the robberies."

"You mean you were the lookout?"

"No, man, no. I wasn't no lookout."

"Well, if the cops were to come by, you would have yelled, 'Look out!'—right? Where do you think the word 'lookout' comes from?"

The suspect laughs.

"How much did they pay you for that?"

"Uh, nothing—five, ten bucks each time."

Now he's in for at least three robberies. Even then, he'll think he's outsmarted the cops because he hasn't admitted to a dozen or two others. In fact, he's already given himself up as a repeat felon.

But I'm not done yet.

"C'mon now, you didn't get those Air Jordans with five bucks. Then again, you might have offed some toothless, old Run-D.M.C. groupie for those."

If you can get them to laugh, you'll get a statement. That's always true. In fact, I'm almost dying for my chance to try this joke on a Hannibal Lecter type: Two cannibals are snacking on a clown when one turns to the other and says, "You taste something funny?"

With the guys, if you talk about sex, they die. I don't know why, but they fold.

You'll say, "Let's forget about all this cop shit, we'll talk about that later. Let's talk some more about them bitches. How many you got right now who are giving you blowskis?"

It's all right if they think you're crazy, or a "freakazoid," as they used to say. A little later, you'll say, "A man like you getting all that action has gotta be gettin' paid. So how many of these other robberies you done? Fifteen? Twenty?"

When interrogating a crew of two or more crooks, the detective should always lead the weakest one away to the interview room first—never the leader. The followers may be afraid of the leader, but usually they're also a little bit jealous. Letting them make the first statement gives them power they've never had, and if they feel the leader has ever slighted them—as Franco did about his booth-robbing bosses McClean and Capone—they'll be quick to rat their leaders out.

Not everybody is going to give up the previous crimes just like that. The predicate felon might need a sales pitch. If he can be convinced he's already caught dead to rights on one felony, he may think he's doing himself a favor by talking if I promised to tell the district attorney's office about any cooperation he offers on this and other crimes.

I always made good on such promises, sharing with the assistant district attorney everything the suspect had shared with me. Of course, I hadn't ever promised that the charges would be dropped or reduced—that would be illegal. I have, however, won more than one statement after making a written promise to the interviewee that we wouldn't arrest him that day. We'd spring a guy like that at 11 P.M.—and pick him up again an hour later.

Every detective has a favorite story about winning a statement with a bald lie. Mine involved a big monster of a guy who'd banged me up pretty good when I grabbed him at his home in Brooklyn after another member of his robbery crew had given him up. He had walked from Brooklyn to Manhattan to Brooklyn that night in an attempt to elude us, and now that we had him, he was determined not to talk.

One of my detectives almost broke him down, but not quite. As squad commander, I was the closer.

I was just beginning to get the prisoner warmed up when I suddenly remembered the suppository I was carrying around in my pocket because of a hemorrhoid. I pulled it out and showed it to him.

"Look at your Uncle Jack," I said. "How good do you feel that an old man like me is bleeding out of his ass because you beat me up? How good do you feel that I've got to stick this thing up my rectum?"

He just lifted his head real slowly and said, "I'm sorry, Jack. I didn't mean to hurt you." And then he wrote up a detailed statement admitting he had been the main guy in the robbery earlier that night.

Another time I told a suspect he had not only left his fingerprints on a gun we'd picked up, he'd also left his sweat glands.

"Sweat glands don't lie," I told him.

The minute we left the interrogation room the young cop who was sitting in on the interview said to me, "Boss, you want me to take the gun in for the sweat gland test?"

Like a lot of people, he had fallen into the trap of assuming that cops are honor-bound to speak nothing but the truth. In the interrogation room, we can lie all we want about evidence, as long as we're dead straight about the lies we told when we're asked about the interrogation in the courtroom.

Once the suspect has made an oral statement, the detective has to memorialize it. The best way to do this is to have the suspect write the statement out in his own words on a page topped by the Miranda warnings, with a line or box next to each warning where the suspect can write in his initials. If the suspect balks because he doesn't write well, he should be encouraged to try anyway. If the detective has to do the writing, he or she should include intentional errors and ask the suspect to cross out and initial any changes. This can prove to a jury that the suspect is able to read.

Only when the written statement is done should the detective or assistant district attorney try to get the statement on audiotape or videotape. A video can make all the difference in winning a conviction, but there's a slim possibility that a suspect who was willing to give a written statement will freeze up when the camera's turned on. More often, the suspect warms to the idea that he's worth so much attention.

It can't be left unsaid that of all the tools an interrogator can use to win a good statement, nothing beats having some of the truth already in hand. The more information a detective has, the more creative, authoritative, and effective he or she can be. That doesn't mean a suspect should be sent home without an interview if the cops don't know everything about him. It means a detective has to do everything in his or her power to learn what can be learned about the subject and the crime before the interrogation begins.

From experience, I know what a difference that can make. Bear with me: This is another story that involves a priest.

I was working at Times Square one night when an Episcopalian priest from Westchester County walked into the district. He was carrying a photo of a twelve-year-old boy. "I'm his guardian and he's a runaway," the priest said. "Perhaps you'll be able to find him."

He was right about that. Three days later, I found the kid hanging out in Times Square and listened to the story he told about why he always ran away. I called the detective squad, but they didn't want to touch the case. So I took down every detail myself and called the priest in Rye, which is usually about a twenty minute drive away. About five minutes later, he was sitting with me at Columbus Circle.

"You know, Father," I began, "as happens in a lot of these cases, the child is making allegations."

The priest's gaze was steady. He was in his mid-thirties—just a little older than me.

"Now I know I look like a pretty young sergeant to you," I said. "And the thing is, I was an even younger detective. And the reason I was a real young detective is because I was real smart, and I caught a lot of crooks. And I know when someone's lying, Father—I want you to understand that.

"Father," I said, "the young man is telling me about numerous times he engaged in sex with you, and he has given me specific times and locations. And before I go into his story further, Father, let me explain to you that I intend to go back to every location the young man has talked about, and I'm going to interview people there, and I'm going to show them photos—don't worry, Father, these are photos where you've got your clothes on. But some of those people I interview might wind up calling the newspapers—I really don't know what they're going to do."

As I kept talking, my mind was racing back to all the mornings back at Holy Child of Jesus when one of the priests would walk into our classroom and the nun would bow down as if JEE-sus himself was among us. I had no interest in seeing the last flicker of that belief go dark, but I wanted this man's crimes to stop. Before reciting the Miranda warnings, I offered him just a little solace.

"As you well know, Father," I said, "confession is good for the soul."

The priest sat motionless.

"Everything the young man described," he said, "is true." And with that, he took a pad of paper I offered him and produced a five-page written statement that enumerated his crimes in excruciating detail.

Later, after we had been hanging out downtown for several hours, waiting for his arraignment, he tried to turn the tables on me.

"Jack," he said, "you've been away from the church for a while. Would you like me to hear your confession?"

If he had asked me the same question during the interrogation, I don't know what I would have said. But with his statement already in hand, I felt I could now risk creating a little distance between us. So I told him, as plainly as I could, that the nuns at Holy Child of Jesus had somehow impressed upon me the idea that any guy who'd been blowing little boys was probably not in a sufficient state of grace to absolve me of my sins.

Whether or not the nuns truly did deserve any of the credit, I owed that one to good preparation.

Since about 1988, when I was promoted to lieutenant, I've spent a fair amount of time coming up with systems to make cops, collectively, more effective. Though some of these systems weren't designed solely with detective squads in mind, they established some of the standards for intelligence gathering, analysis, and the type of systematic, relentless effort detectives should be held to.

Most police chiefs wouldn't even think of asking more from their detectives. Most chiefs were never detectives themselves, so they view the detectives as overblown egos dressed in crummy suits who solve the big cases with a combination of blue smoke, mirrors, and the assistance of the press. Though the precinct or district commanders often operate with insufficient resources and limited authority, the chiefs look to their patrol commanders to deal with crime and look upon the detective bureau as almost a necessary evil.

Napoleon, though a brilliant general, felt the same way about the admirals in his navy, putting all his most gifted commanders in the army and leaving the seas to lesser men. But what happened? He paid dearly for his bad attitude about the navy at Trafalgar, where the British navy under Admiral Nelson decimated the French and Spanish combined fleets and ended any hope Napoleon had of further world conquest.

In policing, the chiefs' bias against detectives has meant the recruitment, selection, and training of both the detectives and their commanders receive scant attention. As a result, there is often nobody in a position of authority who knows enough about detective work to make the detective squads more effective or to hold them accountable for results.

Take the way a typical robbery is handled by detectives in a typical American police department:

The call comes in to 911. One or two patrol officers in a radio car respond to the victim's call and take down a cursory description of the event. If these two cops are unusually sharp, they also get a phone number for the victim and type it accurately onto the report that'll be forwarded to the detective squad. The patrol cops may be friendly; they may be rude, but either way they're likely to offer a grim prognostication before leaving. "There's probably not much we can do," they say. "Even if we do catch this guy, it'll probably take a year and a half to go to trial, it'll cost you some time off work, and he'll be back on the street a few days later anyway."

A day to one week later, that robbery report finally hits the desk of a detective. Even that may be expecting too much. When I arrived in New Orleans, the detectives there didn't even look at the report because they considered themselves too overwhelmed by other work to investigate robberies. In most cities, however, the detective will at least dial the number for the complainant that's listed on the initial report.

If fortune is smiling on the case, the phone number is correct and the complainant picks up. But that's unlikely. Detectives generally spend more time trying to track down complainants than they do trying to track down crooks. Later, when the two parties do hook up, the detective asks if the complainant might come in and look at some photos, though he neglects to mention how out of date the photo books are. Or, if showing photos is too much trouble, the detective simply goes over the description of the perp that the complainant already gave to the uniformed cops and promises to call back someday if the squad ever happens to stumble upon a robber who fits the description. Finally, before the good-byes, there's the same discouraging prognostication as before. In the mind of the detective, the work on the case is done.

That was the way robberies were handled in the NYPD and Transit Police in the late 1980s, when robberies in New York were surging again after falling back from 1980's all-time high of 107,000. Every month, some 100 subway riders experienced firsthand the rise of the wolf-pack robbery, a crime we at Transit defined for statistical purposes as any robbery involving four or more perpetrators. Transit's decoy squad had been disbanded in 1986 amid a media-driven controversy about the quality of arrests made by other plainclothes units, and the department had fallen into total retreat.

Before robbery's comeback, the NYPD had made some headway against pattern robberies beginning in 1981 with the establishment of the Robbery Identification Program. Though the idea may sound old-fashioned, the principal weapon of detectives in the RIP units were the photo books of robbery recidivists that the program put together so that victims could sit down and finger their assailants. Even so, the RIP photo books were usually outdated and incomplete, and even successful identifications left loose ends everywhere: Detailed statements weren't taken, accomplices weren't pursued, and if the primary suspect wasn't found where the detectives expected him to be, he wasn't hunted down either.

In September 1988, I was put in charge of a new squad called the Repeat Offender Robbery Strike Force, where I had twenty-four cops and four sergeants, many of whom had worked with me in the decoy squad. Our assignment was to identify pattern robberies, set up in the field, and catch crooks in the act. This meant there were two significant restrictions on our work. First, in order to avoid turf battles with the Transit detective squads, we weren't allowed to do any investigations into robberies that had already taken place. Second, we were starting out with no system in place to tell us where and when we might find the crooks we were supposed to be catching. In short, to be successful, we had to learn to make cases by paying close attention to a couple aspects of the job that most detectives don't even think about. To put ourselves in a position to make arrests, we had to get better at crime analysis. To make our cases against the crooks as strong as they could be, we had to strive to provide every victim of a robbery with efficient, one-stop service.

That policy ought to be a departmentwide commitment. The police ought to be able to promise crime victims "same-day service," just as Jiffy Lube promises to do every oil change in ten minutes and Domino's guarantees delivery of every pizza in half an hour.

In that ideal scenario, the first cops on the scene of a crime—whether they're patrol officers or detectives—become marketing representatives for the entire department. They have to sell the victim and witnesses on the idea that it might be worth a quick ride in the patrol car to see if the robber is still in the area and certainly worth a trip to the station house to talk to one of the detectives. "Give us a chance," they should be confident enough to say. "We might be able to catch this crook today."

The detectives at the station house have to be, as we know, well prepared to carry out the next steps in the case. For one thing, since the best chance of getting a positive identification on the robber is that the victim or witness can pick out a photo, the detectives had better have sets of photos that are complete and up to date.

You'd be surprised how few departments maintain decent photo files and how infrequently those that have good photo files bring victims and witnesses in to view them. Mug books date back to at least 1880, when New York's Chief Byrnes stitched together his "rogues' gallery," but more than a century later the department cared so little about mug books that it took two years for parolee portraits to make it from headquarters to the precincts. Newark went four years without distributing new photos to the precincts because the department had an asbestos problem in its darkroom. The New Orleans police had almost no photos at all at the district station houses.

Today every police department should invest in a computerized system like Kodak's Photo Imaging, which keeps all mug shots in a central file server that can be accessed from every station house and can sort the photos using selected information about the suspect—including age, appearance, method of operation, and the location of previous arrests. A good system of sharing Polaroids would do, though that would be more expensive in the long run. The important thing is that every station house have up-to-date photos on file at least for everybody with an arrest record—including new parolees and former juvenile offenders—who lives or has been collared in that precinct.

In the interviews with the victim or witness, the detectives want detail. What exactly did the suspect or suspects look like? Any tattoos? Scars? How about their M.O.—what exactly did they say when they put the gun to you? Where were you coming from? Did the robber have some way of knowing you had money on you? What exactly was stolen? Did you have any engraving on that ring? Do you have a serial number written down somewhere for that cell phone?

In old cop movies like *Detective Story* and *The Naked City,* the detectives compiled stolen-property lists so they could make a case if the stolen property popped up at a pawnshop or was found in the possession of a burglary or robbery suspect. In New York, a serial rapist who eventually became the prime suspect in attacks on fifty-one women between 1993 and 1999 was caught only after police reviewed the records of a Bronx pawnshop and found that distinctive necklaces belonging to one of the rape victims had been pawned there a day after she and a friend were attacked. Pawn records and stolen-property lists should be compiled and compared daily or at least weekly using computer databases, but in the vast majority of departments, both of those chores are lost arts.

Throughout the interview of the complainant, meanwhile, the detective should always keep one thought in the back of his or her mind: Is this part of a pattern?

If there's a chance of finding the crooks out on the street or back at his watering hole, the detectives should go back out with the victim or witness at a time and day when the suspects are likely to be seen again.

If not, the best thing the detective can do is carefully memorialize the victim or the witness's answers.

But fattening up the case file doesn't catch the crooks if the file is just going to sit in a drawer. The cops need a system that can put all the information to work.

One night soon after the creation of the Robbery Strike Force, I sat down at the River Cafe, under the Brooklyn Bridge, to consider the problem while gazing out on a million-dollar view of Lower Manhattan and the Statue of Liberty. This time my elixir was a Nureyev, which was a vodka-and-champagne cocktail the great dancer and playboy had come up with while hanging out at the bar with Andy Warhol.

In the Decoy Squad, there'd been many times during the interrogations when the crooks we'd caught doing bag or chain snatchings made inculpatory statements for past crimes we hadn't even known about. It would happen sometimes just because we'd pressed the right buttons. But there was no doubt we could have tied the suspects into even more crimes if we'd had enough information about past crimes to question the suspects closely on the ones that looked like their work.

To focus the field operations of the Robbery Strike Force, we needed the same information organized in a way that would help us decide who to look for and where and when we might find them. It had been easy enough for police to recognize a "chronic condition"—meaning a location where crime is high because the conditions for crime are particularly favorable—but it wasn't always easy to spot a "pattern"—meaning a series of crimes committed by a single individual or crew. A guy dressed like Captain America might do only two robberies before every tabloid reader in the city got wise to the pattern, but a kid in an eight-ball jacket with a silver gun might do thirty-five along one subway line without anybody ever noticing a link between the crimes.

How could we spot him sooner?

Twenty thousand years earlier, some other cave dweller had scratched lines onto an ox bone to mark the passage of time because he was trying to anticipate the seasonal migration of bison, reindeer, or salmon. By doing so, he invented writing. All I needed to come up with now was a crook-tracking system that could isolate an individual shark or pack of sharks as they swam through the world's largest subway system and track their movements by location as well as time.

I called my solution "The Charts of the Future."

In our little office in Lower Manhattan, the charts surrounded us. They ran from floor to ceiling and around desks and chairs across fifty-five feet of wall space. If you spun your head around like an owl, you could see every one of the 430 stations in the system represented and at which ones the different train lines intersected.

I assigned a code number to each of six categories of robbery. One was a gun robbery, two was a knife robbery, three a strong-arm robbery, four a wolf-pack robbery, five a bag snatching, and six a booth robbery. For time of occurrence we used colored pencils, with, for example, green representing a robbery committed between 4 P.M. and midnight and blue indicating a robbery committed during the midnight shift. Next to each entry was room for a brief description of the perpetrator or perpetrators and their method of operation.

The charts gave us our marching orders. A streak of green twos would light up across seven or eight stations, so we'd look closer and see five of them were committed on different nights but all within the same three-hour span by a pair of male blacks, one nicknamed "Drac." "OK," the charts were saying, "go out and get 'em."

Sure enough, when we spread out across the same stations during those same hours, we'd eventually spot a guy missing four front teeth, and if we followed him and his pal, we'd be able to grab them as they moved on another victim. Later, when we finally got our own detectives assigned to the unit, they'd consult "The Charts of the Future" again before doing an interrogation, pull out the pertinent files, and the crook would wind up giving up several other robberies.

In the past when these characters had been arrested, they had been pleading out to petit larceny and they'd be out robbing again in two to three months. With our charts now in the game, they were being sent away for heavy time.

To the detectives, the charts demonstrated why some often-neglected aspects of the trade deserved greater attention. If they gathered detailed information through thorough interviews of victims and witnesses, if they complied and analyzed that information by using the charts, if they ran background checks on the perps, and if they pressed for statements in the interrogation room, they could solve a lot more crimes and send crooks away for longer stretches of time.

In most police departments, unfortunately, there is no set of standardized procedures detectives are expected to follow on each of their cases. In Newark, New Orleans, and Philadelphia, I've recommended using a series of checklists, one of which has to be included in every case file. These enable the squad commanders to see whether their detectives are touching all the bases on every investigation or apprehension, from sitting in on the autopsy in a homicide to running checks through all the proper computer data systems for a carjacking.

Some of the detectives whine that a checklist is an insult to their intelligence and professionalism, but you know what? Airline pilots, who are highly trained professionals paid to perform the same task every day, fill out checklists before every takeoff. They do it because it saves lives. If you looked in the files of all the investigations that have gone cold, you'd find missing steps were common to most of them. In the file for a shooting, for instance, a patrol cop might have dutifully jotted down the license plates of all cars parked within two blocks of the crime, but nobody ever bothered to run the plates to see who owned them. One car might belong to a violent felon from across town; another might be a car stolen earlier that night that could open up a whole new avenue of investigation. In New York City, the "Son of Sam" serial killer was finally caught because of a parking ticket left on his car at the site of one of the slayings.

Detective work may be a game that rewards individual creativity, but systematic effort creates more opportunities to use that kind of individual talent.

And just as there are systematic approaches to identifying suspects before they're caught and to interrogating them after they're caught, there is a systematic way to track them down when they've gone missing.

On the morning Sonny Archer, Eddie Norris, and Jimmy Nuciforo pulled up in front of Brooklyn's Seventy-Fifth Precinct, it was time to close the circle.

My instructions to Norris, Archer, and Nuciforo had been brief. One minute they were sitting behind desks at One Police Plaza. The next minute they were heading for East New York under the stipulation that I was not to see their faces again until they'd grabbed their thirtieth fugitive.

As I've said, Archer is a great tracker—good enough to know that he had to sneak right back into One Police Plaza while I wasn't looking so he could do the job right. That's because the hunt for fugitives always begins on paper or a computer screen. In New York City, there were nineteen computerized data systems that a detective might use to track down a crook. For various reasons we would have to address, Archer was one of the rare detectives who knew how to make most of those systems talk.

In the rest of the detective bureau and in cities since, too many cases hit a dead end when the detectives or a court-administered warrant squad check the most recent address listed in the suspect's file and discover that their fugitive hasn't lived there in years or—would you believe?—had made up a street number. In New Orleans, 40,000 people were wanted for crimes or for skipping court appearances and the squad commanders tried to tell me the detectives couldn't do much about the crooks who'd lied. "Is that right?" I'd say. "The crooks aren't playing fair?"

The computer hunt would begin with a name. In many New York City precincts, there wouldn't even be a photo attached to the want card. That meant even if the precinct got a gift from heaven in the form of a phone tip on the location of one of their fugitives, the responding officers wouldn't be able to pick the guy out of a crowd when they got there. A more common lapse in the system made it possible that a fugitive could be arrested in the same precinct where he was wanted, but the squad wouldn't hear about the collar until days after he'd been fingerprinted downtown and released.

Archer's first rule is that he tries to never hit the street without a photo to go with the name. That precaution eliminates the possibilities that he arrests the wrong man, or finds himself talking to his man and doesn't know it. Data from the computer systems begins to fill out the rest of the portrait.

When a tracker goes out, he needs to be able to tell who's lying to him, so he should have a pretty good idea of who the fugitive is. Who are the fugitive's parents? His brothers and sisters? Does he have a wife or girlfriend? Does he have children by an old girlfriend? What kind of criminal activity has he been involved in before? Who were his accomplices? Who was he in prison with? Who'd he call the last time he was locked up? Where has he lived? Where does he hang out? Does he drive a car?

In the NYPD of early 1994, not many detectives had access to all nineteen data systems, due in part to concerns that corrupt cops might sell information back to the criminals, but mostly because catching crooks was not the department's top priority. In the ideal department, all detectives or their commanders would have access to every existing data system—state, local, or federal—that might contain the subject's arrest, incarceration, and parole records, his narcotics files, his warrant files, his warrant status, his Department of Motor Vehicle records, his parking ticket history, and his welfare and public housing files. The detectives would also have access to one or two proprietary people-seeking systems like AutoTrack, which collects numerous public records and allows individual searches by name, date of birth, Social Security number, address, or phone number. Additionally, all investigative files would be kept in computerized systems that would allow detectives to punch in a name and call up every case in which the subject was named as a suspect, a complainant, a witness, or sometimes even as a confidential informant.

Archer and others like him develop a feel for which information is likely to be most reliable. Records created before the suspect's criminal career began, like Board of Education documents and the family's public housing application, are more likely to contain honest answers. If by chance there has been a previous warrant search for the suspect, the city's Warrant On Line File, or WOLF, will detail every step of the chase and thus provide a shortcut to useful contacts and addresses.

Any phone number that pops up can be critical to the hunt. Just like regular people, crooks tend to call their moms and their girlfriends, and records are kept of all numbers they dial while in custody. Likewise, they have a tendency while out on the loose to check in with their loved ones around Mother's Day, Father's Day, Christmas, and birthdays. Either AutoTrack or the phone company can usually attach an address to any phone number they're given.

If only old addresses come up, the first person Archer visits is likely to be somebody like a superintendent or building manager, rather than family. The fugitive might run if a warning comes from his family. With a superintendent, Archer can show two or three photos and play like he has no clue if he's picked up the trail of any of them. If, however, the superintendent turns out to be truly cooperative, Archer will take every bit of information he can get.

One of the want cards the squad commander turned over to Norris, Archer, and Nuciforo was for a stickup guy named McBee. (The Seven-Five squad begrudgingly accepted help tracking down robbers and shooters, but they held on to their homicide wants to limit the potential for embarrassment.) Even though he wasn't a murder suspect, McBee was believed to be pretty dangerous, so even with the clock ticking, my crew took the precaution of sitting for a day on the address they had just to get a sense for the comings and goings. They hit the house at about six the next morning.

When I say "hit the house," I don't mean busting down doors. They knocked and woke up McBee's younger sister. "I saw him last night, but I don't know where he is," she told them. A search of the apartment came up empty, but didn't prove that the second half of her statement was true.

Moments later, as they watched from the street, the sister came out of the building with her coat on and headed for the housing projects nearby. Outside one of the towers, she stopped and called up to a window, then turned back home.

With his computers, Archer linked McBee to a phone number in one of the Housing Authority buildings, then determined the phone belonged to McBee's girlfriend, who lived in an apartment there with the couple's two young children. My guys were outside that door early the next morning.

The kids were up already, watching TV, and the voices of a man and a woman could be heard through the steel door. When Archer knocked, all went quiet.

There is a place in policing for battering rams, but a want chase is definitely not one of them. Even with an active court warrant, you want to shmooze the door to open. With just a want card, you can't even arrest your guy until he's stepped out of his home. But if you arrive at his door once and let him go, he's not going to be there the next time you visit. So you shmooze, you wait, you shmooze, you wait. And if shmoozing doesn't work, you try being annoying.

Archer kept at it with the knocker. Norris rapped the door with a quarter. Nuciforo tapped with his detectives' ring. All three started singing out the fugitive's name. "Mc-BE-EEE. Mc-BE-EEEEE." One hour passed, then two, then three. "Mc-BE-EEEEE." The girlfriend was the first to break, and she led both children out the door.

"Mc-BE-EEEEE."

Four hours after their arrival, McBee finally gave himself up, and Archer, Norris, and Nuciforo wrapped him up and dropped him off at the Seven-Five's squad room for his debriefing.

I don't remember exactly how long it took those three to catch their thirtieth crook out there, but I do know they had reached fourteen by the end of week one. I soon had them working their magic in a number of other spots throughout the city, but that first week's total was all I needed to change one important aspect of the way the detective bureau operated.

"Gee," I'd say to Joe Borelli, the chief of detectives, "my Naugahyde squad caught fourteen crooks in a week working out of their cars in the Seven-Five. Imagine if we had sent some real cops to do the job."

I had been a little unreasonable in my demands on the Seven-Five detectives, but they achieved more than reasonable results. Soon they were tracking down fugitives, spotting and solving patterns, and making bigger and better cases by interrogating all their prisoners. From that point on, I could point to their success when I was torturing other squad commanders and ask how it could be that the Seven-Five was able to do all those things despite having three times anybody else's caseload.

As for Borelli, he earned a special place in the history of the department as the chief who made his detectives understand that every crime is a big crime.

The detectives were beginning to perform up to their full potential. Now the department was ready to take a big run at crime.

FIVE

GET SMART
Accurate, Timely Intelligence

Imagine a darkened room high in police headquarters in the largest city in America. One hundred and fifty top police officials, resplendent in brass-button dress blues or Madison Avenue suits by way of Filene's Basement, sit in rows along the walls or lean over a string of tables illuminated by green-shaded lamps and piled high with crime and administrative data. At the front of the room, where the line of tables opens, a precinct commander stands alone at a podium beneath computer-generated street maps filling three eight-foot-tall projection screens. Chief of Patrol Louie Anemone and I sit directly opposite the podium, each of us grilling, commending, or soliciting lessons from the commander about the number of dots speckling each screen.

It is a Friday in 1994. It is 0700 hours.

Imagine now that Anemone, the perennial MVP of the New York Police Department in the closing years of the century, would have been up most of the night pouring over the weekly crime figures and case files while I was out late at a shooting or just hanging out with Miller—smoking cigars, downing espresso, and never doubting for a moment that everything Louis and I would need to ask the right questions would be right in front of us when we took our places across from that podium. Imagine, finally, that before the meeting started, I would have had to remind Louie for about the sixteen-hundredth time that no, I'm not at all jealous of the four stars on each of his epaulets or how the Glock pressing up under his ribs punctuated his Pattonesque air of command—because at my weight I'd look like Ralph Kramden in a uniform and, besides, men who wear suits rule the world.

This was the original Comstat meeting, the cornerstone of a management and anticrime process that has been studied by police departments throughout the world and replicated in the cities that are leading the way to historic declines in America's crime rate.

Of course, not every Comstat meeting in every city and every station house can be chaired by the guy I built my original concept around, but all the faithful reproductions share with the original a fundamental set of objectives and an Anemone-like central figure with the dedication, talent, and temperament to animate the cops or commanders across the room with a healthy dose of professional anxiety.

One way to look at a Comstat meeting is as a live audit of overall police performance, one in which the leadership's goals sometimes border on the unreasonable because that's the only way to ensure at least reasonable results. But before that, a Comstat meeting is a way of sharing crime data that recognizes why the first step to crime reduction itself—the gathering and analyzing of accurate, timely intelligence—has to be quickened by the heat of accountability.

The reason is simple: Most people in the world learn things faster when they know they're going to be tested on them. Cops are no different. If we had been satisfied to just sit in a circle and chat about the intelligence we all had (which is the way some departments run their knock-off versions of Comstat), a lot of cases in New York would never have been solved and a lot more people would have been victimized.

In mid-1995, a little more than a year after we started Comstat, a homicide case came up at one of the meetings that'll give you an idea what I mean.

In a typical homicide, the cause of death falls into one of only a handful of categories. Shootings account for the vast majority of killings in any American city, though the exact number varies from place to place according to the relative availability of guns. In New

York City, where gun ownership isn't very widespread, gunshot wounds were the cause of death in about two-thirds of homicides, with most every other victim dying from a stabbing, a bludgeoning, or some other simple use of force. A homicide by any other means couldn't help but win a second look, or at least a double take.

In this particular case, the cause of death recorded by the medical examiner was "ligature." The victim was a forty-six-year-old prostitute who'd been found hog-tied and gagged in a room at a hotel near Times Square called the New York Inn. She'd been tied with clothesline and strangled with a pink towel, and the New York Inn didn't supply its patrons with either. Even in the most dangerous profession a woman can work in, the circumstances of this murder were unusual. It didn't look like the work of an angry pimp.

Sergeant Gene White of the Comstat unit had been keeping a daily count of the city's homicide cases, and the Times Square murder also looked unsettlingly familiar. Checking back into our files, he found an unsolved murder of another prostitute from several months earlier. Sandra Lasure, thirty-eight, had been found lying facedown on a bed at the East Village's St. Mark's Hotel in mid-February. She too had been hog-tied; she too had been strangled with a pink towel.

Immediately, Manhattan Homicide was alerted to the pattern, but five months later, with both homicide files still open, the killer struck again. This time, the victim was a twenty-one-year-old prostitute found hog-tied in a bathtub in a hotel on East 27th Street. She too had been strangled by her attacker, but she had survived to recount what she could remember of the moments before she lost consciousness.

The woman recalled arriving at the hotel with a pock-faced john who was wearing a beret and carrying an orange gym bag. He had been easygoing at first, she said, and so she had consented to his request for a special performance. She was to stand at the other side of the room and twirl like a ballerina, then dance backward toward him with her arms stretched out in front of her. But when she danced within his reach, he wrapped clothesline around her ankles and pulled out a gun. The last she remembered, she was lying in the bathtub with a rope tightening around her neck. And when she awoke, she discovered that all her belongings were missing.

At Comstat, a captain from Manhattan Homicide told us he saw no evidence of a pattern.

This guy had to be kidding. "Are we saying we suddenly have several people out there who are strangling prostitutes?" I asked.

A more reasonable assumption was that our killer sometimes went to the watering hole hunting for prey but didn't make a kill. For every crime a predator commits, whether a bag snatch, a robbery, a rape, or a serial killing, there are usually a few targets who got away. (Even lions have a hit rate of only 30 percent.) So we decided right there at the meeting to get some people out on the streets in Midtown and the Lower East Side to canvass prostitutes and find out if any of the others knew our man. Quickly, they found one who only a month earlier had been raped at gunpoint in her building's elevator, then taken by her pock-faced attacker to the roof, where he'd wrapped a rope around her neck and sodomized her. Just before she went out, the rope slackened, $30 was pressed into her hand, and the man fled. She told our investigators she was willing to help, and several days later she flagged down a patrol car on the Lower East Side to point out her attacker, who happened to be carrying an orange gym bag with a rope and gun inside.

The captain who had refused to recognize a pattern in the first two homicides led the press conference announcing the arrest of this suspect in connection with the two homicides and several other recent assaults on prostitutes. We knew, however, that he'd let months slide by while refusing to even acknowledge the likelihood that we had a serial killer out there.

Maybe the captain truly believed there was no connection between the cases; maybe he felt that the slaying of a prostitute was a "misdemeanor homicide"; most likely, he was desperately trying to keep the investigations from attracting any further attention from his bosses.

You can call it human nature, but that little habit can quickly block the free flow of critical information within a large organization. Rest assured that captain was watched closely from then on to make sure his failure to recognize or report a pattern wasn't part of a pattern too.

The leaders of a police department must make it clear that intelligence about the bad guys has to move from the top of the organization to the bottom, and laterally, across bureau and division boundaries. The Comstat meeting is one way to model and uphold that principle, but the attitude has to be lived out at every level, at every moment of every day.

THE BLUE WALLS OF SILENCE

As slow-footed as the police work was on that 1995 strangler case, the NYPD of that moment had made great strides toward being smart about intelligence. Obviously, some people still had to be pushed in the right direction, but in many large departments neither the executive corps nor the detective commander would have had any knowledge about those two homicides. Because we held commanders accountable to follow their detectives' cases, at least this captain could answer questions about the stranglings and maybe learn something from the outcome of the investigation.

A year and a half earlier, we were like most other police forces in the world: The crooks were out there, working overtime—they'd chalked up 600,000 violent crimes in the twelve months before we were sworn in—and the effect within the department of the crooks' Herculean efforts was . . . well, it hardly registered.

Police departments in the United States run through police chiefs at an average rate of one every two years, so a department's old guard always have a strong motive to keep their chief executives focused not on crime but on developing "five-year strategic plans" that never come to fruition. The less the chief or commissioner knows about everyday operations and anything connected to the dreaded "C" word, the less anybody has to change.

They tried the same trick on us. About ten days into the Bratton era, Bratton himself turned to me and said, "Things are pretty quiet around here, wouldn't you say?"

Quiet? I thought the commissioner was kidding me. About fifty people had already been murdered on our watch and he called that "quiet." We were trying to create a department in which every single cop was a crime fighter and, therefore, always had crime information at the forefront of his or her mind. But it was becoming obvious that keeping even our own inner circle completely up to date on the crime was going to take some serious effort.

For about seventy years, the way the score has been kept in policing is through the FBI's Uniform Crime Reporting Program. Every month police departments send in their UCR crime numbers, and every six months the totals are published. The numbers that count most are the Part I offenses, or "Major Index Crimes"—murder, rape, robbery, felonious assault, burglary, grand larceny, auto theft, and arson. Police chiefs have always sweated out the results, but about the only tactics they used to bring the numbers down involved crossed fingers or erasers.

I wanted the crime counted and mapped daily.

First, though, I put in a call to the Operations Division. I wanted them to beep me any time we had a homicide and any time a cop shot somebody. Operations already distributed a daily log of murders, special events, officer suspensions, and accidents involving radio cars, but my request must have taken them by surprise. When a boss called in to find out what was happening in the city, their pat answer went something like this: "Not much happening, Commissioner. We got a water main break on Fifth Avenue around 20th

Street, there's a candlelight vigil for the hansom cab horses getting started in Central Park, and the FDR is jammed up due to the President's visit." Of course, very rarely any mention of crime.

Anyway, they seemed to underestimate my appetite for timely information. "Do you know how many homicides there are in this city?" the sergeant asked. "Do you know how many shootouts we were in last year?"

I knew the numbers by heart—there'd been 1,946 homicides the previous year and about 115 incidents in which police gunfire had killed or wounded somebody. But we needed to get the pulse of violent crime in the city and see how our people were responding to it. And we didn't have much time: Before our first week was over, City Hall was already acting cranky about having a police commissioner who got better press than the mayor, and we'd already learned to tuck a phone book or two in the seats of our pants when we were called in for meetings with the mayor or his staff.

We were playing against the clock now. The two-minute warning had already sounded.

I have to hand it to those Operations guys. They were cute. I got a lot of beeps waking me at three in the morning for homicides that had been reported five hours earlier. But Miller and I were rolling on all kinds of jobs. If it was after three in the morning, he'd call me from his car as he pulled up outside my apartment. If it was any earlier, we'd just excuse ourselves from our table up at Showman's or Elaine's and head out to Johnny's Crown Vic with two espressos to go. "Whatsa matter"—somebody would call out as we ran the gauntlet of journalists, movie stars, and wannabes—"your crime strategies not working so good tonight?" "Nah," another wiseguy would chime in. "Rudy must be running a bed check." Miller would save his retort for our return, when he'd put on his best network voice and say, "It was a tough run. We were robbed, shot at, stabbed in the back. And that was just from City Hall."

I'd always have to say a few Hail Marys on those runs on account of Johnny's driving, but so what? Nothing replaces being at the scene for evaluating the training, operation procedures, attitudes, and available resources of the cops who actually do the job or for getting the facts about each incident without any sugar coating.

One thing we quickly discovered was that the timely communication of intelligence did not come easily for many people in the organization. At complex shooting scenes, for example, the detective in charge of the case generally had to work the scene without having any idea what kind of intel other detectives were already developing from interviews at the hospitals or interrogations at the station house.

The simple solution? The squads needed mobile phones.

In policing, even the smallest communication breakdowns could have fatal consequences. One bitterly cold night in Queens, a plainclothes cop fatally shot two men sitting in a car when a tactic his partner improvised apparently took him by surprise. A shootout with a third man had initiated a chase of the vehicle, but the partners made the stop not knowing that the shooter had somehow slipped out of the car while it was momentarily out of sight. Unable to see any of the passengers clearly, the officer who approached from behind decided to smash the car's tinted rear window with his flashlight, apparently not considering how the flash of light, the shattering glass, and the startled movements of the passengers would affect his partner. Standing just outside the driver's side window, that second cop must have guessed he was being fired on and immediately answered in kind. When Miller and I got there, the commander of Queens Homicide had told us immediately it "looked like a good one," meaning the officer had been justified in firing. Not until the end of his story did he finally mention that no weapons had been found in the victims' car.

"When," I asked him, "are we going to get to the 'good' part?"

This lieutenant was, perhaps, the best squad commander in the city, and he'd been right that the two cops, given the totality of the circumstances, appeared to be guiltless (though, as in all police shootings, that would be for the district attorney and a grand jury to decide). But there was sad comedy in his attempt to put an upbeat spin on the situation. Just like the captain who saw no pattern in the strangler case, he was afraid to tell us the bad news.

Several days later, when a pair of cops in Staten Island shot at a couple of car passengers in a replay of the first incident, we realized the bad news about smashing in tinted windows was, in fact, something every member of the force had to hear about before any more shootings arose from some harmless-looking trick with a flashlight that the cops had probably seen work in a movie.

Tactical problems like that one are going to pop up no matter what the leadership does, and most can be quickly corrected through realistic training—as long as the leaders are getting out in the field enough to discover them.

But we also ran across evidence that breakdowns in communication between various members of the force were not at all limited to the frantic moments surrounding a shootout or a car chase. For instance, much of the intel about crime that the department had in its possession was as good as lost to most of the people who could use it. The sorry reality is that the most formidable "blue wall of silence" in policing is the cops not talking to each other.

Four weeks after we were sworn in, Previn Shah, the fifty-eight-year-old owner of a newsstand near Penn Station, was shot dead behind his counter during a midmorning robbery attempt. A day or two later, when we met with the Midtown South squad commander to discuss the investigation, I asked if his detectives had come up with any suspects by calling up crime and arrest reports through the department's Computer Assisted Robbery System.

CARS, as it's called, is a computer database that contains information on just about every felony arrest and all homicides, robberies, and sex crimes reported in New York City since the mid-1980s. For almost a decade, then, investigators with access to the system had been able to use one or more scraps of information from one crime—a description of a perpetrator, a weapon type, a nickname, the method of attack—to sift through hundreds of thousands of past crimes and felons for potential suspects. CARS, you could say, was a New York detective's best friend.

Unfortunately, the Midtown South detectives didn't have direct access to CARS. Nor could the squad log directly into CRIMS, NITRO, WOLF, BADS, or about a handful of other computerized database systems down at headquarters that could fetch everything from court histories and motor vehicle records to narcotics rap sheets and fugitive investigations. Most of the hardware they needed was right there in the squad room, but the department's Management Information Services Division, living up to its reputation as an enemy of management, information, *and* service, was holding back on the access codes. The standard excuse was that opening up access to the systems would open up opportunities for corrupt cops to sell information to the bad guys.

We figured if we had bad cops, we'd root them out with stings and arrest them. There was no need to handcuff the good cops. So before our meeting was over, I phoned MISD and told them to turn all these systems.

MISD got cute on me too. About a week later, I asked a roomful of detective commanders from around the city if opening up these systems had helped them. They were bewildered. They had no idea what I was talking about. Apparently, MISD had turned the systems on only at Midtown South and left the other seventy-five precincts in the dark ages. MISD was immediately extended an invitation to join our meeting. "What do I have to do?" I asked them. "Make seventy-five phone calls?"

Knowing not every detective in the city was going to stay up late every night to learn all the intricacies of the new tools we'd just handed them, I asked Louie to put out an executive summary of each system's capabilities—then we started grilling the detective commanders at Comstat to see if they understood how to use them so they'd appreciate why their squads ought to be using them too. We also knew that our warrant squads were filled with people like Sonny Archer and Jimmy Nuciforo, who'd mastered all these systems in the course of hunting for fugitives. A fair number of detectives were therefore reassigned to the warrant squads and told they couldn't return to their old squads until they'd caught a few crooks and demonstrated their mastery of the intel systems.

Sometimes you have to force people to learn.

You wouldn't think detectives would have to be told that information already captured somewhere in the criminal justice system could be useful to an investigation, but they often don't know what's on these systems and they're almost never trained how to go in and get it. That's why in every city I go to, one of the first things I do is find out what kind of intel systems are available to the police and whether anybody is using them. Not only do we then distribute a summary of what's on the computers, but the checklists we give to the detectives include checkoffs for the systems that should be used in each type of investigation.

Different departments have different tools, so they all would benefit from looking into each other's toolboxes. In Birmingham and New Orleans, for example, almost everything bought or sold at a pawnshop is fed into a police database, so a patrol officer or a detective taking a robbery or burglary complaint can punch in descriptions of the stolen goods and see if they've been pawned, and if so, by whom. The cities' stolen goods records are stored too, so if the detective is talking to a suspect who's wearing a Yale University ring or a watch with a serial number on it, the detective can find out if those items were stolen in a recent crime. In Philadelphia, the detectives can look up a prisoner in the state corrections database and pull up the names of every visitor he's ever had.

Many of the systems, I'll admit, aren't very user-friendly, but that's symptomatic of a major problem with intel: Police departments like to create specialists, and specialists think they're special, so they have trouble working with anybody else. Sometimes even at the precinct level, there'll be a special stolen-property guy, a special robbery guy, a special auto-crime guy—each of them with their own personal stockpile of intel. What's worse, many of them are at the mercy of special computer guys, who buy the hardware and software they see at a glorified Tupperware party and forget that the user they ought to have in mind when they set up these systems is the cop or detective out in the field who's trying to catch a few crooks.

The kind of data systems the police and other law enforcement agencies should be using would tear down the obstacles to information sharing. "Case management systems" store all investigative files in their entirety, thus allowing users to plug in a name or keyword and pull up every file in which that word or name appears. If Fatty Arbuckle has been a witness to four shootings and two murders, a detective should know that before talking to him. If somebody just did a stickup at a Ground Round, it would pay to check if any other Ground Rounds have been hit over the past several months. Unfortunately, systems that can search through the entire text of every case are rarely used in law enforcement. Why? Because cops and prosecutors simply don't like it when anybody else is looking over their shoulders.

Maybe the Mac Daddy of all "blue walls of silence" is the one that normally separates the Narcotics Division from the Detective Bureau. Every day the detectives catch drug-related homicides and start their investigations from scratch, even though a guy down the hall in Narcotics might have several files filled with background information on the shooter, on the victim, and on several witnesses who were interviewed during the detectives' canvass. If you asked the detectives if they talked to Narcotics about these cases, they'd stroke you by saying, "We work very, very closely together." In reality, they only work together on what they perceive to be "big cases," and not many of their "big cases" involved small players in the narcotics business.

In New York City, we were eventually able to establish a drug motive in about 25 percent of all the city's murders, but we knew that a lot of other people were being gunned down in street disputes in which the drug connection was never firmly established. In the end, the consensus was that, at the very least, 40 percent of the city's homicides were by-products of the drug trade.

We couldn't just present this evidence to the detectives and Narcotics and ask them to play nice together; we forced the issue. Into each borough's homicide squad, we introduced a "narcotics module," consisting of a supervisor, six narcotics investigators, and two undercover officers, who could do buy-and-busts into the drug crews targeted by the investigators for questioning about the homicides.

In their first year of operation, the new modules helped solve 113 homicides.

In New Orleans, we accomplished the same effect by taking the detectives and narcotics investigators working at central headquarters and placing them all under the authority of the city's eight district commanders.

That same year the clearance rate on homicides rose from 30 percent to 72 percent, and New Orleans led America with a 24 percent decline in violent crime. The next year (after they'd warmed up) the clearance rate on homicides reached 87 percent, and the double-digit violent crime decline continued.

THE POWER OF MAPPING

Improving the department's use of intelligence wasn't just a matter of making people do a better job of sharing intel we'd already captured somewhere within the organization. The cops out in the field needed intel of a kind they'd never dreamed of before.

They needed to borrow a trick from an old cave-dweller. They needed "The Charts of the Future."

Outsiders often assume technology drove many of the changes in policing that we modeled in the NYPD. What a joke. A faith in timeless ideas like mapping came first, and we worked our way around or over the technological hurdles because we knew the results would be worth the trouble.

It's easy to lose sight of the power of mapping. Maps are superior to numbers or narratives as a means of communicating to individuals at every level of an organization the immediate challenges in front of them. Maps tell a story in a way numbers and narratives simply can't.

Numbers, of course, do a good job of describing volume and are indispensable for assessing trends or performance over time. But if a cop were sent out into the street knowing numbers only, he'd be equipped to make only the following type of judgment: "There's a lot of crime out there" or "There's not much crime out there." That kind of knowledge is only so useful.

Narratives are good at describing individual events. A cop needs the information from narratives for descriptions of the crooks, their tactics, and the types of victim they prefer, but narratives generally have little to say about how crime is concentrated.

Maps are ideal for focusing attention on the greatest concentrations of crime. A map that plots crime events over a given period of time makes the past present. For the area it depicts, it says these are the crime conditions *now*. It says maybe we haven't plotted any new incidents since last night, but judging from events of the immediate past, this is where Yellow Top crack is being sold, this is where Red Top is being sold, this is where house burglars have been active from 3 P.M. to 6 P.M., and this is where bag snatchers are preying on morning commuters.

A crime map prompts anybody who's looking at it to ask, What are the underlying causes? Is there a crack spot there? Is it a bus stop? A shopping center? If the cop can easily retrieve more details about each of these patterns from the pertinent narratives—like physical descriptions of the perpetrator or perpetrators, their mode of operation, the weapons they've used, and common characteristics of the victims—he now has a chance to do something about the pattern, even if the bosses in the department are doing nothing more creative with deployment and tactics than distributing officers evenly across the city.

Maps also highlight possible correlations between crimes or types of crimes. If, for instance, there's been a shooting on a corner where both Red Top and Yellow Top arrests have recently been made, there's a good chance the shooting is related to the drug trafficking and a good number of the buyers or sellers out there may know the identity of the shooter.

In short, there is no better tool than mapping for zeroing in on a target.

Think about it.

In 1940, the Germans had more bombers and more pilots than Britain's Royal Air Force, but Britain had been quicker to appreciate the value of radar. When German planes took to the air, the Brits instantly mapped out their progress on a war table and sent up their Spitfires to turn back or gun down great numbers of the invaders. Despite their losses, the Germans still had a chance for victory weeks into the air battle, but their own intel wasn't accurate. Believing they had already destroyed Britain's airfields, they turned their attention to bombing civilians in London and gave the RAF time to regroup.

If your objective is to get lucky rather than gun down a German bomber, you do the mapping in your head. Once you learn that all the babes are at the China Club on Monday nights, you're not going to wait until Wednesday to go to the China Club and waste your Monday night at Moomba. On Monday night, you will be at the China Club. (The tactics and follow-up on what you do there will be discussed in my next book.)

I've heard some people say that reducing crime isn't brain surgery. And it's true—brain surgeons only save one person at a time. But even brain surgeons have an MRI map of the brain to look at before they begin cutting through muscle, skullbone, and the dura mater to get at the problem itself. In fact, the surgeons keep a map in front of them throughout the operation in the form of a monitor display that shows the area of the incision at about ten times actual size.

In a police department, leadership has to get behind the concept of mapping to get a system up and running. But there are always some other heroes backstage.

In every city I work in, I try to find at least one person in the crime analysis division who's ready to knock down walls to pull together the crime data we need. In New York, it was Sergeant John Yohe. In Birmingham, it's Lieutenant Ellison Beggs. In Newark, Megan Ambrosio; in Philadelphia, Chief Vincent DeBlasis. Some have long experience on the streets, some have none at all, but every one of them has almost a sixth sense for the kind of information that helps catch crooks. Megan, a small-boned academic who does all her crime-fighting from behind a desk, once cracked a string of Jersey City carjackings and a string of Newark gas station holdups at the same time by digging up dozens of closed auto theft cases and phoning each of the victims. By matching new details about the stolen vehicles with witness accounts of the holdup crew's getaway cars, she was able to pinpoint a Jersey City neighborhood where the crew had launched each of their misadventures. When she heard a radio report about another stolen car from that neighborhood that had crashed in Newark, she tipped a detective to the possible link, the detective raced over to meet the passengers at the hospital, and the driver gave up the whole game.

John Yohe was the pioneer. Like the others, he was a bit of a computer buff, but he had also been a good street cop, so among other things, he understood how a crime became a report and how a report became data that we could capture. When I asked, he was able to pull together the NYPD's first weekly crime numbers and then its first weekly crime maps not because of any new technology but in spite of the technology we had.

When the process started, kids in the suburbs were doing their homework on Pentium machines, but Yohe was punching in crime data from all seventy-six precincts and writing his own code for a simple spreadsheet into a borrowed 386. When we started moving from hand maps to computerized mapping, Yohe quickly found out that even the best mapping software around couldn't plot multiple crimes at any single address. Here we really relied on Yohe's creative ability, because he was able to devise a way to get around the software's logic and make our hot spots look like hot spots.

Around that time Bratton was putting together informal sit-downs for his executive corps with some of the top corporate executives in America, including the CEOs of American Express, Johnson & Johnson, Morgan Stanley, Motorola, and General Electric. Some of them treated Louie and me like kids from the Fresh Air Fund—real charity cases—but we had kind of a meeting of the minds with Jack Welch of GE. Welch had come in talking a language we could hardly comprehend—secretaries who were buying boats with the proceeds from their incentive packages, research and development budgets running into the millions—but when I pointed out that we were attempting to turn around an organization that literally had to go begging just to buy the acetate sheets we needed to put our original maps on an overhead projector, he acknowledged we had chosen the right path amid difficult surroundings. "You go with what you have," he said. "You can't wait for the R&D to catch up with you." And that had been our philosophy from the beginning. If it had been up to MISD, we would have all been sitting around the Old Policemen's Home before they found a system they liked and could make operational.

In the beginning our crime maps were produced with pushpins and paper, but today a police department of almost any size should make the investment in mapping software. Off-the-shelf mapping software for every station house now costs about the same as having a water cooler for a year, and teamed with a PC and a portable machine that can project onto a large screen, the maps can be used at every Comstat session, every roll call, and even can be carried from place to place for use at community meetings.

The police can't be afraid to share the crime maps with the public. Citizens deserve to know about the crime so they can make informed decisions about where to buy or rent a home, when not to walk alone, and which way to send their children to school. In fact, the maps should also be made available to the local media for broadcast or publication, on a World Wide Web site maintained by the department, and at kiosks in the station house. Any visitor to the Web site or kiosk would be able to follow the commands on a computer screen to call up just about any information about crime incidents that the police have. If the police know, for instance, what kind of coats or sneakers are being targeted that season by school-age robbery crews, they should make a point of sharing that information too.

The guiding idea for the cops has to be: What can we do to reduce the number of people victimized by crime? One way is to give the public every advantage in steering clear of the crooks.

If a department flat-out can't afford the technology right away, they should follow Jack Welch's advice and go with what they have. When the NYPD's precincts were mapping with pushpins in 1995, New York accounted for 68 percent of the nation's total crime decline. Any other department can do equally well, provided the maps in every precinct are up to date and displayed where everybody in the precinct can study them. In New York, we ordered every precinct to create a "crime information center," where the various pin maps were accompanied by the pertinent crime reports and by photos of suspects and fugitives. But the maps have to be kept under glass: If they aren't, playful cops will rearrange the pins any time the bosses aren't looking.

WHAT TO MAP

What's important is not the mapping technology, but how even the most primitive maps help cops see the city or neighborhood they are paid to protect and serve.

A. The Existing Landscape.

First, we sketch in the permanent and near-permanent features of the manmade terrain, paying special attention to the watering holes—abandoned houses, schools, public housing projects, homeless shelters, methadone clinics, subway stops, schools, parks, check-cashing businesses—and to potential fences—like pawnshops, jewelry stores, scrap yards, and auto body shops. Many of these locations show up on off-the-shelf software that maps all the commercial establishments listed in a city's Yellow Pages. That information can also come in handy in unexpected ways, like when a robbery crew starts targeting Laundromats, gas stations, or Arby's restaurants.

On top of this permanent landscape, we will be dropping in various overlays of other information. We want to be able to see the correlations between crimes and their surroundings or between one type of criminal activity and another.

The first overlay we add are the chronic locations we'll be trying to clean up, including drug spots—which should be differentiated by type of drug sold and "brand" name—and all quality-of-life hot spots—prostitution strips, gang hangouts, truancy hangouts, and corners where there are regular dice games or drinking. Street intelligence can identify many of these locations, but the precincts should also map arrests and complaints to determine if there are any trouble spots being neglected.

B. The "Customers."

The citizens who live, work, and hang out in the neighborhood are the cops' customers. The majority, of course, are law-abiding people who deserve nothing but the best but who make only infrequent demands for direct service. They'll show up on the maps—if at all—as victims or complainants.

Victims and complainants are usually the people who need good police service more than anybody else, but occasionally, the cops come across "serial" complainants. These people might be working insurance scams, they might be making false accusations against their enemies, or they might simply be a little nutty. In New York and New Orleans, cable TV boxes were routinely being reported stolen because customers had discovered they could fence the devices for a few bills and ask for free replacements from the cable companies. Any time the police are analyzing a crime pattern, they have to look at victimology, and they should have the capacity to check if a complainant is popping up with suspicious frequency.

But the clientele a cop really has to get to know are the "problem customers," because unlike in most other businesses, where the loyal customer is king, in law enforcement, it's the problem customer who merits the most attention.

In our business, the problem customers are the people who've been locked up before and the people suspected to be members of ongoing criminal organizations like street gangs or drug crews.

Various studies have shown that about 40 percent of the 700,000 people in America on parole wind up back in state prisons within five years, and half of those are back within six months. Nearly half of all state prisoners were on probation or parole at the time of their last offense. And that's with the local cops having no intel about who the parolees in the area are, what they look like, and what the restrictions are on where they can go and whom they can associate with.

What should happen when a parolee gets out of prison is he should be required to stop first at the local police precinct to have his picture taken and distributed—along with a brief summary of his criminal history and parole restrictions—throughout the department and to every cop in the station house. A commander or detective should then sit down with the parolee and offer a greeting that can be repeated in a follow-up letter sent to the parolee's home:

"Welcome back, great to see you. We're confident you will be making a fresh start here in our community and we want you to know we're here to help keep you on the straight and narrow. We have your photo, we know why you were in, we know you were a member of this or that gang, and we know your parole prohibits you from doing *x*, *y*, and *z*. So keep your nose clean, kid. We'll be watching."

In many states, the cops would also know the parolee's DNA. DNA profiles developed from the blood samples of prisoners, parolees, and probationers are constantly being added to a national network of law enforcement databases. As use of the network grows, more and more crimes could be solved if the technology isn't neglected because the DNA of blood, semen, or saliva left at a crime scene matches a sample already on file.

The gang members and drug crews are usually known throughout their neighborhoods, so there's no reason the cops shouldn't know all about them too. All of these characters, as well as anybody wanted on an outstanding warrant, should have their current addresses and past arrest locations mapped. When the cop is looking for suspects, he'll think first of these characters he's come to know, then check these maps to see if there's anybody he's forgotten.

Photos of these individuals should be kept by affiliation and by corner in books left at the precinct's crime information center or, better still, on Photo Imaging machines, which can call groups of suspects up by Zip code for review by victims, witnesses, or the cops. In Transit, we once had a robbery witness pick from a mug book a suspect who was so distinctive in appearance that the detective said he looked "like a taxicab with the doors open." The rest of us just called the suspect "Big Ears," and when the story of his crime spree hit the press, one sympathetic reader volunteered to fund cosmetic surgery to improve the poor kid's self-image.

One last source of intel on the problem customers can be studied right out on the street: Because gangs often leave a significant information trail right under the cops' noses—in the form of graffiti—the cops should be trained to decipher the scrawls they drive or walk past every day. Half the time, all an interpreter needs is to recognize distorted letters, know a few gang symbols, and figure out when the symbols are being dissed by rivals. Once, a couple of other cops and I found a robbery suspect we knew only as "Money Love" by following a trail of his tags up a public housing staircase and knocking on the thirteenth-floor door where we found the biggest of them all.

C. The Crimes.

So far, the maps in the cop's head show a stage set and a crowd of the usual suspects faces from central casting. Now we get to the main event—the crime itself.

We begin with Part I crimes—murder, rape, robbery, felonious assault, burglary, grand larceny, grand larceny auto, and arson—and add separate categories for shots fired, for shooting victims, and for narcotics complaints and arrests. And we're not interested in looking at six-month-old data the way the FBI would; we need the crime numbers at least weekly. At the precinct level, we'll look at it every day, just like checking in on the Dow Jones Industrial Average.

Icons or color coding will identify each crime by type and time of occurrence, but each incident should also be entered into the computer so it can be called up by date, by day of week, by weapon, by vehicle, and by the perpetrator's description and method of operation. In locations like schools and public housing complexes where crime numbers can pile up quickly, the crimes should also be coded to indicate whether they occurred indoors or out. (Advanced departments can even make use of software that maps three-dimensional views of such structures.) Car thefts should be mapped once to indicate where the car was stolen and once to show where it was recovered and whether it had been stripped or left relatively intact.

Now our maps are ready to go to work. With just a few keystrokes on the computer, any cop can take a closer look at all the Friday- or Saturday-night burglaries inside the Thomas Jefferson housing complex or all the knife-point street robberies involving a red car or a stocky man with a blue cap.

The possibilities are endless. The surprises are endless too.

In New York, mapping showed us that 60 percent of the city's grand larcenies occurred in just three precincts. It showed us that robbers in one Lower East Side precinct worked one side of the neighborhood by day and shifted to the opposite side of the neighborhood at night. It showed us that a rash of rapes in Queens had all taken place within a couple blocks of one subway line, allowing us to set up stakeouts and take down our man. It proved, when we mapped the home addresses of robbers arrested in Midtown, that the old adage was true: "Manhattan make it, Brooklyn take it." As a result, we started asking Midtown victims to look at more photos of Brooklyn crooks.

The mapping sometimes even told us what door to look behind. In a housing complex near the East River where a lot of senior citizens lived, we'd had a long series of elevator robberies. When we mapped all the parolees in Manhattan, two lonely little dots popped up inside that complex, and the Comstat unit dug up backgrounds on them. At the precinct's next Comstat meeting, Louie pounced on the robbery squad commander when he said they were having no luck solving that pattern.

"What about the Hernandez brothers?" Louie shouted. "Has anybody looked at them?"

The commander almost choked on his tongue. How could the chief of department know about the Hernandez brothers, and who were they anyway?

They were our two little dots on the map. And they turned out to be the guys we wanted.

SMARTER COPS, SMARTER STOPS

One of the many beauties of mapping is it helps make bosses smart about crime and blind to political considerations.

All dots are created equal. When the dots come up on the maps, they tell us what questions have to be asked, but they don't tell us whether the victim they represent was Leo DiCaprio or a sweatshop seamstress making $2 an hour. We'll want to look at the victims' background when we go to solve the cases, but when the dots come up, all that matters is that the commander at the podium knows if they are part of a pattern and has a plan for preventing any encores by catching the perps or at least forcing them into retirement.

For the cops out there who are actually facing the criminals, the maps can be as good as a guarantee that the intel they need to protect themselves and the public will be shared with them in a timely manner.

But that's only in a department where the crime meeting is not just a once-a-week spectacle suffered only by the department's top commanders. The meetings have to take place at about four levels, depending on the size of the department, all the way from the Louie Anemones and the eight-foot screens down to the daily roll calls for every tour in every precinct, with questions asked in excruciating detail. At the precinct level, it would be the precinct commander grilling patrol, narcotics, and detective commanders. At the next level, it would be the tour or platoon commanders grilling the sergeants. And at roll call, the sergeants would be sharing intelligence about current crime conditions, passing down specific crime-fighting instructions and, last but not least, quizzing the officers to see how well they're adhering to the four steps: "Quigley, tell me about these auto break-ins we had on your beat last night. . . . What are you laughing at, Johnson? How come we had another push-in robbery in your sector yesterday?" Or "Harris, does the name 'George Washington' mean anything to you? Nice try, but I wasn't thinking of our first President. George Washington is some ne'er-do-well in your sector who's got ten new narcotics complaints on him. What's the story? How's George making his Benjamins?"

When these questions are being asked at every level, the maps have put everybody in the department literally on the same page. And the knowledge that the process distributes to the far reaches of the organization tips the balance in favor of public safety at a moment of truth for the department—when the average cop makes a stop on the street.

A poorly informed cop may stop a stickup man who's carrying a gun and lose even the gun possession charge when the case goes to court because the cop can't articulate the cause for "reasonable suspicion" that would justify the frisk. An informed cop would be able not only to explain how the suspect's demeanor was consistent with a gun-carrier's, but how details of the stickup pattern—the perpetrator's description, style of dress, M.O.—contributed to reasonable suspicion. If that cop stops an innocent passerby, the cop will also have a better explanation in way of an apology.

In Upper Manhattan one night, a couple of cops pulled over a car on a routine stop. If they had worked at a time before the department mapped crime and stressed the importance of accurate, timely intelligence, they would have just written up the ticket for a minor traffic violation and sent the car on its way.

But this was a new era, and they knew there'd been a string of violent house robberies in the area. This was serious business. The crews carried radios and would rappel down the sides of buildings and kick in the doors of the apartments they'd targeted. They'd rape the women they ran across and escape into the night, carrying huge sums of cash. They carried guns, but also, they always carried a roll of duct tape on a stick to speed the work of gagging and binding their victims. Their targets all appeared to be drug houses, but the maps don't give robbery and rape victims demerit points for bad behavior. They were dots like everybody else, and the patrol force up there had been told all about them.

The robbery crew would have had a real good laugh when they

drove off if the cops who stopped them didn't have accurate, timely intelligence. But visible inside the car was a stick wrapped with duct tape. That, along with the fact the passengers matched the general descriptions of the perps, gave these cops probable cause to arrest the car's passengers for at least one of the robberies.

When the contents of the car was vouchered, the cops found guns, radios, and duffel bags in the trunk. The crew, it seems, had been on their way to their next house call when they ran into a couple of well-informed New York City police officers.

THE MISSING LINKS

Unfortunately, some of the intel the cops should be paying close attention to is not available to them.

If a delegation from Mars came down tomorrow to study our criminal justice system, they'd be surprised to learn that the cohort of crooks we know to be both the most violent and the most likely to repeat their crimes are the ones the cops have the least information about.

As long as a gangster gets an early start—in some states even seventeen-year-olds are treated with kid gloves—he can usually resume his criminal career later with full confidence that, thanks to the juvenile justice system, the cops have no photo, no fingerprints, and none of the other documentation that routinely would aid in the identification and arrest of a repeat offender.

If we are ever going to save those most "at risk"—the innocent victims—those rules have to change.

Schools contribute to our ignorance about juvenile offenders by failing to report many of the crimes that occur behind their doors. I once asked the head of all high school principals in the New York City public school system if he thought a school would report a robbery when three kids jump a schoolmate in a stairwell and take his Air Jordans.

"Probably not," said the school executive.

"Well," I said, "what would you call it if you walked out your front door one morning and three teenagers smacked you in the mouth and took your shoes?"

That didn't change his position, but the NYPD is now standardizing the reporting of violence in the schools. The cops understand that the same kids who do stickups in the stairwells are the ones who do stickups in the streets and subways.

Child welfare files represent another intelligence cache that should be opened to the police. In most cities, a case involving child neglect that hasn't reached the level of a criminal offense is handled by a child welfare bureau and the police know nothing about it. But the adults accused of neglect should appear on one of our maps, because these are people the cops would want to talk to in the event a child is attacked, threatened, or abducted in that area.

The cops could do even more to ensure kids' safety if they were allowed to review all child neglect and child abuse cases before the cases were referred to the city's child welfare agency, rather than the reverse, which almost guarantees a slow response to criminal acts against children.

Of course, the cops have plenty of their own blind spots to overcome, but the FBI could push them a bit by adding a few items to policing's unofficial scorecard—the UCR reports.

First, the category for rape should be expanded to include all felony sex crimes. As the definitions stand, if an attacker holds a gun to a woman's head and sodomizes her, the incident won't be counted as a Part I crime because it's not considered rape.

Next, narcotics complaints—though subject to suppression—should be tallied in every city so the public can keep closer tabs on the severity of local drug problems.

Finally, unsolved missing persons reports should appear high on the city-to-city comparisons. Because a very large percentage of missing persons cases are solved by the voluntary return of those who were reported "missing," most departments don't pay much attention to the whole category. The problem is, many of the missing persons cases that don't solve themselves are probably homicides that nobody has ever investigated.

If departments started treating unsolved missing persons cases as seriously as homicides, there'd be less of a chance that a serial killer like John Wayne Gacy could bury two dozen bodies under his house before anybody noticed.

SIX

"PUT COPS ON DOTS"
Rapid Deployment

In the spring of 1997, Eddie Compass, a thirty-eight-year-old police captain who had grown up within a holler of one of New Orleans's notorious public housing developments and had spent his summers amid the barbed wire, broken glass, and shattered spirits of another, took command of the police district that kept watch over his old neighborhood.

New Orleans's First District sits just outside the city's French Quarter but enjoys almost none of its famous neighbor's charms—wrought-iron balconies, fresh seafood, or street corner brass bands. History remembers the area as home to Storyville, a neighborhood where prostitution was legalized and jazz was incubated, but Storyville's legendary houses of pleasure had been torn down in the thirties to make way for the sprawling Iberville Housing Project, which, along with the Lafitte houses, soon became a couple of the city's most proficient nurseries of crime. If tourists wandered into the district at all, it was to gape at one of two ancient graveyards or because they took a wrong turn at 3 A.M. when they stumbled out of Donner's, the Funky Butt, or one of the transvestite karoake bars on Rampart Street, the northwest edge of tour-guide New Orleans.

The First didn't get many tourists, but it did raise its share of crooks. From Lafitte and Iberville, the hoods had only a short walk to some of the city's premier late-night feeding grounds, like Jackson Square or Pirates Alley next to St. Louis Cathedral, where Jean Lafitte's crew once sold their ill-gotten loot and today's bandits play the same tired game day after day after day:

"Bet you twenty dollars I can tell you where you got your shoes," they'd shout out to a tourist.

It was a setup; a sad joke. "You got 'em on your feet in New Orleans," the crooks would laugh. Then they'd strong-arm their mark if he didn't hand over the twenty voluntarily.

The First was in a rut. In the early months of '97, six of the city's seven other districts were racing toward numbers good enough for the largest violent crime reduction in the nation, but the district where Compass had grown up was stuck in gumbo, and deployment was a dish their commanders seemed to think was best served cold. Morale itself wasn't bad, thanks in part to a recent reorganization of the entire department, but results in the First belonged to the demoralizing days of the recent past, when the city's murder rate led the nation and its undermanned, underpaid police force was best known for corruption and for generating a pretty high murder rate of its own.

The department as a whole had a few things going for it. Its chief, for one. Richard Pennington, a former deputy chief in Washington, D.C., had been sworn in as superintendent on October 13, 1994, to the worst welcome imaginable. That same day a mother of three was executed on her front lawn in a hit ordered by a New Orleans police officer named Len Davis. Davis's motive: The victim had filed a "confidential" complaint with the department a day earlier, accusing Davis of pistol-whipping her neighbor.

Several months later, a twenty-five-year-old city cop working as a guard at a Vietnamese restaurant was shot several times and killed after unlocking the door for a colleague on the force who sometimes moonlighted at the place herself. Officer Antoinette Frank and the eighteen-year-old punk who was with her made off with $10,000 in the robbery, but not before Frank also shot two of the owner's children in the head while they kneeled on the kitchen floor and begged for their lives. When the crime was called in, Frank herself was one of the officers who responded to the scene, and Pennington was there to see her lead one of the survivors out of the restaurant.

"What happened?" Frank asked the trembling young woman.

"You saw what happened," the woman replied. "You shot my brother and sister."

Pennington was like Gary Cooper in *High Noon.* Soft-spoken but strong-willed, he proved more than a match for the bad guys—beginning with those who wore badges. Though New Orleans already had fewer cops per capita than most any other large city in America, Pennington didn't hesitate to clean house. Blowing up his own Internal Affairs Division and bringing in the FBI, the chief fired, suspended, or demoted more than 200 officers during his first twenty-eight months and accepted the resignations of 36 others who stepped down while under investigation. In New York, this would be equivalent to dismissing or punishing 6,000 cops, but with the skeleton crew he'd left standing, at least there was a pretty good chance they would all be playing for the same team.

By the time Compass was given his own district, it was clear that Pennington wasn't the NOPD's only significant strength. Its eight district commanders—the midlevel executives closest to the problems on the streets—were, for the most part, very good cops. With Compass taking over the First District and an aggressive detective commander named Louis Dabdoub moving into the top seat in the Second, Pennington had pretty much filled his lineup card with a group of strong leaders at the most critical level of the organization.

Compass came to his new post after making his name in the department as an expert in "community policing," an idea that truly could make every city in America a safer place—if Americans everywhere were willing to double or triple the size of their police forces and if police executives everywhere were ready to admit they've been faking its implementation almost since it was dreamed up. The First District, for example, had close to a dozen federally funded Community Oriented Police Squad officers among its total patrol force of seventy-two when Compass moved in, but the COPS cops weren't doing any of the wonderful things community policing officers supposedly do, like walk beats, solve crime problems, or improve the quality of life. I know, because in the summer before Compass took over, I strolled the housing projects where these cops were supposed to be known on a first-name basis and even though I was wearing a police windbreaker instead of my usual attire, the residents looked at me like I was from Mars. One woman sitting on a porch that looked over an overgrown, garbage-strewn courtyard laughed when I asked how often the cops come by. "Honey," she said, "they don't come in here."

As in most every other city that claims to do community policing, the First District's COPS cops spent most of their working hours answering 911 calls. On paper, they had "beats." In reality, they stayed in their cars until the radio started going, then ran from call to call to whatever corner of the district the calls took them.

The community policing officers were not the only ones working "off post" in the First District. Every district in the city also had several people assigned to a special "task force" that had formerly been charged with investigating all crimes other than homicides, rapes, and child abuse cases. But since these investigators hadn't even been bothering to go out in the field on robberies, all these units were relieved of investigative responsibilities and the districts were told to transform them into proactive street-crime units that could be sent from hot spot to hot spot to help clean up problems as they arose. In the First District, however, this unit was still a refuge for cops who didn't like to leave the office.

Despite these lingering symptoms of dysfunction, Compass walked in on his first day with a kind of confidence that can't be taught. Maybe it was because he understood that for all the deployment issues he had yet to resolve, the reorganization of the department had already given him additional resources—and far more authority than he would have had as a district-level commander in any other city in America. Maybe he simply understood that he had been put in better position than anyone else in the world to bring down crime in New Orleans's First District.

Clearly, his moment had arrived. He'd known many of the

crooks in the First District since they were bullies in the school yard, and he was certain they would cut and run like the Iraqi army the instant they were confronted by a police force with a plan.

Now all that was required of him was to lead. Because aside from the somewhat unteachable characteristics of good leadership, the principles of effective deployment aren't very difficult to grasp.

And Pennington, along with my business partner John Linder and I, had already applied those fundamental principles to a redeployment plan that gave quarterbacks like Compass all the resources he needed to call a good game from the field.

I remember well one of my first visits to the First District.

It was well past midnight on my first date with a woman fifteen years my junior, and she'd decided a tough guy from New York might like to venture out of the French Quarter to hear the music in the bars where tourists dare not go.

"Wow," she said, "I've never been with a man who was so unafraid."

"Gee," I thought, "now I can't tell her I feel like I'm gonna shit in my pants." She was Esmeralda and I was a cross between Quasimodo and Orson Welles, but if she wanted to see me as Captain Phoebus, I wasn't about to shatter her illusion.

I wasn't carrying a gun because I didn't think I could afford to look any heavier than I was, but at least I had some good intel on how the crooks were deployed. I could see the dots in my mind as we walked along—a rash of stickups on that corner, a couple shootings on the next block.

"Why are you putting your watch and rings in your pocket?" she asked.

"In case I have to defend your honor, my dear," I said, meanwhile thinking about how the flash of a bait fish always draws predators in for the kill. I was glad I hadn't yet had a single drink, because I knew they also looked for the slightest stumble.

One of the musicians we heard that night offered this personal greeting from the stage: "You two ain't gonna make it to the parking lot alive." I could chuckle at that, because I knew from a Comstat meeting earlier in the day that the First District had just started posting a cop outside. When my date suggested we settle in at one of the places where the aging transvestites started their lip-synch contests at about 3 A.M., I reflected happily back to a line graph the department had put together that showed street crimes dropping to nothing near dawn as the crooks drifted off to their beds. Before long, I figured, the witching hour would be over.

New Orleans was testing me. For the past twenty years or so, I'd been tortured by fellow New Yorkers about my taste in clothing, so I had been hopeful that one benefit of taking an assignment in New Orleans would be that my two-tone shoes and homburg would finally blend into the background. I was dead wrong. In the after-hours joints, I looked like an easy mark. Inside the New Orleans Police Department—where the detectives arrive for work in polo shirts instead of pinkie rings—I was still the nut with the funny wardrobe. Well, maybe not "the nut"; I'd graduated to "eccentric."

But this time I was also sometimes viewed as a carpetbagger who'd made it big on some snake-oil strategies I'd sold in New York.

"Whayuh you from, anyway—Hahvud?" one skeptical homicide commander asked me. "What the fuck does some boy from up Nawth know 'bout fighting crime in N'Orlins?"

It was a variation on a refrain I'd hear everywhere I went. Every city thinks its crime problems are unique—as if the hump selling crack on the corner is any different in New Orleans than in Washington Heights or as if their car-breaker-inners have a special little pirouette they do before they knock the glass out of the rear window. At least this commander had fire, though. If there were 100 more like him in the department, I knew we could turn things around. But there were plenty of others, I'm sure, who whined behind my back because they were under the mistaken impression, like just about everybody else in the country, that the fix I was peddling rested solely on:

1. computers
2. community policing
3. "zero tolerance" quality-of-life enforcement, or
4. the temporary suspension of the Bill of Rights

Of course, they had a point if they were also wondering how the success of the NYPD could be replicated in a department with less than half the manpower per capita. For a couple days, even I was thinking about dumping Comstat and my "Four Steps to Crime Reduction" to pitch a new twist on the "Broken Windows" theory of policing. In New York, the biggest quality-of-life problem had been the squeegee men; in New Orleans, it was the heat, and I was sweating out of places I didn't even know I had. The real snake-oil salesmen had been conning the public into believing that murders had gone down in New York City because we'd driven the squeegee men off the streets, so maybe I could convince people that all we had to do to knock down murders in New Orleans was build a tennis bubble over the entire city and turn on the A.C. I'd call it the "Central Air" theory of policing, and I was willing to bet it would do more to lower crime than fixing broken windows.

Unfortunately, my contract would probably have expired before the cooled air ever kicked in, so as a half-measure, I hunted down a place where they sold this great talcum powder in a gold can and I returned to the principles that had worked in New York. "Deployment is more important than numbers," I would say.

Of course, more numbers better deployed is the best of all worlds, but since we were going to have to wait more than a year before any new recruits could join the force, improving deployment was the only thing that could help us right away.

All right, was Mayor Marc Morial's answer, but first tell us how many cops we'd need in the best of all worlds. Given the city's growing national reputation for violence, the political will was there to restore the force to its former strength—and beyond.

There are a lot of variables to consider in trying to come up with the optimal size of a police force. How bad is the crime and how much or better had it been over the past twenty or twenty-five years? How many calls for service does the department handle? Is the drug problem unusually bad? What features of the city might require additional police staffing? Is there a subway system? Public housing? Legalized gambling? Any major tourist destinations or commercial shopping areas? How about work rules? Are there one or two cops in every patrol car? How many of a cop's patrol tours are lost to court appearances? Is training adequate or does every member of the force have to spend more days each year sharpening his or her skills?

It's an inexact science, for sure, but you use the answers to those questions to help make comparisons to the manpower in similar cities. For New Orleans, I arrived at a figure of 2,000, then explained how the department could get the same effect with just 1,700—which was about 400 more than they had but only about 220 more than they were already budgeted for.

In the business world, smart companies no longer hire as many full-time employees as they really need—they hire about 85 percent of the number they need and make up the difference with temporary workers or independent contractors who can be trimmed relatively painlessly during the slow times. I wouldn't ever want to see Kelly Girls working as cops, but overtime can be used in a similar way to make a department leaner and more productive.

Even while waiting for the new recruits, the department could have substantially increased its effective size by increasing overtime. Then, to ensure the time-and-a-half pay isn't being wasted, those overtime hours would have been used exclusively for cops answering calls in radio cars—where productivity is easy to measure—while the officers cut loose from the radio would have been free to go after the crooks.

In the end, the city council gave Pennington only a fraction of the overtime budget he asked for—and then started cutting back. The bottom line was that for the next year or so, we were going to have to prove the part of my mantra about deployment being more important than numbers. In fact, we were going to have fewer cops in 1997 than the department did in its dismal 1996.

The main principle of deployment can be expressed in one sentence: "Map the crime and put the cops where the dots are." Or more succinctly: "Put cops on dots."

The abbreviated version has a certain advantage. If you repeat it slowly enough and often enough while keeping your eyes locked in a blank stare, you will soon be hailed as one of the great gurus of policing. And rightly so.

Of course, there are a few more details to consider.

First, there's the element of time. The phrase "where the dots are" has to be understood as a question not just about location but also about the time of day, the day of the week or month, and the season when the targeted offenses are taking place.

Then, even before we consider tactics themselves—in other words, what the cops will do when they get to where we're sending them—there are a number of legitimate questions that would probably come up if you simply told a roomful of police officers to take all the intel they'd been given and "go where the dots are."

"How many of us should go out?" they might ask.

"How should we split up?"

"Should we take a car or should we walk?"

And a question not to be dismissed—"What should we wear?" In New York, before we changed their wardrobe, all patrol cops assigned to fighting narcotics had to wear uniforms everywhere they went. In New Orleans, there were no cops in plainclothes at all. That's a great advantage if you're a robber, because you never have to worry that your target or the bum looking on from the corner might really be "five-oh."

The hardest thing for most police departments to figure out is that not all of their patrol officers are needed for answering calls for service. If the patrol division does nothing but answer 911 calls, they're just report-takers, not crime fighters, and it probably means the cops answering the calls or the deployment of the cars isn't efficient enough.

Despite its low staffing, New Orleans wasn't completely overwhelmed by the demands of the radio. Newark, even with twice the police manpower per capita, was much worse. Before Joseph Santiago took over as police director there, the average response time for a robbery was two hours, not only because their dispatching system was a mess and a lot of cops were hiding behind their desks, but because the department had failed, as most do, to align the work schedules of the cops with the work schedules of the crooks. Past midnight, it wasn't unusual for half the city to be covered by a single patrol car.

New Orleans had no major problem with response times for robberies—but they may have been helped by the fact that the people responsible for investigating robberies didn't even bother to respond. The patrol force's trouble with 911 calls was more typical: They answered more calls than they should have and stayed too long when they got there, especially, I'd noticed, when the calls came from Hooters or one of the strip joints.

In 1995, the department had responded to one and a half times as many calls for service as there were residents of the city, and 56 percent of all those calls were not crime-related. Almost half of those runs were for false burglar alarms or for callers who hung up before speaking. Years earlier, the city had established a series of fines for repeated false alarms, but the fines weren't enforced.

The problem with false alarms is nationwide. Burglar alarms account for at least 15 percent of the calls for service in many cities, and only about 1 percent of the alarms signal an actual crime in progress. That means about 15 percent of the work done by the nation's patrol force is wasted. Somehow the people who own alarms have to reduce the costs of that wasted effort, either through the imposition of escalating fines for multiple false alarms or by laws requiring that the manufacturers of alarms provide first response every time one of their products sounds off.

Every police department has to look for ways to limit the time lost to those unnecessary calls for service, but it has to pay even more attention to ensuring that its deployment of radio cars fits the demand. The only way to do that—though few departments do—is to look at the radio runs every week by precinct, day of week, and time of day, then realign deployment accordingly.

In the First District, Captain Compass discovered the main reason the radio units wasted valuable time was because they were allowed to. As long as the cops on radio assignment knew the next call to the district would be picked up by some other car, even if that car belonged to COPS officers who were supposed to be out walking foot patrol, nobody worried about how much time the cops spent on each response. To free up some cops for crime-fighting, Compass simply told his platoon commanders that there would be no more help from other units and that the commanders themselves were expected to be the first line of defense whenever their people needed help keeping up with the calls. Efficiency increased immediately, meaning there were now more man-hours that could be dedicated to crook-catching.

Now it was time to tell the cops freed from the radio how they were supposed to split up.

There's an old military maxim: "He who would protect everything protects nothing."

Over the past decade or so, the rise of a particular brand of community policing has caused many people to assume the best way to deploy a large group of patrol officers is to divide a city or neighborhood according to some kind of a grid and put one cop into each box to handle whatever crime or quality-of-life problems might pop up there. In a city where each beat is small enough to be patrolled on foot, the idea is an honorable one, with its principal advantage being that foot cops can get to know the crooks on their watch extremely well. The cops can't just drink coffee with the precinct council leaders; they have to get to know the good, the bad, and the ugly.

But even leaving aside the fact that no department in America, least of all New Orleans, has the manpower to put a foot cop in every beat every day—and most couldn't even provide that kind of fleeting blanket coverage with patrol cars—the idea of community policing is full of holes. A thin blue line of inexperienced, undertrained, and undersupervised cops doesn't stand a chance against the hit-and-run tactics of the criminals. If they all spread out and aren't following a game plan, they're nothing but scarecrows—to borrow a metaphor from John Timoney. And the thing about jailbirds is, they ain't afraid of scarecrows.

The giveaway that community policing was hatched by academics is how the model devalues the role of supervisors. Everything is left up to the individual cop, including the hours he or she is going to work, which explains why the community policing officers in the old NYPD mostly worked ten to six and took weekends off. Their supervisors, meanwhile, had been told that they were to act as mentors and coaches rather than bosses.

Having a coach or mentor may work at an ad agency, where the only adversary anybody will ever face may or may not be armed with a staple gun, but when you're engaging repeat offenders and predatory criminals armed with 9mms, you need a field commander to get out front and show the rookies, by example, how to stand their ground and make arrests without anybody getting hurt—including the crooks. On Christmas Day, 1982, I showed five-foot-one Vertel Martin how to take a gun off a suspect—left hand on his gun, right hand pointing your own gun at the ground, partner perpendicular to you on the other side of the suspect—and we came up with not just a gun, but also a camera whose film contained snapshots of a couple vics he and his crew had robbed and left tied up in a nearby Midtown hotel.

The first piece of wisdom a smart supervisor will impart to his or her charges is that the crooks usually work in teams. You can't expect a five-foot-one cop who weighs 110 pounds to chase off a couple guys who are built like Mark McGwire and hopped up on some dangerous brew of testosterone, blunts, and crack. If corners where there've been drug dealing and quality-of-life problems need clearing, the smart supervisor grabs a van, picks five or six foot-patrol cops off their posts, hits the corners one by one, and loads up the van with anybody they arrest. When we talk about the value of foot patrol, we have to be clear that much of the value is lost if there is no supervisor out in the field with them deploying them for maximum impact.

At an NYPD Comstat meeting, we once questioned the commander of an Upper Manhattan precinct about some persistent quality-of-life problems he was having along Broadway and why so few tickets were being issued.

The commander hesitated.

"Captain," I asked, "could it be that your officers are afraid to give out tickets?"

He acknowledged we might have hit the heart of the matter.

"All right, then," I said. "Just send them out in teams, with a sergeant there to supervise. Better yet, go yourself."

And as if fear weren't a powerful enough inhibitor, there's also the little matter of human inertia. If 10 percent of the people in any business do 90 percent of the work, 90 percent of the cops wouldn't accomplish much of anything if left to their own initiative. But when they're working in a team setting, under a demanding and inspirational leader who, in turn, is being held accountable by his supervisors and the community for the team's performance, a much higher percentage of the cops will work to their fullest potential.

The supervisor of a patrol unit also has a responsibility to ensure that members of the community are aware of all the crime problems they face and that they provide constant feedback on how the cops are doing so that all the community's needs can be addressed. The average community policing officer doesn't have the experience, the juice, or the desire to handle those aspects of the job.

There's one last important reason why a supervised team of cops, rather than the individual cop, ought to be seen as the basic building block of an effective police organization: When police commanders identify a crime or serious quality-of-life problem in their community, they should never be satisfied just to "keep a lid on it"; they should send enough people to take it out. Otherwise, the crooks win.

As we looked to redeploy the entire department, we wanted to be sure that every district commander was going to be able to call upon that kind of concentrated enforcement capability. We weren't going to be able to do it by adding cops to the force. For the next year or so, the difference all had to come from a restructuring of the entire department.

If you took the command structure of most departments and replicated it in the private sector, here's what it would look like:

A customer at McDonald's asks to see the manager: He has a complaint about the french fries. "Sorry," says the manager. "The fries guy answers to somebody downtown. He's with another unit."

"Oh," says the customer, "and who can I talk to about the ketchup dispensers?"

"Heinz handles the ketchup," says the manager. "I'm not sure how you get in touch with them—maybe their phone number is written on the back of their take-out packets."

A ridiculous scenario, right? McDonald's couldn't survive with that type of management structure. But those are the kind of answers you'd probably get if you walked into a neighborhood police station house with a complaint about an antidrug operation or to report that your brother or friend had been killed.

The departmental structure Chief Pennington had inherited was typical in the way it fractured responsibility. Detectives and Narcotics worked downtown and answered only to themselves. If a district commander had a serious problem with a violent drug crew, he had to petition headquarters for help and then sit and wait until Narcotics got around to it. But Narcotics didn't set priorities the way a district commander would. They tended to judge jobs according to how strong a case they could develop and how many guns and drugs they could throw on a table when their seemingly neverending investigation was done.

The detectives didn't even have desks in the districts. A district commander might have concerns that a recent homicide could spark a series of retaliation shootings, but if the original homicide wasn't a priority downtown, there was nothing the commander could do to speed the investigation.

When I sat down to talk to Pennington about these problems, he got the benefit not only of our experiences in New York, but also of my rapidly growing library of books for military nuts. Since the spring of 1995, when I picked up a copy of *The Knight's Cross,* a biography of Erwin Rommel, the German master of desert warfare, I'd been boning up on the secrets of history's greatest military leaders and strategists, and many of them included terrific wisdom on deployment.

I know some people get uneasy when parallels are drawn between warfare and policing—they prefer we use the vocabulary of modern business management. But you know what? Most of the big business gurus get their audiences pumped by talking about "going to war" with the competition or getting "down in the trenches" with front-line workers, and nobody gives them a hard time. When the Catholic Church confirmed me, the bishop slapped me on the face and told me I was now "a soldier in the army of Christ," and my parents didn't think to complain about the imagery. Besides, the policing profession is a little more like armed combat than most. What else could it be when fifteen to twenty thousand people in America are being killed by the opponents every year and another 400,000 are victims of gun violence? If it eases anybody's mind, we can call policing a "rescue mission" and hold on to the military analogies, because there's nobody better schooled in rescue missions than the armed forces.

Anyway, there's a great story told about Sun Tzu, the ancient strategist credited with authoring *The Art of War,* the world's first military treatise and a favorite of the business academics.

A king who had come to admire Sun Tzu's principles had asked to see the ideas put to a test, so two or three hundred women from the king's inner palace were brought out and assembled before Sun Tzu. Sun Tzu divided the group into two companies, outfitted them with armor, helmets, and swords, and selected two of the king's favorite concubines as company commanders. He then instructed the entire group in a few basic field maneuvers, making certain they understood how to advance, retreat, turn left, and turn right according to the sounding of a drum.

When all were in place, he gave his first order by the sound of the drum: "Right turn!"

The women fell into fits of laughter, so Sun Tzu patiently reviewed their instructions several times more.

Again, he gave a command: "Left turn!"

Again, the women just giggled.

"If the words of command are not clearly understood, the general is to blame," he said. "But if his orders are clear and the soldiers still fail to obey, their officers are at fault."

With that, he ordered the beheading of the king's two favorites and installed two other women in their places. This time when he barked out orders, the two companies whirled and spun and stopped and started as if they had one mind, and Sun Tzu said to the king, "Your soldiers are now ready. You can send them through fire and water and they will not hesitate. They can settle all things under heaven."

Sun Tzu was no madman. He wrote that a general should treat his soldiers like his sons and held that the supreme military victory was one in which no men were lost because no fighting was necessary. Translated to policing, that means crime prevention is preferable to arrests, because arrests only happen when there've already been casualties.

But Sun Tzu also understood that an army has to move with singularity of purpose and that subordinate commanders have to believe in and act with absolute faith in the vision of the leader.

Bratton had been almost as ruthless at the NYPD, immediately dispatching four of the five "superchiefs" to the Old Policemen's Home and bestowing less-than-lateral transfers to a third of the precinct commanders within a year and a half of the department's first Comstat meeting. Many crime fighters, though, won huge overnight promotions, demonstrating that the new NYPD was, like the French army in Napoleon's youth, an organization aggressively "open to talent." Loyalty to the leader's vision was indispensable, but successful innovators were rewarded.

The great leaders, it seems, have always understood that the secret to achieving decisive victories lies in the ability to establish unity of command over all manners of striking power.

Hannibal, the great enemy of Rome, famously stormed over the Alps with a pack of elephants leading his heavy cavalry, but the key to his remarkable victories on Roman soil lay not so much in these precombustion-driven tanks as in his ability to synchronize each of the varied movements of infantry and cavalry in his multiracial and multilingual army. At Cannae, he faced an army almost twice as big as his own, but by drawing the Roman infantry into combat with his weakest soldiers—just as a police commander can lure the crooks in with decoys or undercover buy-and-bust operations—he was able to envelop the enemy from the sides and rear with his stronger African infantry and finally his Gaulish, Spanish, and Numidian horsemen. When the day ended, only one in eight Roman soldiers had survived.

At Trafalgar, Nelson achieved one of naval warfare's most spectacular victories thanks to daring deployment—a perpendicular blow across the French and Spanish line—a tactic made possible by a new flag-signaling system that allowed him to pass heat-of-the-battle orders to every ship in his fleet.

It is said of Patton, whose World War I tank division took the French village of Cheppy in the first offensive coupling of tanks and infantry, that nobody understood better the value of combined arms. And he learned it by reading Napoleon.

Lucky for me, I had in New Orleans a true warrior on my side who fully appreciated the importance of establishing unity of command. At fifty-five, Terry Ebbert looked like Dorian Gray, not because he'd made a pact with the devil but because he ran about 200 miles a day and he was an ex-Marine. He was the real deal. One Easter Sunday he was standing in the finishers' area after running a ten-kilometer New Orleans road race when a young lawyer from Baton Rouge walked up and shook his hand. The lawyer had been a Marine lieutenant in Operation Desert Storm, and he wanted Terry to know that on the night before the Marines crossed the Iraqi line, the lieutenants there all had gathered in one tent and braced themselves for battle by sharing memories of the things Terry had taught them. Besides winning the Navy Cross in Vietnam and ascending to the right hand of Corps Commandant P. X. Kelly, Colonel Terry Ebbert had been the commanding officer of the Marines' officer training school at Quantico from 1987 to 1989. "A leader can't sit back and say, 'Charge!,' " he would remind me. "A leader says, 'Follow me.' "

The businessmen who'd created the New Orleans Police Foundation had brought Terry in as the founding executive director, and when the old war hero set up his office on Poydras Street, he found a special place in his filing cabinet for a copy of the general orders George S. Patton, Jr., had issued to his commanders when he took over the Third Army in 1944. Patton's officers were expected to make daily visits to the front ("to observe, not to mettle"). For me, Terry pulled out a small paperback he had helped to write for the Marine Corps. It's called *Warfighting*.

The NOPD had a few things in common with the Marines. Both organizations were small, both had to get by without the best equipment, and both counted their losses in bodies. I like to tell Terry he stole all the best ideas in *Warfighting* from Sun Tzu, but really, that slim paperback may be the best synthesis available of some timeless military concepts about leadership, deployment, and strategic thinking that are most relevant to policing.

The Marines believe in maneuver warfare, as opposed to warfare by attrition, which means they need to be quick and nimble enough as an organization to exploit opportunities that may come and go in a flash. To accomplish that, they push decision-making authority down the chain of command so that the soldiers and commanders in the field can devise and implement tactics on the run to accomplish whatever mission their senior officers have set before them. One of the reasons they can pull this off is because their people are so well trained, but beyond that, the organization has recognized that as long as subordinates operate with a firm appreciation of the "commander's intent," or desired end result, accepting occasional mistakes or flaws in their field strategies beats the hell out of making everybody wait around for communications to travel up and down the chain of command.

At the same time that individual initiative is expected and required of every soldier, the Marines entrust overall command of any given operation to a single leader, whose job it may be to draw up mission tactics that will best exploit the combined power of land, sea, and air forces. When the Marines are operating in the same theater with other branches of the armed forces, the Marine Corps and all the other branches submit to the leadership of a single joint commander. This is because the alternative would not only be inefficient, it would limit the operation's ability to use one tactic to either reinforce or exploit the effects of another. As Napoleon said in his time about the various forces at his disposal: "Infantry, cavalry, and artillery are nothing without each other. Nothing is so important in war as an undivided command."

I was happy to be able to tell Terry that our talks about creating unity of command were reinforcing an idea we'd fully embraced in New York. In policing, the challenge is to unify command not over land, sea, and air, but over uniformed patrol, narcotics, and the detectives. We weren't there long enough to implement the idea across the entire city, but the last thing we did before Bratton stepped down was to take the ten precincts and two Housing Police districts in the police borough called Brooklyn North and unify the command of all 4,000 of their patrol cops, narcotics officers, detectives, and associated supervisors under Joe Dunne, a brilliant field commander who'd headed the Seven-Five back in '94 when Bratton came on. Traditionally, a borough commander, like the precinct commanders, had no direct authority over the detective squads, the narcotics units, or the housing units, who answered up their own chains of command to the chief of detectives, the chief of narcotics, and the chief of the Housing Police.

Just as in the Marines, the decentralization of decision making sped up the tempo at which our forces moved, allowing Dunne to do things like move narcotics investigators into detective squads—or detectives into narcotics units—to clear up rashes of shootings or home invasions. At a moment's notice, he could move quality-of-life enforcement, warrant squad, robbery, anticrime, and auto crime units into a precinct to take out a pattern of carjackings. He could even pull narcotics units off their regular beat so they could help the precincts keep down the number of street-corner stabbings and shootings that usually accompany the spirited, weeklong buildup to one of the summer's biggest parades.

Dunne's expanded authority did not come at the expense of the precinct commanders. Whenever he put any of the boroughwide units to go into a precinct, those units were to answer to the precinct commander, and they were expected to get a full briefing on crime conditions in the neighborhood before they hit the streets. From above, we held Joe accountable through Comstat. Doing so ensures that the commander is carrying out the commissioner's intent and not turning into Marlon Brando in *Apocalypse Now*.

The initiative worked. Deployment in Brooklyn North became rapid, concentrated, synchronized, and focused. In the first ten months of the initiative, crime in Brooklyn North dropped 50 percent faster than it did in the rest of the city for the entire year.

Terry and I looked at what we had to work with in New Orleans and gulped. There were no auto crime units, no street crime units, no robbery units, no citywide narcotics squads, and almost no foot cops. About the only people we had to give the local commanders were the detectives and narcotics units at central.

On Labor Day weekend of 1996, 13 people were murdered in the city of New Orleans—the equivalent of having 182 people murdered in one weekend in New York. If that ever happened, I told Terry, the Marines would be parachuting into Central Park and storming the beaches of Coney Island. Days later, Chief Pennington, John Linder, and I released a fifty-five-page report recommending dramatic decentralization for the NOPD.

Some of the business people Terry worked for didn't like the idea that one of the consequences of the plan would be to put more cops in the bad neighborhoods instead of the French Quarter and the central business district, but Terry could wow them with the Marine analogies. Besides, he told his bosses, *Time* magazine and the television networks aren't that interested in litterbugs. They come to New Orleans to tell the rest of the nation about the murder rate. Gary Cooper—I mean Chief Pennington—closed the deal by going out on a limb and publicly guaranteeing a double-digit decline in violent crime and a 15 percent reduction in murder within one year if awarded support for the strategy and substantial pay increases for his troops.

Our plan for the NOPD wasn't an exact copy of the Brooklyn North initiative. In Brooklyn, we knew the idea would work; here we were throwing a Hail Mary pass. With the NYPD, we had an organization that was like General Motors in 1923—a huge conglomeration of quality brand names and parts makers with no unifying management structure; with the NOPD, we had the Apple Computers of 1996—a tarnished brand name with a tiny market share whose machines had been bursting into flames. With Dunne, we had a proven field commander, supported by subordinate commanders, who had tasted success in 1994 and 1995 and who were ready to take the first step toward burying the traditional function-based command structure. In New Orleans, where the entire department was smaller than Dunne's Brooklyn North, we were moving authority down yet another level and putting almost all the department's resources in the hands of eight untested district commanders, some of whom couldn't even recognize the outlines of their own districts when we first showed them their maps.

But we didn't have the luxury of keeping any people in reserve at headquarters to use as roving troubleshooters, so we decided to send just about every detective and narcotics cop we had out to the districts, where for the first time they would have to answer to the district commanders. At headquarters we kept only enough investigators to handle sex crimes, child abuse, major narcotics cases, and to establish a cold case squad. And knowing that the chief executive has too many other obligations to focus around the clock on operations, we plucked a smart young major named Ronnie Serpas out of Special Operations and made him an overnight three-star general. As the first to hold the title of chief of operations, Serpas was to be what Timoney and Anemone were to Bratton. He would become the Grand Inquisitor at Comstat and the force driving the entire department in its day-to-day fight against crime.

Over time, the district commanders could anticipate the arrival of new recruits, and so I also laid out what I still believe should be the standard units under the direct command of every precinct or district commander in the country. Every morning when that commander looks inside his or her tackle box, he should find the following crook-catching equipment ready for use:

- a detective squad, which would, of course, investigate all homicides, shootings, robberies, burglaries, domestic violence incidents, assaults, and so on, but also interrogate every person arrested in the district to help win convictions and make new cases
- a narcotics unit, which would identify drug spots, drug crews, and violent gangs, take them out with buy-and-bust operations and other arrests, develop confidential informants, assist the detectives with shooting and murder investigations, and pass intelligence to the major case narcotics unit at headquarters
- a robbery and burglary unit, which, like my old robbery squad in Transit, would identify patterns or hot spots and go out with decoys and stakeouts to catch the crooks in action
- a fugitive apprehension unit, which, like the guys who tracked down James McBee in the Seven-Five Precinct, would run down everybody wanted on bench warrants, arrest warrants, and parole or probation violations
- a quality-of-life unit, which would, among other things, enforce laws relating to public drinking, pissing on the street, drunk driving, noise, graffiti, prostitution, curfews, truancy, and aggressive panhandling

In life, and especially in the life of a consultant, you never get everything you want. While waiting for new recruit classes, each NOPD district has been making do without the last three items on my list and by using one small task force to pick up some, but not all, of those tasks.

The important thing was that the decentralization unified command of most patrol and investigative functions, making commanders like Compass the masters of their own destinies.

Without gifted commanders—like Louie Anemone, John Timoney, Joe Dunne, and Ronnie Serpas—the other principles of good deployment are nothing.

Eddie Compass was a leader. He just had the look, which is something you come to recognize as soon as you see it. I can tell you 100 things about the qualities of a leader, but there's still something intangible in the way a leader carries him or herself that make other people willing to follow.

Confidence has a lot to do with it. As Henry Ford once said, "Whether you think you can or you think you can't, you're probably right." A leader has to truly believe the brass ring is within reach and has to make everybody else see it too. Compass not only believed he could reduce crime and fear in the First District, he believed his district could be better at reducing crime and fear than any other district in the city.

There are certain attributes of leadership that can be prescribed. In policing, bosses often lose respect because they turn away from the streets when they're given desks. Most fire departments don't have that problem. Their bosses not only share the danger and hardships of their subordinates, they are always the first into the flames. As a result, they are revered. Not everybody loves them, necessarily, but at least they're awarded respect.

In policing, the exact parallel to entering a burning building is hitting the door of a wanted criminal. Ever since I was a lieutenant and had my own fugitive unit in Central Robbery, my rule has been that a boss always goes to the door. In routine cases, that meant a sergeant. In cases where the fugitive was known to use a gun, I had to be out front. At that moment, it's just like a first date in New Orleans: No matter how a-scared you are, you don't let your fear show.

Another advantage is that if anything goes wrong, the boss has a better chance than anybody else to bring the situation quickly back under control. As a sergeant, I once had to ask a hyped-up NYPD entry team armed with helmets, jump boots, and automatic weapons to sit out an apartment search because I was worried about some kids I'd seen upstairs in the building. Wearing nothing over our suit jackets but thin trench coats, another sergeant and I went in instead and shmoozed out of hiding the cop shooter we were all there looking for.

The simple truth is, as Patton, Terry Ebbert, and many others have said, you can only lead from the front, and Compass must have known that in his bones. When the radio got hot, he and his second-in-command, Lieutenant Bob Gostl, would jump in a patrol car and start answering calls themselves. At 0300 hours, when most commanders would be fast asleep at home, Compass would be helping take a gun off some character outside the Iberville Housing Project. The good ones are all like that. As chief of patrol in the NYPD, Louie Anemone was the first one in the door when an Emergency Services unit stormed a barricaded bicycle shop to haul out a robbery crew who had already shot both the store's owner and Officer Ray Cannon, the first cop to respond to the scene.

Maybe the most important test of leadership Compass faced in his first few months was when a couple of guys with a gasoline can torched the district's satellite office inside Iberville. Another commander might have closed the office, citing concerns about the safety of his officers. Not Compass.

"We're not gonna let those bitches run us out of the development," he declared. The First District cops loved it. When a commander has made it clear to every one of his subordinates his firm belief that cops must follow honorable rules of engagement at all times, showing a little passion for the fight can never hurt.

Compass also let his platoon commanders know that they too had to be seen—night and day—by their subordinates out in the field. The troops have to know that the bosses care not only about their performance, but about the conditions they work in—the hot days, the rainy nights. They should be made to feel that their commander will be their strongest advocate when resources are needed or when their work merits recognition. They should feel that the only boss they need to worry about pleasing or crossing is the one they report directly to. A good leader calls attention to their accomplishments and backs them even when they make mistakes—as long as the mistakes were honest and came about in carrying out the commander's intent.

This works best if the leader's vision is shared by each of his or her subordinate commanders. Just as Pennington could see in Compass a natural disciple of the new crime-reduction emphasis, Compass filled his district's most critical positions with subordinates who were also true believers.

Lieutenant Gostl took command of the detective squad and soon came up with a district-level Comstat meeting that kept every investigator up to date on patterns and, through the use of video, helped ensure that important crime information from the meeting was shared at roll calls with every patrol officer on every tour. Sergeant Mark Mornay took over Narcotics and devised creative new ways to combine them with other district personnel to solve burglary and auto theft patterns. Sergeant Michael Glasser completely overhauled the "task force" into an efficient street crime unit, casting out the paper pushers and bringing in young athletic cops who could back up narcotics on a search warrant or use quality-of-life laws to clear a corner where guns were often used to settle disputes. In the Lafitte Housing Project, Compass installed Sergeant Ruben Stephens, a friend from childhood who believed as strongly as Compass that the families who live in the public developments were overdue for some effective policing.

First, Stephens moved his entire unit out of the district station house and established a twenty-four-hour command post inside the development. Then he made sure his foot patrols were legit, walking the complex himself to see that his cops were checking stairwells and abandoned buildings, patrolling the courtyards and the periphery. Most importantly, he executed the fundamentals of crime-fighting the way the rest of the district did: He spotted patterns, identified possible suspects, set up stakeouts, and took out the problems. The last time I checked, there hadn't been a robbery at Lafitte in more than ten months.

The overall effect began to restore the community's faith in their cops, and within six months, calls were pouring in to a citywide hot line from Lafitte residents who were willing to supply the most detailed complaints imaginable about one of the development's most intractable problems—a drug crew, based in one of the courtyards, that controlled the crack trade for the whole project and several surrounding blocks. The callers reported where the crack was cooked, where it was stashed, and the names and vehicles of several of the players, including the leader of the crew, an ex-con in his mid-twenties named Tyre McMasters.

Stephens had all the intel he could ever want. What he needed now was a game plan.

McMasters's crew was sophisticated enough to dodge the uniformed cops in Stephens's own unit—their lookouts used radios and a simple series of whistles to pass warnings to the dealers. But the business was not exactly a model of discipline and order. Before Compass put Stephens in the development, the crew sold out in the open, and long after they were chased inside, the trade continued to contribute a swarm of prostitutes, robbers, and burglars to the fabric of the neighborhood. When the crew started using young kids on bicycles to deliver drug orders to customers, Stephens really got angry.

If pressed, a uniform patrol unit can do a lot on its own to disrupt a drug crew, but it makes sense to bring in a unit that can do buy-and-busts in order to build the strongest case. Knowing Compass's resources were limited and hoping to send a strong message to the community, Stephens decided he wanted to bring in the FBI. To nobody's surprise, Compass immediately went to bat for the federal help and got it.

Stephens's unit quickly came up with a confidential informant who would be asked to do a lot of the hard work. Two or three times a week, the informant would meet with the cops and federal agents at a prearranged location, put on a wire, and head into the dealers' lair to make drug buys. The feds and cops would monitor the transactions from a distance.

In the end, the operation worked beautifully. About six months after the first buy, federal warrants were put out for McMasters and six others, and Stephens's people were able to sweep all seven up off the streets in just two days. Five pleaded to reduced charges in exchange for cooperation in a case against a supplier higher on the ladder, while Tyre McMasters and his own chief of operations, Theron Roberts, faced trial on federal racketeering charges.

We must learn, however, how to move these investigations more swiftly. About the time this one started, McMasters's girlfriend became a mother. But she would not live to hear her child's first words. Several weeks into the FBI investigation, she was at a club on North Claiborne Avenue one night when a gunman came in looking for McMasters. McMasters wasn't there, so the execution became hers. She took one bullet in the head.

Her death was nobody's fault but the killer's. Still, it shows why it's critical for the police to move rapidly on all fronts and why commanders like Compass have no quarrel with the pressures that come with increased authority.

In early 1998, Compass was attending a nineteen-day senior management seminar for police supervisors at Harvard University's Kennedy School of Government when the chief who was teaching the class let slip a comment about the Comstat process being overly adversarial.

Compass objected.

"It separates the weak from the strong," he said. "I'm given the task. I'm given the power to do the job. I can't blame anybody but myself for my failures if I fail."

What he neglected to mention is that the Comstat process is just a tool. In the hands of the mediocre, it's useless. In the hands of a great leader, it can be Excalibur.

Later that year, when a bunch of upstarts at Lafitte tried to fill the vacuum created by the McMasters takedown, there was no wait in the response of the First District cops. Calls from the residents gave the district enough to obtain a search warrant, and within a day, the cops led by Compass's old pal Ruben Stephens had knocked out the fledgling crew by seizing their guns and cash.

SEVEN

THE TOOL BAG
Effective Tactics

In a big city or a bad neighborhood, crime doesn't feel like a simple problem. It feels like the humidity in New Orleans—relentless, incurable, everywhere.

Take the worst corner in any precinct in any city in America. Everybody who lives in the neighborhood knows the corner is dangerous, but the solutions may be as hard for them to imagine as the connections between each new report of violence or theft. When you're sleeping in the bathtub to protect yourself from the nightly gunfire outside your windows, it's kind of hard to tell who's doing all the shooting.

The obvious center of the action might be a corner convenience store with a few apartments above it. Drugs are sold from the building—that much would be clear from daily parade of double-parked Cherokees and Pathfinders with out-of-state plates. And the drug trade might also explain why there was a shooting on that corner last week, why there are addict prostitutes trading tricks on the next street over, and why there's always a loud intimidating crowd on the sidewalk drinking beer, pissing at the curb, and blasting their radios. The neighbors phone in complaints about the spot time and time again, but the only response they see is a patrol car sent through on a drive-by. The uniforms rarely make arrests, and if there are any undercover units, all they do is sweep up a bunch of buyers every once in a while and then declare victory.

But if it's truly the worst corner in the neighborhood, there'd be more to the picture than that. There may have been seven shootings, five homicides, thirty robberies, and thirty-five burglaries within a block or two of that intersection within the last three months. Every morning there'd be a string of cars somewhere nearby each with its side rear window punched out. There'd be a handful of older residents who won't dare go out anymore, even to sit in the park, cash their Social Security checks, or shop for food. There might even be a thirteen-year-old math whiz at the nearby junior high school who just started carrying a gun in his backpack wherever he goes because he's tired of being yoked by the wolf packs waiting in the boys' room or at the bus stop a block away from school. Last Thursday maybe he went home without his sneakers.

Sounds pretty hopeless, doesn't it? Not that long ago, even the police didn't think they could do much about an area like that. But if the cops are properly deployed and are gathering and analyzing the crime every day, they can turn that neighborhood around in about a month.

It wouldn't be one lone tactic that'd win the day. Success would be achieved through a combination of tactics simultaneously employed. Tactics are like the isolated actions of all eleven players running a play in football. Some may be blocking, some may be sprinting downfield to receive a pass, some may be acting as decoys; a few are allowed to run the ball or throw it. In one sense, there aren't that many types of action a player can engage in, but the combinations are just about infinite. If the offense becomes predictable, no plays will work. If, on the other hand, the play-calling is varied and enough of the players perform their jobs well, the offense should be able to move the ball at will.

Since crime prevention is always the ultimate objective, one critically important police tactic is to keep the public informed and sufficiently on guard. For now, though, I want to focus only on tactics that directly affect the bad guys.

Our main objectives?

1. to arrest them early in their crime sprees
2. to pressure them into abandoning their worst behavior
3. to take away their guns

TACTIC ONE—QUALITY-OF-LIFE ENFORCEMENT

In early 1996, Queens Homicide was having trouble with a couple of six-month-old double murders—one of which had been a source of great embarrassment for the whole department. That first twin killing had happened inside an Elmhurst nightclub, and because the joint was locked up and quiet by the time any cops arrived, the report was initially classified as "unfounded." Half an hour later, a second call came in adding important new information: The victims referred to in the previous call were now lying dead in the street.

Both double homicides had been professional hits involving drug players a few steps above the street, and not much progress was being made toward locking anybody up for them. Mindful that our killers might not be through killing, Louie Anemone and I finally arranged to sit down with the Queens detectives and a DEA unit, called REDRUM, that was also working the case.

"Look," I said after getting a brief update, "why don't we just do the quality-of-life on these guys?"

From every corner of the room, I got shot a look like I must be intellectually challenged.

It wasn't that they didn't understand my meaning. Over the past two years, the NYPD had been demonstrating that assertive enforcement of quality-of-life laws, like those against public urinating, public drinking, loud radios, turnstile jumping, and truancy, can knock down more serious crime problems if each resulting stop or arrest is treated as an opportunity, potentially, to lock up a fugitive or shake out new intel about various unsolved crimes.

Perhaps, however, these investigators didn't understand why the idea works. In this situation, I was merely suggesting we ought to grab a few of these gangsters on things that would be easy to get them on—like using stolen credit cards or cloned cell phones. As it was, I had no knowledge that the killers had, in fact, been making cell phone calls on somebody else's bill or shopping with bogus plastic. But I knew they were gangsters, and no matter how much money gangsters are making, they never like to pay for anything they can steal. They can't help themselves.

One of the REDRUM guys finally responded. "Commissioner," he said, "we don't operate like that. These are long-term, sensitive investigations. We work with informants who are deep inside these organizations to build our cases. We gather large volumes of evidence through wiretaps and other surveillance methods to build our cases before we go to take these crews out."

When Lee Iacocca was an executive at Ford, his engineers fed him a line like that. Iacocca wanted to get a convertible out on the market immediately and the engineers told him it would take a year or two just to develop a new platform for a convertible. "You don't understand," he told them. "I want you to take one of our cars and saw the roof off it."

"You don't seem to understand," I told REDRUM. "I wanted these humps locked up months ago."

Poor REDRUM. They were forced to admit that federal law enforcement is so screwed up that DEA units don't have the power to lock gangsters up for cloned phones. That would be a job for the Secret Service.

Fortunately, NYPD officers could make arrests on cloned phones, so with REDRUM's information, including an ID on the nightclub shooter and a license plate linked to his crew, we set up DWI and vehicle safety checks near the Roosevelt Avenue bars where all the hit men hung out.

Sure enough, one night the right car showed up, and when the cops stopped it, they arrested one of the passengers on a single charge: possession of a cloned phone. The maximum sentence on the phone count was only a year and the actual sentence is about ten minutes, but the suspect didn't know that, so he became the first to crack, giving up another of the passengers, a guy named Chino, as the shooter in a couple of gangland homicides.

Chino was a seasoned crook. He'd been a contract killer for the Medellin drug cartel since he got out of short pants and he was the leader of his own assassination crew. But when confronted with his associate's statements, he too folded almost instantly and tried to win himself a deal by admitting to a role in nine killings.

Eventually, forty-six homicides were linked to the rival crews involved in the original double killing. And it's fair to say that the death toll would have been even higher if the cloned phone arrest hadn't interrupted the warfare.

Quality-of-life enforcement works essentially the same way, but the tactic has been a source of widespread misunderstanding, especially among some of those who champion it.

Because the policy reinforced Rudy Giuliani's larger effort to revive civility in the New York City, it often gets top billing among reasons cited for the NYPD's successful campaign against crime. In fact, it was only one piece of the puzzle. In New Orleans, we did almost no quality-of-life enforcement because of the lack of personnel, and the city still led the nation in 1997 with its 24 percent decline in murder, rape, robbery, and assault, then followed that up with two more double-digit declines in 1998 and 1999.

In 1982, quality-of-life enforcement was given a name that put it in lights. That year, James Q. Wilson and George Kelling published an article in *The Atlantic Monthly* that came to be known as "Broken Windows." "Broken Windows" was merely an extension of what we used to call the "Breaking Balls" theory, which is the idea that the bad guys could be discouraged from doing anything really bad, at least on any one beat, if the beat cop used enforcement against minor infractions to chase the crooks and the problems they created into the next district or precinct. Sergeants who didn't like paperwork were always advancing the "Breaking Balls" theory as a way to keep things quiet, but some of us who were "in the game" refashioned the concept into a policy I now think of as "Breaking Balls Plus." We realized that if we phoned the warrant desk every time we issued a summons, ball-breaking could be used to catch robbers, rapists, and drug dealers so that they'd be displaced to where they belonged: the pokey.

The central image of *The Atlantic Monthly* article suggested a more mystical link between minor incidents of disorder and more serious crimes. If a building has all its windows intact, the theory goes, it can sit vacant and undisturbed for an indefinite period of time. But if one window is broken and not quickly repaired, all hell breaks loose. The implication is, if the police would take care of the little things, the big things would take care of themselves.

How sad. That idea was tested in New York's subways in the late 1980s, along with a strain of community policing that encouraged supervisors to be "coaches" instead of leaders. The result was an 87 percent rise in subway robberies from 1987 to the middle of 1990.

While I applaud tactics that reduce disorder and the public's fear of crime, implementing quality-of-life tactics alone is like giving a facelift to a cancer patient: The patient may look better and even feel better, but the killer disease hasn't been arrested.

In 1994, when the NYPD crackdown on quality-of-life offenders like squeegee men was followed a few months later by reports of a dramatic drop in violent crime, many people credited the "Broken Windows" notion that the crooks had suddenly taken to the straight and narrow because they had picked up on the prevailing civility vibe.

That's not how it works.

Rapists and killers don't head for another town when they see that graffiti is disappearing from the subway.

The average squeegee man doesn't start accepting contract murders whenever he detects a growing tolerance for squeegeeing.

Panhandling doesn't turn a neighborhood into Murder Central.

In fact, panhandlers don't work in bad neighborhoods. In Midtown Manhattan, a beggar might be able to act like a bully. In a bad neighborhood, he'd be set on fire. Literally.

Quality-of-life enforcement works to reduce crime because it allows the cops to catch crooks when the crooks are off-duty, like hitting the enemy planes while they're still on the ground. A bunch of young Wall Street analysts doing Jell-O shots during a pub crawl along Madison Avenue may be just as likely to piss in the street as a crew of robbers drinking malt liquor on a corner in East New York. And when stopped by the cops, both should have to clear the same hurdles before they're let off with just summonses.

But only one of those groups is likely to include somebody who's relaxing after a long day of robbing or who's building up the courage to go out and rob. Only one group is likely to include somebody wanted on a warrant or somebody carrying a nine in their waistband.

There is, I have to admit, at least one quality-of-life offense that can lead directly to serious criminal behavior: public intoxication. About 40 percent of convicted violent offenders admit having drunk alcohol shortly before committing their crimes, so laws against public intox should be enforced wherever they exist, at least to keep known crooks off the street for a night when they're found carrying a load.

But for quality-of-life enforcement to make a significant contribution to crime reduction, it has to be supported by a larger strategy. What we needed in the subways in 1990 (besides various tactics of a totally different nature) was "Quality-of-Life Plus."

First, we needed to be more selective about who we were arresting on quality-of-life infractions. When a team of cops fills up a van with arrestees, the booking process can take those cops out of service for a whole day in some cities. The public can't afford to lose that much police protection for a bunch of first-time offenders, so the units enforcing quality-of-life laws must be sent where the maps show concentrations of crime or criminals, and the rules governing the stops have to be designed to catch the sharks, not the dolphins. "Quality-of-Life Plus" is not "zero tolerance."

The rules have to be fair. Every quality-of-life offender caught must meet a set list of standards before winning release with only a summons. If the offender have no identification and the cops can't otherwise establish identification to their satisfaction, the offender has to be arrested. This may sound extreme, but criminals have a penchant for using aliases, and the worse they are, the more likely they are to be carrying false ID. A young pickpocket I once collared knew, for instance, that Albany only checked fingerprints against past suspects in the same age range, so he tried to pass an ID that added about thirty years to his life.

If positive identification is established on a quality-of-life stop, the cops must make a call downtown or run the offender's name through a mobile data terminal to check if he or she is on parole or probation or has any outstanding warrants. The department should also have compiled lists of the 100 or 10,000 people with the most felony or misdemeanor offenses on their records. A farebeater whose name shows up on any of those lists would not be allowed to go home with just a ticket.

The arrest of even one fugitive might reduce crime if it interrupts an active criminal career, but Quality-of-Life Plus is only fully effective if the department is interrogating all prisoners and following up all the resulting leads immediately. If you remember, there should be a series of explicit objectives associated with each interrogation, namely:

- an inculpatory statement about the main crime in question
- statements about any other crimes the suspect might admit
- information about the prisoner's accomplices
- information about physical evidence related to the commission of their crimes

- information about drugs, guns, stolen property, fences, and chop shops, whether linked to the prisoner's crimes or not
- information about any other crimes committed by other people

If all leads are pursued with a sense of urgency, one shark caught for a minor quality-of-life violation becomes a whole school of crooks sent up the river for a long time.

So how many different ways are there to catch bad guys on relatively minor violations? Here are the ones I've found to be most useful:

1. Beer and piss. Trained squads hit troublesome corners and make stops for public drinking, underage drinking, and public urinating.
2. Gambling. The same corners might have illegal dice games going on; other corners may host three-card monte or other shell games.
3. Noise. Most cities have laws against unreasonable noise, whether from boom boxes, car stereos, parties, or clubs.
4. Truancy, wandering, and curfew violations. I'm not a big fan of curfews, because too often they're selectively enforced according to a kid's skin color. But a curfew could be an excellent tool if its penalties are applied only to juveniles on parole, probation, or who otherwise have criminal records. Those offenders should be remanded to court; the other kids who are out unreasonably late should all be brought home. Wandering laws, which prohibit kids from cruising the same strip all night long, should be enforced with the same principles in mind. Truancy sweeps are highly effective, in part because they reduce the opportunities a young person might have to commit a crime. (Before we began a "truancy plus" crackdown in New York, robbers

under the age of sixteen committed one third of their crimes during the hours of the day when they were supposed to be in school.)

5. Prostitution. Unlike, say, public urinating, prostitution is an offense that often does result in increases in other crimes—like robberies, assaults, and even murders. In New York, our most effective tactic against street prostitution was Operation Losing Proposition, in which we'd clear an area for a night by arresting all the hookers and then send in female undercover cops to snare the johns. Forfeiture laws allowed us to seize the johns' cars, and, of course, we gave them a different kind of debriefing than they'd expected.
6. Graffiti. "Artists" caught in the act should, of course, be arrested and debriefed about other crimes, but cops trained to recognize tags and gang symbols can use such written evidence to track down other offenders.
7. Traffic and DWI Violations. You've probably seen movies where a cop knocks out the taillight of the car he's watching, then stops the driver for a broken taillight. I wouldn't recommend doing that, but cops can usually come up with a justifiable reason to stop a suspicious vehicle, including a loud radio or—if the cops are equipped with a translucency meter—blacked-out windows that make the passengers invisible to an observer on the street. They also can justify stopping every car that comes by if they set up a DWI or safety-belt check, which can be extremely effective in disrupting business at a drug location and beginning the interrogation process that will take the organization apart.

The most effective stops usually incorporate a bit of trickery. On a main thoroughfare, there should be a highly visible checkpoint where the cops are stopping every third, fourth, or fifth car according to a preset ratio. (They should also be passing out flyers to inform people why they've set up the checkpoint.) Another unit will set up down a side road or side street to stop every vehicle that turns off to avoid the main checkpoint.

The best-trained cops should be at the secondary checkpoint, because they'll have more opportunities to pick out phony driver's licenses, registration, insurance papers, or Vehicle Identification Numbers. If an arrest is made, the contents of the entire car needs to be inventoried before it's towed away, so these cops also should be trained to spot traps inside the cars—behind the dashboard vents, under the accelerator pedal, or between the truck compartment and the backseat—where guns or drugs are often hidden. The cops should also know all about all cars that have been reported stolen in the city and that have not been recovered.

Departments that can afford additional resources can use dogs to sniff out drugs or try some high-tech handheld tools like the Vapor Tracer, which supposedly can sniff out drugs or gunpowder or Contraband Detector, which uses ultrasound to detect cavities in a vehicle where guns or drugs could be hidden.

A variation on the vehicle checkpoint idea is to create a checkpoint for every truck carrying or towing another vehicle. This tactic can slow down car-theft rings in a hurry.

Another is to target some of the lightest vehicles on the road. Ron Waston, a precinct commander in Brooklyn, ordered his cops to issue more traffic summonses for bicycles after he noticed that two-wheelers were being used regularly in ride-by shootings, probably because the shooters realized that cars have a much more limited number of escape routes. Within weeks, the stops in Waston's precinct took twelve guns off the street, and we soon started looking for steady flow of bike summonses from every other precinct in the city.

The overall effect of Quality-of-Life Plus is that a much larger percentage of the department will be making an impact on the real accelerants of crime, like guns and drugs. Most cops aren't really that good at catching people dealing drugs or trafficking guns. But we do know that many of the gangsters of this era roll around in cars that have blacked-out windows and very loud radios. Are most cops capable of looking for blacked-out glass and listening for loud radios? Yeah, they're pretty good at that, and because those indicators are offenses in themselves, the cops don't have to worry about accusations of inappropriate profiling.

Since the NYPD adopted this thinking in 1994, there've been many violent crimes solved because patrol cops were encouraged to take the small offenses seriously. One of the first came courtesy of a young cop in Midtown who won the nickname "Strategy Man" after he took down a whole ring of criminals by following up on an open-beer violation.

It should be noted, however, that the beer drinker deserves some of the credit too. First, he wasn't carrying any ID, so instead of getting a ticket, he was arrested. Next, while he was being patted down, a crack stem was found in his pocket. That alone could have kept him in the system for three days. Suddenly faced with the prospect of a miserable weekend, the beer drinker sat down to talk with Strategy Man and the precinct detectives, looking to make a deal. What he had to offer were names and apartment numbers for a drug crew that controlled a few single-room-occupancy hotels in Hell's Kitchen. The detectives used that information to obtain court-approved search warrants, and together with Strategy Man they hit those apartments, made several arrests, and seized a number of Uzis and Mac-10s—and more than a kilo of cocaine.

Quality-of-life stops can also catch a criminal on *future* crimes.

On June 4, 1996, a nineteen-year-old drifter named John Royster was wandering through Central Park, humming little songs to himself and engaging strangers in brief conversations about the wonders of nature when he spotted a thirty-two-year-old woman in a checked skirt walking quickly along the path in front of him. Royster dashed forward, grabbed the woman from behind, clutched her hair, and began slamming her face against the cobblestones. He then tried to rape his victim, but fled when another pedestrian happened on the scene. In horribly similar incidents over the next eight days, he beat two other young women and murdered a sixty-five-year-old Manhattan dry cleaner named Evalin Alvarez.

When Royster was tracked down and arrested, one of the New York papers gave me credit for solving the case. In fact, I had retired from the department several weeks earlier and was already hanging out on my boat at the far tip of Long Island.

The credit really belonged to the detective who dusted the window at the dry cleaning place for fingerprints, then matched one of them, using a computer sorter, to a print we already had on file.

A year earlier, it seems, John Royster had jumped a subway turnstile—and had been booked and fingerprinted, in accordance with our new department policy, because he wasn't carrying adequate ID.

TACTIC TWO—QUALITY-OF-LIFE ENFORCEMENT FOR BUILDINGS

Most quality-of-life enforcement could also be called civil enforcement, because many of the violations used to stop or arrest offenders belong to the civil, rather than criminal, code.

When the concept is expanded to include civil codes governing buildings and places of business, a few more good tricks pop up that come in handy when the cops are targeting drug locations, chop shops, fences, gambling halls, and houses of prostitution. These tactics usually require enlisting the help of lawyers, who may be employed by the Police Department, City Hall's legal department, or the local prosecutor's office.

The applicable laws vary from city to city and state to state, but New York laws can be used by way of example.

1. Padlocking. The police can close a building or business location where two or more narcotics or gambling violations resulted in at least one arrest and conviction within the past year. A state judge can order the closing even without the conviction if there have been three gambling or drug violations.
2. Evictions. Landlords don't like to have their properties padlocked, so even if they're a little shady they can be convinced to accept legal assistance in evicting tenants who are dealing drugs. In public housing developments, of course, the government is the landlord, so the city attorneys and local prosecutors can pursue evictions on their own.
3. "No trespassing" orders. A willing landlord can also sign an affidavit making it illegal for anyone to be found in a given building except the tenants listed on the affidavit and visitors who can show they have a legitimate reason to enter. Again, when the city is the landlord, the right to enforce this rule is automatic. In New York, we used this tactic extensively against drug buildings. In one Washington Heights apartment house, a guy arrested on the stairs for trespassing gave up enough information for the cops to get a search warrant, though not enough information for them to know they'd struck gold. Expecting to find the stash of a low-level crack dealer, they instead found a hidden door that led to an adjacent apartment where the drug crew controlling the neighborhood had set up a video surveillance room that looked like something out of the Starship *Enterprise*.
4. Enforcement of health and environmental codes. These are mostly just excuses to get in the door of suspected chop shops, drug locations, and fences. In some cities, a cop might not have the right to inspect records at auto yards, service garages, and convenience-food stores, but the cop may be able to get inside for a look around by teaming up with a health inspector who has a right to check the tuna

salad or an environmental inspector who has the right to look for public health hazards like oil spills on the floor.

TACTIC THREE— TARGETED SURVEILLANCE

In the fall of 1988, Leroy Lawrence was nothing but an apparition. He was a hand reaching out from between subway cars. He was fingers raking across a woman's shoulders. He was a blur of a figure reeling in a bag by the end of its broken strap as the trains accelerated into the tunnels. He was 100 purse snatchings along the Seventh Avenue line, and none of us in Transit even knew if he was one crook or many.

There was no doubt this apparition was good at what he did. In recent memory, there had only been one outbreak of purse snatchings to match this, and that had been the work of one Herbert Cephas. Herbert Cephas was so dedicated to his craft that when he was off-duty, he would hang on to a lamppost with one hand and ask the kids in his neighborhood to grab the other and spin him in a circle. He felt the exercise was necessary to strengthen his snatching arm.

The crime demanded skill and daring, but if the purse snatcher made the slightest miscalculation, he could pull a woman right off a platform and under a departing train. Others had done it before, and I'd been down under the trains to see the results.

If we were going to stop this new rash of snatchings, first we were going to have to make the source of them visible, the way a message written in lemon juice appears when held over a flame. In other words, we had to go looking for him—using the time and location of his crimes to guide us.

Targeted surveillance can mean any number of things. It can mean putting a cop on a roof to figure out the flow of traffic to a drug location or to radio descriptions of the suspected buyers to other cops waiting around the corner. It can mean watching a holster store to spot people carrying guns. It can be watching a scrap yard, a pawnshop, or a jewelry store to see if its proprietor is buying stolen goods. In the subways, it could mean standing in a shallow cutout while the trains roared past inches from your chin, just so you can catch any robbers trying to use one of the tunnels under Chinatown or Little Italy for an escape route.

In the case of Leroy Lawrence, we did our mapping and discovered that the department hadn't even been looking at the right trains. We'd been told our snatcher always rode the local train, but every individual report had put him across the platform on an express. When we looked closer, we saw that the snatchings always happened in the afternoon and always at one of the five express platforms between 14th and 96th streets. With our squad of twenty-four, we had just enough people to put one uniform cop on every express platform and two plainclothes cops on every uptown and downtown train from two to seven every afternoon. It was a logistical nightmare, but our tactic was bold, concentrated, and synchronized, and it paid off in a hurry.

Within a week, my crew had spotted a few characters who looked particularly suspicious, including a thin little guy in his mid-twenties who had a habit of riding between cars with an empty duffel bag over his shoulder. In those days, it wasn't unusual for people to hang out between cars, but this character seemed to ride the trains far more often than the average commuter. We had a pretty good feeling he was our man when his face looked back up at us from a mug book. Leroy "Sugarfoot" Lawrence was his name, and he had a prior conviction for robbery.

Our next break came from an unexpected corner of Manhattan when an off-duty cop witnessed a snatching downtown on another subway line. We had made provisions for surprises, though, by distributing Leroy's picture to other squads so it could be used in photo arrays. The off-duty cop picked him out for the downtown robbery, and soon we were heading up to the Bronx with a warrant for Leroy's arrest.

Leroy lived in a sixth-floor apartment, and when we knocked, he bolted toward the fire escape outside his kitchen window. A member of our unit was out there waiting for him, so Leroy ducked back into the apartment and dashed to a window without a fire escape. When I heard the cop outside the kitchen window hollering for backup, I put my shoulder to the door and burst in.

The window Leroy had gone out of had a little terrace outside, but no stairs or ladder. Leroy, making like one of the Flying Wallendas, was already climbing up on to its railing, and I was already imagining the headlines the next day about the humble purse snatcher pushed to his death by an overzealous Transit lieutenant.

Then he was gone. Sixty feet up, Sugarfoot Lawrence had decided he could fly without a net.

A few hours later, one of the chiefs started in on me about letting Leroy get out the window, but this boss was the kind of cop who'd only seen warrants served on TV, and Leroy had left me with a smile to last the whole day: I was the happiest man in the world when I leaned out the window that afternoon and saw him landing safely on another fire escape one floor down and one long broad jump away.

"Don't worry," I told the chief. "When they make the movie, the fat Transit cop makes the jump too and tackles the bad guy outside the neighbor's window."

If there were any doubts left about Leroy's role in the purse-snatching spree, our search of the apartment had put them to rest. Inside his wife's closet was a collection of patent leather that would have made Imelda Marcos jealous—dozens and dozens of bags, all neatly arranged by size and color. Many, of course, had broken straps.

All of which made it difficult for Leroy to remain a mysterious figure in the subway system. A few days later, he was spotted on a train by one of my cops and arrested.

TACTIC FOUR—WARRANT ENFORCEMENT

We've talked before about the importance of running warrant checks on every arrest or summons, including those for minor quality-of-life violations. We also know that most police departments could do a much better job of chasing down many of the people who are wanted on warrants.

Those two steps alone would reduce crime. Each warrant served not only takes a potentially dangerous crook off the street but encourages the prisoner to share information about other crimes.

Still, the full value of warrants is realized only when investigators also use them to bring in for interrogation the people who are most likely to help solve cases. Detectives should chase down many of their own warrants, but if the fugitive has to be taken from home, it's best if the detective handling the case goes out with a squad trained in "hitting doors."

The first warrant squad I put together at Transit could serve as a model for every police department. It was a great crew, and we gave it one of those cool law enforcement acronyms—FIST, for Fugitive Investigative Strike Team—which they wore on the back of their jackets. The name was a small thing, but it probably helped some of the members get over all the talk they'd heard about how chasing warrants wasn't real police work.

In fact, no police work could be more real. Lots of police bosses these days like to sign up for Outward Bound courses so they can fly out West, eat bark in the woods together, and come back raving about the amazing bonding experience. If the bosses need to bond, let them spend a couple of weeks a year in a fugitive squad, chasing down warrants.

I picked John Dove and Vertel Martin to head FIST, because if twenty-five cops under my command were going to be hitting doors at four-thirty every morning, I wanted to be able to sleep through it. John Dove was the character who got cut out of the final screenplay for *The Wizard of Oz*—they kept the ones with no home, no brain, no heart, and no courage, but they drew the line at no personality. Dove, though, was a smart, demanding, disciplined leader, and the only sergeant who might have commanded equal respect among the patrol cops in my squad was Vertel Martin. Which is saying something, because Vertel, at five-foot-one, weighed in at only about 100 pounds. But she too insisted on perfection.

FIST was a high-volume operation—the McDonald's of fugitive abduction. Every morning teams of six to eight of these cops would map out a loop of about a dozen locations each team was going to hit, review their individual tasks in detail, and then roll. The FIST units had a success rate of about 70 percent, so every morning when the detectives came in, they'd already have about ten characters lined up for interviews who were already motivated to give up some other crooks.

A lot of departments forget that anybody who's skipped a court appearance or a parole appearance and has been out of jail at least thirty days can be charged with jumping bail, which is a felony. And the threat of a felony charge is a lot of motivation.

Dove and Vertel later straightened out the NYPD's warrant squads so that they too were hitting dozens of doors every day before breakfast, and Dove went on to become commander of the cold case squad for Brooklyn Homicide, where he demonstrated time and again how much the execution of warrants could do for an investigation.

With my prodding, the NYPD in 1994 had begun routinely running targeted warrant sweeps in order to solve crimes or concentrations of crime. We would begin with a single building address—say, the site of a homicide or a known drug location—then work outward in concentric circles to bring in a number of additional addresses. Next, we'd "WAG" each building, meaning each of the selected addresses would be entered into a computer system called the Warrant Address Generator and out would pop the names and apartment numbers of every person in that building who was wanted on a warrant. Maybe the first guy wouldn't know enough to help us, but the third or fourth might just give up with something. And if our target was a drug location, our parade of fugitives usually could help us piece together the spot's entire chain of command.

One day Dove's cold case squad picked up a homicide case in which the detectives had already established a known suspect. Some months earlier, a Queens man named Glenford Powell had intervened in a curbside argument between a woman he had been dating and her ex-husband. Though the argument had erupted in broad daylight, Powell had chosen to settle the dispute by pulling out a gun and shooting the ex-husband dead.

The trouble for the detectives was that Powell had disappeared.

Though Dove's squad hadn't been given much information about Powell, they did know he had been a midlevel marijuana dealer who managed three or four spots in Brooklyn and Queens. So the detectives called up all the arrest records for those locations and ran those names to find out which ones had active warrants on them.

Six or seven of the names did have petty warrants attached to them for things like misdemeanor marijuana possession, and Dove's squad made the most of them. One by one, the fugitives were picked up and brought in for questioning. The first had nothing to offer, nor did the second. The third guy said he couldn't exactly pin down Powell, but he did know the name of one of Powell's former employees. When the squad punched that name into the warrant database, it came up with two active warrants and six or seven previous arrests, most involving a handgun.

Powell's business associate answered the door when Dove's squad came knocking, and because a 9mm was recovered at the scene, he proved to be very cooperative. Powell, he said, had moved to Houston and changed his name.

But Powell was hardly laying low. The detectives soon had the names of a few clubs he frequented and an assurance that the women in those places would know Dove's suspect by his reputation as a lover and the nickname that came with it—"Fabulous."

Needless to say, "Fabulous" made his return to New York in handcuffs. In the courtroom, they just called him Glenford Powell.

TACTIC FIVE—THE EXTENDED CANVASS

Common detectivespeak: "We solved this case using information developed through investigation."

Usual translation: "Somebody called our tips hot line and told us exactly who did the crime and where we could find him at that very moment."

Cops are so worried about appearing to be professionals, they often forget the only thing that matters about catching a crook is that the crook gets caught. Instead of trying to do things the hard way, detectives should use every opportunity to generate and exploit random tips, whether that means publicizing evidence through TV, radio, newspapers, and the Internet, blanketing a community with sketches of suspects, or following up every single phone tip left on a citywide twenty-four-hour drug hot line.

It's not unusual for a hot line caller to give up a crook using an exact name and address—but it's been standard practice in many police departments to file that kind of information away before anybody even looks at it.

If pride is keeping the investigators from using these tactics, maybe they can get over it by thinking of all these tactics as "an extended canvass." There will always be a need to knock on doors, but the cops also need to think about bringing the investigation into every other living room in the city by way of television.

John Miller was the best chief of detectives the NYPD has ever seen. True, he wasn't officially a detective chief at all; he was the department's top press guy. But during his fourteen months as deputy commissioner for public information, Johnny probably solved more cases than any chief of detectives since Thomas Byrnes, and observers of Byrnes's success credited much of it to pioneering applications of "the third degree."

Miller, as an experienced TV reporter, had a sixth sense of how a story plays out in the media, but he never thought of himself as just a mouthpiece for the department. He thought like a crime fighter.

At around ten o'clock on a cold morning in March, a van carrying about a dozen Hasidic students was inching along on a crowded entrance ramp from Lower Manhattan to the Brooklyn Bridge when their schoolboy chatter was suddenly cut short by gunfire, shattering glass, and screams. Four of the teenagers were wounded, including sixteen-year-old Ari Halberstam, who'd caught a bullet in the back of the neck. Halberstam, who was said to be a favorite of the ailing spiritual leader of the worldwide Lubavitcher community, would not live to see the end of the week.

Here was a tragedy that had the potential to tear the city apart, and the longer the crime went unsolved, the more the tensions would grow. Local TV stations were cutting into their regular morning programming to broadcast news of the shooting and Miller, figuring there must have been hundreds of potential witnesses on the bridge or entrance ramps, argued for and won approval to go before the microphones with the few details we had about the shooter.

We knew he had damaged his dark Chevy sedan in a collision on the ramp, then shot out his own window while firing at the students' van. We also knew he had an olive complexion.

Before long, details were pouring in from witnesses now scattered around the metropolitan area, including a partial license plate number on the Chevy. By the time Miller held a second press conference at midday, he had lined up about $41,000 in reward money and he had convinced Bratton that the moment had come to announce a new easy-to-remember phone number that had just been set up to handle citizens' crime tips.

About two miles into Brooklyn, in an auto body shop under the

Gowanus Highway, a repairman who'd been threatened with a gun that morning heard some of the details from Miller's news conferences and realized he had important information to share.

Just after ten that morning, a driver from a nearby car service had pulled a damaged Chevy Capri into the garage and, holding the gun to the repairman's ear, had recommended that the repairman replace the driver's-side window and smooth out the dents before he got his head blown off. The repairman did as he was told, but later in the day he walked into a precinct station house and told a lieutenant there everything he knew—the driver's first name, the cab company he worked for, and the location of an apartment where these cabbies kept a stash of guns. Detectives immediately set up surveillance across the street from the car service, waited until the suspect arrived and pointed out the suspect, then swarmed on him. With a big assist from the media, we had the car, we had the gun, and we had our shooter, all well before the sun went down behind the Brooklyn Bridge.

Miller had a hand in solving a number of serious cases. In the murder of Previn Shah, the 34th Street newsstand owner who was shot during a midmorning robbery, the break in the case came several weeks after the crime itself when an informant who knew the shooter walked into a squad room claiming he'd been haunted into taking action by the victim's picture, which Miller's people had posted at every newsstand in the city.

In another case, a pair of robbers shot a Maryland couple while they were shopping for their daughter's wedding dress at designer Vera Wang's exclusive boutique on the Upper East Side, and the bride's distraught fifteen-year-old sister gave the nightmare a perfect page-one headline: "I HATE THIS CITY!" Six months later, Miller heard that detectives had just come with a grainy video of the two well-dressed crooks doing a stickup at an Upper East Side hotel, and he demanded that the footage be made immediately available for broadcast. Days later, we had names on these guys and enough related information to scoop them up at a pool hall in Queens. The crooks didn't seem to mind—in the Nineteenth Precinct squad room, one of them treated us to a fair impression of Sinatra performing "The Summer Wind."

But the extended canvass isn't for high-profile suspects only. The public should routinely be made aware of crime patterns in their neighborhoods, both so they can take precautions and because they can often help solve the crimes. If the local TV and radio outlets aren't interested in a particular crime pattern, maybe a neighborhood paper will pick up the ball. The Internet is a perfect medium for posting daily information about crimes and crime patterns, though some members of the public don't have online access. And the cops can always hand out or post flyers.

Sketches of suspects are drawn up a lot less frequently than most people would imagine. In the NYPD, we had plenty of good sketch artists, but the detectives seemed to think they needed a really special reason to justify spending $40 of the department's money on calling a sketch artist in. That's crazy. In '95, we had a guy doing numerous robberies on the Upper East Side and I had to keep torturing the detectives to put out a sketch even as the number of victims were mounting. Finally, the sketch was distributed throughout the borough, and our suspect was picked up immediately by two cops working across town in the Thirteenth Precinct.

Of course, New York is one of the art capitals of the world, so maybe the NYPD gets a better breed of sketch artist than most other police departments. But no need to worry about that anymore. There's a computer software program available now that allows any detective with a little bit of training to create a good likeness of any suspect by plugging in the features one by one—nose, eyes, eyebrows. It may be nothing more than Mr. Potato Head for detectives, but the images the software program produces are fairly accurate, and it's even able to search a database of mug shots to create instant photo arrays of suspects with similar features.

TACTIC SIX—HIGH-TECH FISHING NETS

Many times when we talk about advanced technology, all we're talking about are file-retrieving systems that work at lightning speed. But speed increases volume, and that can change the dynamics of the chase. It can mean the difference between fishing with a spear and trawling with a milewide net.

Take ballistics. For almost a century, we in law enforcement have known that every gun leaves unique markings on its fired bullets and spent shell casings and that a suspect therefore has a lot of explaining to do if a gun found in his possession is matched with bullets or shell casings found at a crime scene. Until recently, however, the same suspect could be guilty of having fired the same gun in dozens of previous crimes and yet there would be almost no chance he'd be linked to those earlier crimes by ballistic evidence—even if the police department that caught him had the evidence in its own files.

In most cities, that's still true: Nobody looks for a match on the ballistic evidence unless a detective working one of the cases follows a hunch and makes a specific request that the evidence in one case be compared to the evidence in another. Before 1994, the NYPD brought in tens of thousands of guns, bullets, and shells as evidence every year, but an average of only fifteen requests were made to check for a match. That's a disgrace, even though comparisons then had to be done one by one by a technician looking through a comparison microscope.

Today imaging analysis technology has made it possible for a gun's ballistic signature to be entered into a national computer database from which it can be retrieved almost instantly. If you recover bullets or shell casings, you stick those right into the imaging machine. If you recover a gun, you bring it to the range and fire it, then put the bullets and shell casings into the machine.

With this technology available, ballistic evidence gathered in every criminal investigation should be checked against the database to see if the gun used in one crime has been fired in past crimes. A "hit" can be the key to solving two or more cases that nobody would have thought to connect. It can mean a violent felon will finally be put away. Sometimes it can show that a single gun has circulated among a number of crooks, maybe even as a rental weapon.

Unfortunately, the FBI and the DEA each have their own ballistic systems, and each agency is hoping its technology will become the standard in the industry. In a few years, we'll know which one was the eight-track and which was the cassette, but now that question is up in the air and we're not getting the most out of either technology.

Fewer than thirty American cities now use the ballistics imaging technology and contribute to the national databases, but every police department in America ought to. Then it'll be up to the leadership of each department to make sure there are enough trained people on staff to prevent processing delays. The technology is worth a lot less if an investigation is several months old before anybody gets around to checking the shells and bullets against the database. But that's what happens if leadership falls asleep.

Ultimately, the databases should include not just those guns that have been used in crimes but every gun legally manufactured or imported into the United States. If before its initial sale, every gun was fired and its ballistic signature captured in the national database, the cops would be able to begin the investigation of almost every gun crime by tracing the gun back to its last legal owner.

Given ongoing technological advances and the computer's ability to sort quickly through huge stores of data, we're likely to hear about more and more crimes being solved by "cold hits"—as opposed to old-fashioned investigations. Ballistics is only one arena in which these small miracles will come true. Fingerprint recognition software has been in use for years, and DNA samples from crooks around the country are now accessible through a national network of computer databases.

But none of these systems will meet expectations without human effort. The tools' potential will be wasted unless law enforcement leaders make certain that the information held in the databases is limited only by legitimate concerns about privacy, not by our own laziness or lack of vision. First and foremost, police departments can't allow themselves to fall behind in entering and analyzing the data as it pours in.

TACTIC SEVEN—STINGS

One thing you can say about stings: Cops never complain that they aren't "real" police work. Cops get boners just thinking about acting as a decoy, wearing a wire, conducting a buy-and-bust, or taking part in still more elaborate ruses—especially if danger or comedy is part of the package. Even Billy Courtney, the guy who I had play a transvestite in my old Transit decoy squad, would probably put on his mom's bra again today if he was told it was the only way he could hold on to the memory.

Probably the most common sting operation in policing is the buy-and-bust, meaning an operation in which an undercover poses as a customer to initiate the arrest of somebody who's selling guns, drugs, or other contraband. It's the meat-and-potatoes work of most narcotics squads, or at least it should be if the unit's focus is on taking out drug spots instead of running up overtime by arresting buyers. With a buy-and-bust, you instantly obtain strong evidence against a suspect, and if the evidence doesn't immediately put the suspect away, it will probably motivate him or her to give up other members of the crew. If, instead, you arrest a buyer and send him or her back in on a "control buy," you not only put that person at risk but you invite potential credibility problems with the main witness in your case.

As with any tactic, sometimes a buy-and-bust won't work as planned. That just means the cops have to try something else until they find the trick that works.

Out in Bushwick, Brooklyn, a few years back, there was a heroin dealer working out of the basement of an abandoned brownstone who had sold several times to undercover cops trying to get him on a buy-and-bust. But they could never grab him. He wasn't a big player himself, but because he handled a lot of volume and was connected to a larger operation, he had a network of lookouts on the block who would give him a warning over his walkie-talkie anytime the cops tried to follow up the buy by coming in for his arrest. By the time the cops got to the door, he'd have slipped out the back somewhere.

Finally the precinct stopped worrying about actually catching the dealer and just started chasing him out of his hole. Every other day or so they'd rush in, find the dealer gone, put a ringer in his place, and start selling baking soda packaged just like the regular bags of heroin. The junkies didn't like that at all. However they come by their money, they work hard for it, and they weren't about to keep spending their twenty or forty bucks at a location where they were getting beat heroin every other day. And on the days when the undercover guys weren't running the location, the precinct threw other obstacles at the buyers, like a uniform cop posted outside the entrance or a two-ton pile of snow, courtesy of the Sanitation Department, dumped right on the doorstep. In about two months, the precinct had shut the spot down completely.

Stings almost always make cops look clever, but as I've said, all that matters about any tactic is that it works. That's why the sting I'd most like to try someday is absolutely moronic.

It came to me one weekend when I was holed up at One Police Plaza with a number of the superchiefs, all of us working feverishly to bang out the final details of a comprehensive citywide gun strategy.

"What I think we've got to do," I told them, "is pick up a dog at the pound and have him sworn in as a member of the K-9 squad. But this wouldn't be the regular drug-sniffing dog, this would be our special gun-sniffing dog. We'd have to make that very clear. He'd have to wear a little sweater with 'GUN-SNIFFING DOG' in bold phosphorescent letters, and we'd also put a little helmet on his head with a flashing red light on top."

The rest of the sting would run something like this: Led by a uniformed officer, the Gun-Sniffing Dog would parade up and down the nastiest streets on the busiest nights until he'd gotten the attention of everybody in sight. Then, as they passed an undercover cop carrying a quarter-pound of hamburger inside his pocket, the dog would make a dive for the ground beef, the uniformed cop would press a little button, and the light on the dog's head would start flashing. Panicked, the undercover would start to run, the uniform would tackle him, and a gun would pop out onto the sidewalk.

As long as we always had enough other plainclothes cops on the block to grab everybody else who decided they'd better make a dash, we could disarm every knucklehead in New York in about a weekend.

Call it a failure of nerve, but I just wasn't sure New York was ready for the Gun-Sniffing Dog in 1994.

Maybe the next time I get the chance.

EIGHT

RUST PATROL
Relentless Follow-up and Assessment

John Timoney arrived in Philadelphia like Jesus to Jerusalem.

Never had there been a man more deserving of the opportunity to lead the police department of a major U.S. city. To describe him in a word: grand. At forty-nine, he quartered a brogue as thick as it was the day he stepped off the boat from Dublin into John Kennedy's America, and his face would do credit to Mount Rushmore. Experience had hewn him half street cop, half scholar, and he bore his successes with a winning blend of audaciousness and humility.

Back in the NYPD, of course, Timoney had been our Eisenhower to Anemone's Patton. While it was left to Louie and me to press the field battle against crime, Timoney had the depth and breadth of vision to see that every other aspect of running the organization—budget, training, transfers, promotions, disciplinary matters—supported and contributed to the victory effort.

The Philadelphia press immediately fell for him. The day before he took over the department in March 1998, *The Philadelphia Inquirer* led a front-page story with an anecdote about how, even after he'd become a captain, he still liked to make a sport of letting crooks loose after he'd grabbed them, just so he could run them down again.

That idiosyncrasy aside, John Timoney was the person my parents wanted me to grow up to be. In my school's Christmas pageants, he would have been Joseph.

"I've never failed in my life," he told the *Inquirer*'s reporters.

But Timoney understood well that running down crooks isn't the only talent by which a chief is judged. He never had to be reminded that if he gave anything less than relentless attention to all facets of the operation, Philadelphia 6,000-member force could quickly march him to his Waterloo.

Or was it a 5,400-member force? Thanks mostly to a rule that allowed members of the city council to hand out transfers as if they were blocks of surplus government cheese, nobody could say in the beginning where 600 of the city's 6,000 police officers were working.

Finding talented subordinates looked like less of a problem.

Among a handful of rising stars in the department, none shone brighter than the thirty-four-year-old commander of West Philadelphia's Sixteenth District. This captain was brash, he was aggressive, and he was hailed as a savior by many members of a community battered by drugs and violence. Timoney wanted to talk about crime reduction? This hotshot was eager to jump into the conversation. For the first three months of 1998, he bragged to the papers, robberies in the Sixteenth District had fallen 80 percent against the same period a year ago.

At the patty-cake crime meetings recently initiated by the former commissioner, numbers like that probably would have fueled the young captain's continuing rapid ascent.

But Timoney appreciated that the principles of accurate, timely intelligence, rapid deployment, effective tactics, and relentless follow-up and assessment needed to touch every corner of the organization—even the math department. Within days of his arrival, he established a "quality-assurance" unit to make certain the department's crime numbers were accurate. And because the Sixteenth District was leading the city in crime reduction, he soon targeted for one of the unit's first audits.

Vincent DeBlasis, the man Timoney chose to head the quality-assurance unit, knew his way around crime reports. As the city's former chief of detectives, DeBlasis understood that an increase in "unfounded" calls could be hiding a variety of serious crimes. He saw warning lights flashing when a district's thefts were up but its robberies were down, when its reports of hospital stays were up but its aggravated assaults were down, when its "lost property" numbers were up but its thefts were down. All were indications that the corporal responsible for assigning each of the district's crime incidents to one of several fixed categories was, due perhaps to real or imagined pressure from above, downgrading the seriousness of many offenses.

Timoney had also impressed upon him that when a crime was downgraded or made to disappear, it meant the victims and the general public would suffer a commensurate downgrade in police service. Even in a department striving to treat all cases as if they were press cases, a stolen wallet will get more attention from a detective squad than a lost wallet.

On a first pass, DeBlasis and his team found warning lights everywhere in the Sixteenth District's coding. By pulling every incident report the district filed in March and reading closely through each incident's detailed description, the auditors came up with 40 percent more Part I UCR crimes than the district had reported on its own.

Timoney kept a cool head, telling DeBlasis to retrain the captain and his subordinates on proper coding. This one's on me, he was telling the young captain; the next one's on you.

Several weeks later, DeBlasis completed a new four-month audit of the district. Again, the results were sickening. Not only hadn't the problem gone away since the warning, it had gotten worse. Timoney faced a choice: risk bringing immediate discredit on the department or accept that he and the other 5,999 members of the force might as be wearing badges issued by the Land of Make-Believe.

Timoney didn't disappoint. Like Sun Tzu, he cut off the captain's head—and when further audits revealed comparable disparities in a second district, he relieved that captain of his command as well. At the end of the summer, Timoney announced that the fourth-largest police force in the country would not be sending the FBI any crime numbers for the first six months of the year, because its arithmetic couldn't yet be trusted.

The Philadelphia Police Department had been playing with its crime numbers since before the Liberty Bell got its crack—in fact, if the bell had filed a complaint against the clapper, the cops back then probably would have coded the crime as disorderly conduct instead of aggravated assault. Under Timoney, cheaters don't have a prayer. DeBlasis's quality-assurance team constantly audits incident reports and computer printouts of radio runs to see if all calls are handled in a timely fashion, to check the unfounded rates, and to watch the rates at which the original code assigned to each 911 call is changed by the time a corporal at the district level signs off on the resulting incident report. The department, like New Orleans's, has also begun conducting integrity tests to find out what happens when 911 gets a call from a kid on a corner who says his North Face jacket was just stolen. Does the complaint show up accurately in crime reports a day later? Does the kid receive courteous service?

After truth became a factor in gauging performance, Timoney began identifying his authentic stars. In North Philadelphia's Thirty-Fifth District, murders fell by almost half by year's end, and the captain there, twenty-six-year veteran Joe O'Brien, wasn't playing any games with his numbers. Every day he personally reviewed the five or six hundred reports filed in the Thirty-Fifth during the previous twenty-four hours. If half his day was needed to keep up with all the crime occurring in his district, I'd still say the labor was worth the rewards. In fact, every precinct or district commander should initial all crime reports daily and check them against the initial reports on the department's computer-assisted dispatch system. But O'Brien does it all in about an hour.

Getting the numbers right came at a cost. For 1998, the city would show a dramatic statistical increase in violent crime instead of the decline Mayor Ed Rendell had boasted about just before Timoney's arrival. But Timoney had done the right thing. And he still had one number left that hinted at the true impact of his first nine months as commissioner: Murder numbers have always been more resistant to fakery than any others, and murder in Philadelphia was down 19 percent for the year.

For a chief, follow-up means something slightly different than it does to a cop or a field commander.

In the street, follow-up is tracking the last lead down the last dark alley until the last crook is locked away. From an upper floor at headquarters, the idea of follow-up only begins with the obligation to ensure that the field commanders are making the cops track the last lead down the last dark alley until the last crook is locked away.

But that first objective is critical. As we know, murderers get away with their crime half the time, and arrests are made in only one in four robberies and one in six burglaries or car thefts. To win, the cops have to get their batting averages up.

That can be accomplished through oversight—with the crime meetings, which are the most visible expression of the principle, but also with the deployment of "quality-assurance teams" that should be rechecking everything from the crime numbers, to fugitive apprehension rates, to open homicide investigations.

Policing has another term for the quality-assurance teams that review open investigations. They're called cold case squads.

In most cities, cold case squads pick up old cases here and there as the spirit moves them or the bosses, but the squads really ought to be asked to review every case that remains unsolved after a predetermined expiration date, such as three or six months.

With that mandate, the cold case squad becomes a pair of eyes looking over the shoulder of every detective. When people know their work is being reviewed, they try harder to succeed and, failing that, to document the magnitude of their effort. In that sense, cold case squads reinforce the contribution that would be expected from a demanding supervisor with long investigatory experience.

Around 1990, one of the trains that picks up cash receipts from the token booths in the subway every day was held up by a couple of hoods who made off with $27,000 and the guns belonging to the train's guards. A beeper was found at the scene, and I told my detectives to trace it. They balked, anticipating a dead end.

"Amuse me," I said.

I was playing the role of a cold case squad; I was their conscience.

Starting with just the serial number, they traced the beeper back to a Texas manufacturing plant, which led to a jobber, which led to a hole-in-the-wall business downtown on Canal Street. The shop looked like the kind that does most of its business for cash only, but it came up with a sales slip that identified the buyer with half a name more than nothing. "Shafeeque" gave us something to run against our databases and narrowed the search to about four possibles.

The one we liked was an ex-con who had just put in for a parole transfer to Saint Croix, and when my detectives caught up with him that same night as he was entering a Bronx rooming house, he answered their salutation—"Police! Don't move!"—by spinning around and opening fire. Abdulawali Shafeeque had already wounded one of our guys and was still shooting when his leg was shattered by the last round in Sonny Archer's gun. A homemade pipe bomb was later found in Shafeeque's room. He had been doing stickups up and down the East Coast, and it looked like he had been about to move up in weight class.

Sometimes a case doesn't need the eyes looking over the detectives' shoulders. It just needs a set of fresh eyes or a little more time than any precinct detective can give it before fresher crimes push it into a back drawer. Even thorough investigations often fail, and a second start can sometimes be the difference between success and another unsolved crime.

For about nine years, Nicholas "No Socks" Facchiolo lived on the lam. "No Socks," a small-time hood from Queens, had gone into hiding after a witness identified him as the shooter who had opened fire during an argument inside a wholesale produce market, missing his target but striking and killing a father of seven who had stopped at the market to buy oranges for his waiting family.

When John Dove's cold case squad picked up the file, they quickly discovered that some years after the shooting, "No Socks" had been arrested for trying to shoplift some cold medicine from a drugstore in Upstate New York. He'd been bailed out by a businessman from that area, however, before the state completed a fingerprint check.

Playing a hunch, Dove's squad decided to tail the businessman on his next visit to New York City, and after a long day and rain-soaked night of small disappointments, they followed their marker into a pool hall in Woodhaven, Queens, and recognized "No Socks" despite a baseball cap, a ponytail, and a full beard that hadn't appeared in his old mug shots. Throughout his years in hiding, "No Socks" had been meticulous about guarding his identity, but he'd never disguised his enthusiasm for billiards. In fact, the "No Socks" who wore a ponytail had put a new felt on the table inside the One-Oh-Three Precinct.

In another murder case handled by Dove's squad, the victim was a Bensonhurst heroin dealer who'd been stabbed about fifteen times by the perpetrators of a brutal push-in robbery. An impressive number of the dealer's friends, customers, and associates had already been interviewed by the original investigators, but the very first name Dove's squad pulled out for a second interview belonged to a young woman who had an unusual opening line when Dove and Detective Pat Lanigan paid her a visit: "You want to know about the homicide," she declared. She was already trembling.

On the night of the killing, she told the detectives, her boyfriend Anthony and his brother Joseph had gone out to score some heroin and had come back hours later carrying eight bags of dope and a few hundred dollars in cash. Anthony had returned in bare feet despite the cold, and he was wearing his coat inside out. She noticed dark stains on the sleeve. "Wash this," he had told her.

A couple days later, she confronted Anthony about his role in the dealer's death, and he confessed to her. Unfortunately, she made the mistake of letting Joseph overhear her threaten to turn her boyfriend in. Joseph offered to kill her immediately, but Anthony objected, arguing that he alone should bear the responsibility of killing the mother of his child. So he asked Joseph to escort the child outside and he ordered his girlfriend to strip off her clothes and get into the shower. She did as she was told, but collapsing in fear beneath the knife in his hand, she threw herself at his ankles and won his mercy.

Two years after the fact, her story was still chilling, but it wasn't going to be sufficient to convict the brothers for murder. The detectives needed evidence, and their best hope was a down-filled coat the girlfriend said had been sitting in storage at her grandmother's home since Anthony was locked up on a separate robbery charge.

The medical examiner took one look at the pristine coat and declared the chances of finding blood on it to be zero, but Lanigan insisted the tests be run anyway, and traces of the victim's blood were found still clinging to the down lining.

Both brothers were convicted. Such are the rewards of relentlessness.

Cold case or quality-assurance squads aren't the only ways to raise a department's batting average in solving crime. Oversight can take many forms.

It can be a boss who shows up half an hour early for a 7 A.M. stakeout to see if the cops get started on schedule, or who drops in on his detectives to watch a few interrogations, or who joins a beer-and-piss squad out in the field to observe how they're making stops.

It can be both the broken-record repetition and the constant surprises that bosses at every level should bring to their performances at the crime meetings. In New Orleans, the detectives were all starting to feel pretty good about the squads' soaring arrest clearance rates until we unveiled a new series of maps showing solved and unsolved murders, shootings, and stranger rapes for the year to date and for the past six months running. Without those maps, clusters of unsolved crimes can too quickly fall off the department's radar.

In New York, the commander of a Rockaway precinct once stood before us at a Comstat meeting and swore his patrol cops were canvassing neighbors after every reported burglary, just as we had recently ordered every precinct to do.

"As you well know, Captain," I said, "you can only expect what you inspect. Are the cops memorializing the canvasses on the initial burglary complaints as we recommended, and are you personally initializing each of those reports after reviewing them?"

About twenty minutes later, we called him back to the podium.

"There must be something wrong with one of our fax machines," I said. "We just called your precinct and had them send over the reports from your last twenty burglaries. The funny thing about these faxes is that on none of those twenty reports did either a memorialization of a canvass or your initials come out. Have you ever had this problem with your machine before?"

Of course, oversight only works when somebody has to answer for the results. Even in a department that's doing everything else right in terms of mapping crime daily and holding precinct or district commanders responsible for crime reduction, domestic violence and narcotics complaints are often neglected when it comes to follow-up. Police departments around the country have gotten much better about taking domestic violence seriously enough to make arrests when the responding officers find the offenders still on the scene. Still, though, the patrol cops have to learn to check every kid in the house whenever they get a domestic complaint, and the detective squads have to be pushed to follow up swiftly and make arrests on the cases in which the offender wasn't immediately apprehended.

Similarly, narcotics complaints can't be allowed to fall off the map as soon as a patrol car drives past the given location. Whether it falls to patrol or an investigative unit, every drug complaint has to find its way to somebody who can be held responsible for clearing up the problem.

Follow-up for the chiefs isn't all about putting the sweat on subordinates. The crime meetings, for instance, were always intended in part as a mechanism for sharing good ideas throughout a department and for keeping good ideas from ever being forgotten. If we had thought about it a little more in the beginning, we would have started a *Book of Big Ideas* at the NYPD so that innovative cops and commanders would be rewarded by having their names forever linked to the tactics they invented or advanced while the sprint was on.

A chief has to constantly be seeking ways to identify and disseminate best practices. In his or her own inner circle, there should be a small group of trusted people who travel around the region and even the nation to observe innovative strategies firsthand. But the group probably shouldn't include anybody who really loves to travel.

In the detective squads, young investigators should be paired with senior investigators to accelerate the routine acquisition of all the many little tricks that can solve a crime or snare a missing suspect. In fact, a database should be created so that, just as lawyers use Westlaw to retrieve court decisions that can bolster their arguments, detectives could type in a keyword or phrase—like "cell phone," "credit card," or "DNA sample"—to find out how other detectives have made cases with similar evidence or leads. Ideally, the database would gather examples from across the nation, but even systems used only within a single department would spread a lot of light.

Part of the mind-set of a chief also has to match that of the owner of a used, forty-seven-foot, steel-hulled tugboat, which is a mind-set I've recently come to understand quite well. On a steel boat, rust is the enemy, and it can't be allowed to find a hold in any crease or seam of the vessel. If you've sandblasted off a rusty patch, you'd best be sure you've eliminated all of it, you'd best have put down two barrier coats and three or four primer coats, and you'd better not ever think that the rust has been beaten. Every year you have to haul the entire beast out of the water to go over it inch by inch, and in the meantime, your routine rust patrol must be systematic, comprehensive, and relentless. A spot that may have been clean two months ago could now be a budding corrosion that will one day sink the whole ship.

In the streets, crime is the rust; inside the department, the rust is human slippage. The most effective operational systems in the world will fail eventually if they're not relentlessly tested to prevent the inevitable slippage from destroying them.

If a chief can act with that frame of mind, the job half does itself.

But chiefs have yet one more obligation to the principle of relentless follow-up.

At any level, the essence of follow-up is to see a story through from its beginning to its end. And since the story of crime neither begins nor ends with the police, it falls to the chiefs to think strategically about how the efforts of the cops should fit within the context of the larger stories.

In America today, as has been the case for much of the past four decades, the biggest stories in crime are drugs, guns, and gangs.

As a nation, we have the capacity to wipe those problems out.

But to do so, police chiefs, other law enforcement leaders, and the occupants of high elected office have to come together behind comprehensive strategies that track each of those stories from beginning to end.

NINE

AMERICA'S MOST WANTED

Guns, Gangs, and Drug Crews

Several years ago, a character came to my attention who could be a poster boy for strategic mobilization against guns and drugs. This was during our first year at the NYPD, and word had reached headquarters that contracts had been put out on the lives of a State Supreme Court justice, her family, her personal assistant, a prosecutor, a detective, and several key witnesses who were about to testify in a major drug trafficking case the judge was then trying in a Lower Manhattan courtroom.

On the street, according to the informant, the hired gun was known as "Freddy Krueger."

Whatever his true identity, Freddy Krueger had no business being out on the street. By one accomplice's count, this feared enforcer had already had a hand in the murders of at least twenty-five people, and even before he had killed for the first time—quietly taking out a suspected turncoat in October 1990—Krueger had already established himself as co-manager of a bustling crack, cocaine, and heroin spot in the Bronx that rewarded him a weekly cut of about $10,000.

His second killing was more spontaneous in nature, but it was the one that seemed to launch him into a new career. In March 1991, the twenty-four-year-old Krueger was accompanying his supplier on a business trip to Washington Heights when a local heroin addict pulled a gun and started shooting. Grabbing a gun from his wounded boss, Krueger quickly returned fire, following the wounded addict into the middle of Amsterdam Avenue before delivering the bullet that finished him off.

That summer Krueger really got busy. He cut down a welcher in a drive-by, he teamed up with another hit man to take out a rival crew's gunman, and he did a favor for that fellow enforcer by popping a small-time seller in another drive-by. Come December, he helped a group of allies light up a notorious Bronx drug spot in an ambush that took four lives and, just days before Christmas, ventured only a block from his own operation to rub out a personal rival.

The new year would be more frenetic still. Among Krueger's seven murder victims in the first seven months of 1992 were a fifteen-year-old soldier for a rival crew, a boss named Dred who caught his death from the back of a passing motorcycle, a Manhattan heroin dealer whose primary offense was underpricing the street brands Krueger represented, a home raider whose execution came by way of a $15,000 freelance deal, and another rival dealer Krueger had been tracking for almost a year.

That last victim died in a cab just as it hit a tie-up on its way across the Macombs Dam Bridge from Manhattan to the Bronx. Krueger, carrying an AK-47 in one hand and a nine in the other, came running up to the cab from behind. Spending twenty-one bullets, he sprayed his victim's brain and blood all over the interior of the cab, then lowered himself into a car that had spun out into opposing traffic to clear its getaway route back into Manhattan.

At the end of that incredible run, the NYPD hadn't even heard of Freddy Krueger.

Two years later, when I was new to the department, our detectives uptown still didn't know who the nickname belonged to.

Fortunately, Freddy Krueger didn't commit another murder in New York City after 1993—as far as anybody knows—and he was eventually apprehended in his native Dominican Republic. But his story is worth reviewing—if only because it never should have gone on as long as it did. And the problem wasn't that we didn't have dedicated and talented investigators working on any of those murders in the early 1990s. (The story never could have been pieced together without the efforts of detectives and the assistant district attorneys assigned to Walter Arsenault's Homicide Investigation Unit at the Manhattan District Attorney's Office.) The problem instead was that individual detectives were being asked to unravel the inner workings of some fairly complex criminal organizations without the constant support of everybody else on the team that wears the white hats.

The good news is, the story of Freddy Krueger could never be repeated in New York City today, even though the NYPD and the city's other law enforcement agencies have only gone halfway in implementing the strategies I'm about to lay out. If communities everywhere were to implement these ideas, crime as we know it would end in less than five years.

Let's start with the guns.

Even after several years of moderate crime declines nationwide, some 12,000 people a year are killed in America with firearms, and eighteen times that many people are wounded by gunfire, shot at, threatened while looking down the wrong end of a gun, or hit over the head with one. Those 12,000 deaths account for two-thirds of the nation's murders, and there surely would be more if some of the shooters had better aim or if our hospitals weren't first-rate MASH units.

The amazing thing is, killers really seem to need these guns to do their murders. It's not like when you forget your toothbrush and you just use your finger: In any city where crooks have been convinced by assertive policing or tougher penalties to leave their guns at home, murders immediately plummet.

Freddy Krueger probably would have been far less prolific if he'd had a harder time arming himself, and every gun he held in his hands represented several missed opportunities to keep it away from him and several more to take it away.

To begin with, Freddy wasn't the type to fashion crude zip guns out of household objects he found in his basement. Not many criminals are. Instead, he used some of the finest weapons made, which meant that each weapon was, at one point in time, the property of a law-abiding manufacturer or importer.

This was missed opportunity number one. Many guns used in crimes have had their serial numbers defaced—some so expertly that the numbers can't be raised up again even in a lab. The guns' ballistic "fingerprints," on the other hand, are indelible, which means all we would have to do to trace any gun back to its original owner is take it to a range before it's sold, fire it, and enter the markings on its spent bullets and shell casings into a national ballistics database. To accomplish this, the FBI and ATF have to stop arguing about who has the better technology so the machines can be put in every state and their databases networked.

A simple change in our gun laws, which Congress considered but failed to pass in 1999, could then eliminate a big hole in the records that often opens up after the initial sale. The path of a gun is fairly well documented from importer or manufacturer to distributor to federally licensed dealer to the original buyer. And the buyer is subject to strict background checks. In 1997, for example, more than 50,000 handgun sales were blocked because the prospective buyers turned out to be felons, fugitives, perpetrators of domestic violence, or to be under indictment for felony crimes. (Unfortunately, though filing an application for a gun purchase is a crime punishable by up to ten years in prison for these characters, nobody in law enforcement is moving to arrest them. Nor does anybody check, when a gun is sold back to a licensed dealer, if the weapon was used in a crime or if the seller is a felon. But that's another story.)

In any case, secondhand sales in several states aren't regulated at all, so a crook can pick up a gun at a gun show, a flea market, or through a newspaper ad without having to clear any hurdles.

More commonly, guns used in crimes are first purchased by "straw buyers," who meet all the legal requirements, and then moved by criminal traffickers into the hands of crooks in near or distant markets.

To disrupt those pipelines, local cops can take advantage of the ATF's Project Lead, to trace guns used in crimes back to the retailers and original buyers and to determine if the purchases fit into patterns consistent with criminal gun trafficking. To reduce the number of federally licensed firearms dealers that require monitoring, local law enforcement can team up with the feds, raise the licensing fees, and pay a compliance visit to every person applying for a new dealer's license or a renewal. We did it in New York, and the number of license holders quickly dropped by 73 percent.

All of these efforts might have pinched Freddy Krueger's supply of weapons, but even if those tactics had failed, Freddy was leaving bread crumbs for the cops everywhere. He was never known to skimp on bullets, and he didn't show much interest in disposing of his victim's bodies. My guess is, he didn't pick up his spent shell casings either—because you can't call "Time out" in the middle of a drive-by.

To take full advantage of the evidence Freddy left behind, a department would need the equipment and staffing to put it all into a national databases quickly. And there could be no discrimination against the bullets and shell casings from lesser crimes than murder, as there was in New Orleans until 1996. The whole point of entering the ballistic evidence is to make connections between two crimes or between a recovered gun and any past crime it may have been used for. The guns themselves won't talk about their prior exploits just because they're taken in on a weapons possession charge.

What would the NYPD detectives have found if they'd had those capabilities when Freddy Krueger was shooting up the South Bronx and Washington Heights? It's hard to say, because he might have been unusually diligent about disposing of his guns after each time he'd used them, but guns are expensive—an AK-47 went for about $2,500 on the crook market at the time—so detectives in the various precincts probably would have discovered a link between two or more of the killings or shootings at a much earlier date, moving them a step closer to solving their cases.

Street-level gun interdiction efforts could have made the biggest difference of all. There are no better ways to take guns off the streets than to increase efforts aimed at gun arrests and gun seizures, and that's done by employing some mostly familiar tactics:

- increasing Quality-of-Life Plus in high-crime areas or near popular criminal hangouts
- conducting traffic stops, using cops who are trained to spot phony VIN numbers and traps in the vehicles where weapons may be hidden
- executing warrants on fugitives wanted in connection with gun crimes
- making home visits to ex-gun offenders to check their compliance with parole or probation rules governing curfews, truancy and disclosure of their home addresses
- training all cops how to spot people carrying guns and how to make gun arrests that stick
- debriefing all prisoners about sources for illegal guns
- obtaining and executing search warrants to seize gun stashes
- pursuing all local and out-of-state gun traffickers named during those interrogations
- treating investigations of household burglaries as "big cases," since hundreds of thousands of guns are stolen during household burglaries every year

And doing it all with a sense of urgency

Sadly, successful street-level operations were utterly wasted in the case of Freddy Krueger. Long before he was brought to justice in the Dominican Republic, NYPD cops had him in their hands—not once, but twice. The first time, Krueger was between murders four and five when he was arrested in the Bronx for pointing a .357 at another man and further charged with trying to bribe the arresting officer. But the prisoner, who gave his name as Miguel Perez, had never been arrested before, so he was released on his own recognizance. Six months and at least four murders later, he was stopped with a 9mm Smith & Wesson on a dark street near the George Washington Bridge by a sharp-eyed cop who worked for a special antigun unit. This time the suspect didn't even bother to use an alias. His real name—Francisco Medina—worked as well as any, because it too had a spotless record.

By morning, its owner was free to kill again.

We don't catch enough crooks to let them slip away like that. In New York, at least, there must have been an attempt to check Medina's fingerprint records before his release, but many departments don't hold themselves to that common-sense rule. In this instance, a mistake was made on the records check, but more significantly, the justice system failed the public a second time by treating a gun possession charge too lightly.

Lenient local gun laws and overburdened criminal courts are problems in many jurisdictions. But a blanket solution has been available to real crime fighters for more than thirty years.

In recent years, prosecutors in New York and Boston have used tough federal gun laws that have been on the books since the 1960s to take out gangs like the Flying Dragons, the Latin Kings, and the Intervale Posse. In fact, one Boston gang member was sent away for twenty years for the possession of a single bullet.

But when we asked the federal prosecutors in New York to take on all federal gun crimes, both of the city's U.S. Attorneys balked at the potential workload. The Manhattan office nevertheless found time in 1998 to make a federal case against a few restaurant owners who were selling Cuban cigars to their customers. I would applaud such an investigation—if it had been launched the day after the last illegal "nine" had been removed from the city's streets.

It took an initiative of the U.S. Attorney in Richmond, Virginia, to demonstrate what can happen when prosecutors set up a team to bring all federal gun crimes into the federal courts. In little over a year, the murder rate in Richmond, which routinely ranked among the top five in America, fell by 32 percent.

Richmond's Project Exile works this way: Whenever a gun arrest is made, the arresting officer pages a local ATF agent to determine whether the case can be prosecuted under federal statutes. The cops also carry laminated "cue cards" listing more than a dozen factors that are each sufficient to transform a routine gun possession offense into a federal crime, including evidence that the prisoner:

- is also in possession of drugs
- is a convicted felon
- is a drug user (If asked, he'll usually admit it.)
- is a fugitive who has fled another state
- is under indictment for a felony
- is an illegal alien
- is subject to a restraining order
- has a prior misdemeanor domestic violence conviction

The case can also be prosecuted federally if the gun taken from the prisoner:

- was stolen
- has been sawed off, or
- has, as did each of the two guns Freddy Krueger was arrested with, an obliterated serial number

In Richmond, the U.S. Attorney then takes every gun possession case involving a felon, drugs, or domestic violence to federal court, where bond rules are tighter, evidence rules more favorable to the prosecution, sentences longer, and parole unattainable. The city has translated those realities into a billboard, bus, TV, and print campaign that any crook can understand: "An illegal gun will get you five years in federal prison." True to their word, the prosecutors are successfully opposing bond in 80 percent of the Project Exile cases and the average sentence of those convicted has been better than four and a half years.

The success of the ad campaign comes out over and over again during interrogations. As one exasperated drug dealer explained after repeated questioning about how anybody as big-time as he was could forego keeping a stash of weapons somewhere: "Haven't you heard, man? Five years."

The importance of going federal with every case that qualifies can't be ignored. Because the threat of gun offenders being "exiled" is very real, citizens are inspired to phone in more tips, prisoners are motivated to give up more information on accomplices, and criminals still on the loose are intimidated into leaving their guns at home. Just as we saw in New York, the share of people carrying guns when arrested declined dramatically in Richmond as soon as word spread that law enforcement had gotten serious about gun crimes.

If New York got gun strategy right on the cops, Project Exile got it right on prosecution, and the example set by the U.S. Attorney's Office there should be replicated in every corner in the country. Nationwide, gun offenders prosecuted under federal law are six times more likely to be sent to the pokey than those prosecuted in state courts, and their average time served is three times as long. For taxpayers, the direct cost would be minimal, because the federal prosecutors would be picking up many cases that would otherwise have to be handled by the state courts, and the total U.S. prison population—which now stands at about 1.2 million—would increase by 75,000 to 100,000 at the most. Meanwhile, the lengthy absence of the convicted gun offenders would cut caseloads for cops, state judges, and state and local prosecutors.

Of course, there would also be fewer deaths, fewer injuries, fewer lives crippled by fear, and fewer futures surrendered to the siren song of the gangster life.

In the spring of 1999, President Clinton finally took note of what some of us in law enforcement have been advocating for years when he called on Attorney General Janet Reno and Treasury Secretary Robert Rubin to come up with a plan for increasing federal prosecution of gun crimes.

The President shouldn't settle for any version of Exile in which even John Dillinger reincarnate wouldn't meet the thresh hold for federal prosecution. If you want to go down as the President who ended high crime rates in America instead of as the American who almost made it a high crime to go down on a President, you will demand that:

- gun charges for *all* predicate felons are prosecuted federally
- monthly gun "report cards" are kept for all local jurisdictions, in order to monitor the efficiency and effectiveness of the federal prosecutors
- staffing in the prosecutors' offices and at the ATF are sufficient to track down and arrest the 50,000 ex-convicts and suspects who illegally apply for gun permits every year

And, so that first-time gun offenders don't continue to get off easy, he will urge all fifty states to adopt truth-in-sentencing guidelines to ensure that all gun offenders serve at least 85 percent of their sentences.

Without strong leadership at the national level, federal prosecution of gun crimes only happens with a lot of coaxing and confrontation. In Philadelphia, for instance, where four of every five murders are committed with guns, we had little trouble winning preliminary support for Project Exile from the mayor, the local prosecutors, the U.S. Attorney's Office, and a U.S. senator who came up with $1.5 million for hiring more federal agents and prosecutors to handle the additional gun cases. Even so, the U.S. Attorney took a look at the 4,000 gun arrests made in the city every year and said he wanted to increase the number prosecuted federally to only about 200 a year. In a follow-up letter to the mayor, John Timoney used a little satire to point out what the message to criminals would then be: "If you are caught carrying a gun in Philadelphia, there is a one in twenty chance you'll get five years in federal prison."

In New Orleans, perennial D.A. Harry Connick, Sr., resisted the suggestion that he cross-designate some of his prosecutors to the U.S. Attorney's Office so they could try local gun cases in the federal courts. Harry the Crooner sang a sad old song about how doing so would be "giving in" to lenient judges in the state courts, so he argued that it would be more prudent to wait until new state laws were passed to tighten bond rules and increase mandatory sentences for gun crimes.

I argued that maybe Harry should volunteer to live in the Desire Housing Project for as long as it takes to get those new laws passed.

Then Chief Pennington, U.S. Attorney Eddie Jordan, and ATF Special Agent Frank Surotchak started New Orleans's version of Project Exile without him. Surotchak is one fed who operates with a sense of urgency. The sole flaw in the Richmond program is that federal gun offenders are often released before their cases are put in the federal system and thus get a month on the run before anybody finds them again. In New Orleans, the crooks have no hope of winning release or station house bail because "Quickdraw" Surotchak keeps his agents on call around the clock to write up the appropriate paperwork within hours of each arrest.

Drug crews and criminal gangs aren't one and the same problem, of course, but because the objective in both situations should be to take out whole organizations, the broad outlines of the strategies needed to address the two problems are identical. A few of the individual tactics would vary, but not much else.

The drug strategy I propose is an argument for a ground war. The so-called War on Drugs has been dragging on for about fifteen years, and so far, the results are pathetic. In many of our large cities, illegal drugs are more potent, less costly, and more plentiful than ever.

Nationwide, emergency room visits attributed to the abuse of marijuana, heroin, and crack or cocaine have not fallen along with overall crime rates, which suggests that hard-core users are as plentiful as ever. Among those under eighteen, the rates of drug use have grown.

Money spent in producer nations and on border patrol clearly hasn't done much good, and on our own soil, too many drug-related arrests have been made with an eye on numbers but not on a plan.

In New York, we were ready at one point to go for the win. We had been saying for years that a third to over a half of the city's crime problem was related to drugs, but we had only 4 percent of our personnel in Narcotics. With the merger of the NYPD with the Transit and Housing forces and the recent hiring of several thousand new cops, manpower was peaking in 1995, so we decided the time had come to take the ground back from the dealers and never give an inch back.

The idea was to go borough by borough, starting with Queens, where we were going to send in 800 more cops, all under a unified command, to take out one drug crew after another, from the street-level pitcher, to the midlevel manager, to the owner of the spot, and beyond. After six months, we would leave a standing army of about 600 and slide the others down to Brooklyn North, where we'd need about 900 cops to repeat the same feat in four months. Then to Brooklyn South, where we'd need 600, Staten Island, which needed 200, and so on.

We called our plan Operation Juggernaut, and we'd sold Mayor Giuliani on the idea that it would wipe out crime in one year. If only a page-one *Daily News* story hadn't announced the initiative as "Bratton's Juggernaut," we might have found out then what a winning plan could do when applied to a city of eight million. But City Hall backed out the day that headline hit the newsstands, claiming, suddenly, to be worried that sufficient treatment options weren't in place for all the addicts throughout the city who might suddenly find themselves with no place to turn for a fix. Two years later, with

Juggernaut buried, the mayor created a stir by proposing that the city go cold turkey on methadone treatment.

To understand what the War on Drugs would feel like today if Juggernaut had been allowed to set the standard, you could take a study the Brooklyn North Initiative—the Son of Juggernaut—where Joe Dunne achieved a crime decline in 1996 that was 50 percent greater than in the rest of New York City. Or you might keep an eye on Newark, where the triumvirate of Police Director Joseph Santiago and chiefs Anthony Ambrose and Danny DeLorenzi put the Juggernaut strategy into effect on a citywide basis for the first time in the spring of 1999. In the meantime, we can return to the scene of a hypothetical crime meeting, and listen to what it could sound like if the cops and everybody else in law enforcement worked together to take drug crews out systematically, one at a time.

Again, a precinct or district commander would be standing at the podium below two or three large projection screens, and though the dialogue you're about to read is fictional, you can read it as an example of "what might have been," because the criminals discussed and their methods of operation are borrowed from a real case.

Take particular note when the conversation brings in multiple speakers, because the expanded cast of characters participating in this crime meeting is critical to the overall effectiveness of the strategy. For now, unfortunately, we have to visit the Land of Make-Believe to see them all working so well together.

"Good morning, Captain."

"Good morning, Commissioner."

"Let's start with the crew on Beekman Avenue. Does this map look familiar to you?"

"Yes, sir. It appears to be a map of the shootings and homicides in our precinct, year to date."

"I'm glad somebody in your precinct recognizes it. I dropped in on your command at about three o'clock this morning and I didn't see a map that looks like this anywhere in your roll call room. How are your cops going to be helpful in solving your open cases if they don't know where they are?"

"Commissioner, the reason the maps weren't up is because I'd brought them into my office for a planning session with my commanders that broke up at about 2 A.M. As you know, Narcotics, the warrant squad, and the detectives were recently put under my command as part of this operation. We're calling it Project Stickball, because we want to make these streets safe enough for kids to play on within six weeks."

"All right, then, tell me about this cluster of dots near Oak Terrace."

"Right. That's across from 348 Beekman, where we have a crew selling crack in the courtyard twenty-four hours a day."

"Who's the crew?"

"We call them Red Top, or Lenny's Boys."

"Who's Lenny? Do we have a photo?"

"Lenny Sepulveda. Lenny runs the spot, along with his brother, Nelson. But Lenny's Upstate for a short time on a state gun charge."

"Let's get the photos of both of them up on the screen. Which is the one with the Tasmanian Devil haircut?"

"That's Nelson. Lenny's the one on the left with the wandering eye."

"Aliases?"

"Lenny's known as 'Wooly' on the street. He also uses Lenny Rodriguez. Nelson's nickname is 'Wack.' "

"Let me guess: Lenny's the brains of the operation."

"Exactly."

"All right. Tell me the story."

"The Sepulveda brothers got started at this location a couple of years ago, after their former spot—which was only about a block away—was damaged in a fire and demolished. They call this building 'The Hole,' because it has a second entrance that leads into a basement tunnel and then into an interior courtyard ringed by balconies. Uniform cops can't get in, and neither can robbery crews. Buyers exit through the building's main entrance."

"How good is their radar?"

"Foolproof. They have lookouts out front of the building and on the roof next door—352 Beekman. If they see cops, the lookouts call the managers on walkie-talkies or on cell phones and the managers pull the pitchers into one of the organization's stash apartments. We're told the managers sit down with Nelson or Lenny every day before their shifts and talk about where our narcotics units are operating."

"Fixed shifts?"

"Just like ours. Lenny set up the schedule—midnight to eight, eight to four, and four to twelve—and they have one or two salaried managers for each one. The managers hire the pitchers, who are paid ten dollars for every bundle of one hundred crack vials they sell."

"Let's not make this crew out to be mad geniuses. Keep it simple—do you know how people got around New York in the nineteenth century when rain turned the streets to mud?"

"I'm not sure I understand what you're getting at, Commissioner."

"They walked over the rooftops. If you sent a unit in from above, I'm sure you'd shake up the operation a bit. And you can always post a uniform right at the street entrance; the customers love that."

"We'll try those things, Commissioner."

"What have you got on the members?"

"We pulled narcotics complaints from the past sixty days—some of which gave us the nicknames of the perps—and we came up with fifteen individuals who appear to be members or associates. Of those, we could make identities on four—two of whom have bench warrants and one who's on parole.

"We also ran Lenny and Nelson's names through the Corrections computer and came up with seven names of people who called them or had visits from them in prison. Two of the seven are now dead, three are on probation, one is still locked up, and one is on parole. Four of the five who are still alive appear on our frequent offender list."

"Excellent, Captain."

"There's more, Commish. Just for fun, we ran the priors on those seven, and came up with nineteen named accomplices, including a few mentions of Lenny and Nelson.

"We're putting together a matrix with all the unsolved shootings and murders running across the top and all members and associates of the crew running down the side so we can keep track of what we think they're connected to, plus a few other things we know about them like, do they own or operate a car, are they on public assistance, and how many times have they been named as victims, complainants, or suspects in various crimes.

"We also ran the addresses for a three-block area and came up with a hundred and twenty-six people with open warrants, twenty-three on parole, and ninety-three on probation, of whom eighteen are wanted. That's what we're starting with."

"Now to the good part. What's your plan, Captain?"

"The warrant squad will start each day at four-thirty, and their job will be to bring in about two times the number of usual suspects by focusing on this location and this crew. Detectives who have wants on anybody will accompany them.

"The roll calls for Patrol, Narcotics, and the detectives will be held together, so everybody can review the previous day's operations and what's going to happen next. In addition to the usual briefings on patterns, new parolees, and arrests and offenses from the previous day, there will be special instruction on spotting altered Vehicle Identification Numbers, on spotting traps in cars, and on how a cell phone with an altered serial number can be identified using a little device from Radio Shack that checks the microchip inside.

"We'll use a variety of tactics to bring people in, including 'Quality-of-Life Plus' enforcement with the beer-and-piss squad, truancy sweeps to pick up some of the kids the managers hire, and DWI checks right in front of the drug location. We plan to seize all cars on DWI and drug violations.

"Also, I have people contacting all the landlords on the block as we speak . . ."

"C'mon, Captain—I know what that means."

"No, I'm not kidding. We have two cops contacting the landlords so they'll sign affidavits allowing us to arrest any trespassers. We'll use observation posts to make arrests on the drug buyers."

"You know I don't like . . ."

". . . arresting only buyers. I know, Commish, but we'll use the buyers to help us fill in the crew's chain of command and we're holding Narcotics to a reasonable arrest ratio of buyers to dealers.

"All prisoners, of course, will be interrogated, and anytime they give up guns or drugs, search warrants will be obtained and executed. Either I or my exec will go out on every one of them."

"What about putting prisoners on the . . . ?"

"Photo Imaging machine. Of course. All cooperative witnesses will be put on Photo Imaging so they can pick out faces and help us put together that chain of command."

"Right, but I meant the . . ."

"I know, I know, Commish. We always run all prisoners on the pawnshop database to see if they've pawned anything recently and we'll check their jewelry, beepers, cell phones, and whatever else they've got on them against the stolen property lists.

"We plan to throw a block party on the street in a month—we're not taking our eyes off the ball. We do, though, need a few things from you."

"Ah, here we go."

"We understand there are some cops who trained with the fire marshals and Buildings Department. We'd like to team them up with Narcotics to spot violations in buildings we want closed down or where we run into an uncooperative landlord."

"Done."

"Also, we know that most of the crew doesn't live in our precinct; they live in Washington Heights, mostly between 171st and 174th streets. We may want to go in there, not just to execute wants or warrants, but to make some traffic stops at certain times of the day."

"They're commuters, huh?"

"Lenny has a strict rule against his employees working where they live—to make our job harder."

"OK. I'll call the precinct and see that the commander gives you some people to team up with if you want to run any operations there. And make sure they get photos, sketches, and IDs on whoever you're looking for and that they're sharing that information at roll call."

(Now comes the real "Fantasy Island" scenario.)

"All right. Let's go around the room. ATF, what have you got on this crew?"

"We've recovered seventeen guns in that precinct and traced the bullets or shell casings from another several shootings and homicides to guns purchased by two buyers in Alabama. They've been reporting the guns stolen, but we've tracked them down and one of them is willing to cooperate. We think we've got enough to make a case against a Brooklyn trafficker named Raymond Polanco who may have been selling weapons to this crew."

"FBI, what have you got?"

"We've got a CI from Washington Heights who says one of the suspects the precinct has here is the transporter and a guy with at least a few bodies on him. It's this guy Platano—real name: Wilfredo de los Angelos. The CI names him as the shooter in that murder of a kid in a pickup on the West Side Highway and we're sitting on a location for him in New Jersey. If you pick up Platano during this operation, we'd like to know about it immediately."

"And we trust you'd do the same. DEA, what do you have?"

"We're investigating a drug wholesaler named El Feo who we think may be the Sepulveda brothers' main supplier. His real name is Jose Reyes."

"What have you got on him?"

"We're using a CI to arrange for him to take a big shipment of heroin, but that may take a while. We have information that he ordered a hit in the Three-Four on one of his own pitchers, but it's only hearsay."

"Who did the hit?"

"A guy who calls himself Freddy Krueger is bragging about it."

"Can you get him on anything?"

"Not on the homicide, but we know he's a manager of one of El Feo's spots, at 1770 Andrews Avenue."

"That precinct will be in here next week to talk about targeting some drug crews. If we can't get Freddy Krueger for the homicide, we'll get him on narcotics. Then we'll see what he can tell us about this El Feo."

All right, so maybe Freddy Krueger's name wouldn't have come up in exactly that scenario after only his first homicide. The point is, everybody who's supposed to be on the same team—the cops, the local and federal prosecutors, the FBI, DEA, ATF, Secret Service—should be sitting down together each week, putting up everything they know about one drug spot after another, and then moving on a plan to surgically remove each crew or location from the map. Other agencies should be there to contribute too—the Immigration and Naturalization Service, which would have an interest in deporting some of the suspects, the Department of Agriculture, which maintains a huge cache of information about Food Stamp recipients, the local Board of Education, which usually keeps its own records on crime in and around the schools. Soon the discussions wouldn't describe crews with such lucrative operations or such long histories of violence. They'd be about start-up operations that would show up as a small cluster of drug complaints and could be knocked out in less than a week.

Gangs would be treated much the same. Law enforcement would gather in one room to focus on one gang or one gang cell, rough out a chain of command, map their crimes, map where they live, put everything known about each member onto a matrix, and then swiftly and systematically take them out.

It should go without saying that any intel system useful to investigators in any one of the law enforcement agencies has to be made available to the investigators in every one of the agencies. Sensitive information can be protected by firewalls and passwords, but nobody should have to make fifteen phone calls and recite a novena to obtain information about a criminal that somebody else in law enforcement already has. With gangs, there's no reason not to start out right—with a single database about gang members that all agencies would use.

With each gang or drug crew targeted for demolition, there would come a time to decide where the suspects would be prosecuted—in the state or the federal courts. Taxpayers, I'm sure, could care less which entity would wind up spending their money, so the decision should be made strictly by weighing which route promises to make streets and neighborhoods safer.

The federal route has much to recommend it: Prisoners face higher bail or are denied bail altogether. A suspect can be convicted on an accomplice's statement. Other rules of evidence make it easier to effect an arrest or win a conviction. Sentences, as we know, are longer, and prisoners serve an average 85 percent of those sentences. The threat of longer sentences, in turn, increases the chances a prisoner will want to help investigators lock up other crooks. Penalties for racketeering or ongoing criminal enterprises are particularly tough, and a gangster doesn't have to be an underboss in the Lucchese family to be taken down on those charges: A couple of humps selling smack in the playground are an "ongoing criminal enterprise" under RICO laws.

As I said, every state must pass laws to match the federal courts' tougher sentencing guidelines for adult gun offenders. In addition, gun courts for juvenile gun offenders should be established with their own stiff sentences, as well as an intensive oversight program for probationers and parolees, including drug checks, truancy checks, and curfew visits. Violators would be sent straight to the slammer.

In the meantime, there's a simple choice to be made. If we really want to end violent crime, we should follow up everything else the cops are doing by taking most gun, drug, and gang cases through the federal courts. Every day law enforcement wastes in taking in pot shots at each other over turf is another day an innocent life might be taken in the crossfire between a bunch of known hoods.

TEN

THE BATTLE WITHIN
Corruption, Brutality, and the Wrongfully Accused

On a sunny afternoon not many summers ago, I was driving in Manhattan with my seven-year-old son when we came upon a patrol car triple-parked outside a temporary district headquarters on 58th Street. The trunk of the patrol car was open, and a cop was hunting inside for something, apparently oblivious to the fact that he was forcing all traffic to snake a needle's-eye opening between his front bumper and a freight truck parked against the opposite curb.

Public trust in the NYPD happened to be at a tenuous pass itself. Several days earlier, a rail-thin Brooklyn resident named Abner Louima had recounted from his hospital bed a tale of police brutality almost beyond imagination. And yet it was true: While in the custody of the Seventieth Precinct, Louima had been taken into a bathroom where a wooden stick was rammed up his rectum so violently that it tore through tissue and ruptured his bladder. Two officers would eventually be convicted in the assault, but when reports of the crime first surfaced, the story threatened to discount or discredit all that the rest of the cops in the department had achieved in bringing down crime over the previous few years. By association, the style of policing established during Bratton's tenure was implicated too.

It wouldn't be the last time such a link would be imagined.

As I was pulling up even with the cop in the patrol car, I thought to myself that here was a chance, before I headed to Central Park for the day, for me to do my own small part in easing the current tensions between the police and the public.

"Excuse me, Officer," I said. (I always try to use a respectful tone when addressing a defender of the civil order.) "Do you think you could move your car up a little so people can get by?"

The cop's lips curled. "Why don't you mind your own business?" he shot back.

Maybe my ears were playing a trick on me. "I beg your pardon?" I said.

"I told you to mind your own business."

At that point, my left eye popped out of my head.

"Da-Da, why is the policeman yelling at you?" asked Brendan.

I still can't quite remember when I picked the eye up off the floor of the car and put it back in, but I remember my vision was just fine a few minutes later when I walked into the district, holding Brendan's hand, and announced that I wished to file a civilian complaint. The sergeant and the other cops behind the desk were looking at me, in my basketball shorts and new beard, as if they knew they'd seen my face somewhere but couldn't put it in context.

"Who's in command here?" I added.

The little dash of lingo jarred their memory banks and brought out a lieutenant who couldn't have been more gracious. After a short conversation, I told him to forget about taking a written complaint, but to get the message out to all his subordinates that a badge is no license to treat civilians with contempt.

I was furious about that cop the rest of the afternoon—until I realized I was angry with myself as well. I knew that despite all we had accomplished in our twenty-seven months to make the NYPD the envy of the world, we had run out of time before we'd done enough to change a common mind-set among cops that the general public is at best a nuisance and at worst the enemy.

That attitude feeds mistakes, missteps, and misunderstandings in a business that allows very little room for any of the three.

It isn't the root cause of all police brutality and corruption. But it is to crime within a police force what drugs and guns are to crime in the larger community: It's an accelerant, and it has to be dealt with as ruthlessly as the criminal cops themselves.

The attitude of the cop on 58th Street seems to be one half of a messed-up relationship in which two people who need each other—the cops and the citizens—have stopped seeing each other clearly for whom they really are. Just as cops forget that the vast majority of the public is OK, some citizens lose sight of the fact that, as the Mollen Commission concluded in 1994 after a two-year study of corruption in the NYPD, the overwhelming majority of police officers are honest and hardworking.

Even the extent of the ill will can't be overgeneralized. According to national surveys, only one in ten Americans has a "low" or "very low" opinion of the honesty and ethical standards of police officers, which means the cops have about a third as many detractors on that score as newspaper reporters and about a quarter as many as lawyers, Congressmen, and labor union leaders. Almost half of all Americans rate cops as having high or very high ethical standards, and another 40 percent peg them as being of average honesty and integrity.

Still, the lack of mutual empathy between cops and citizens is widespread enough that it can sometimes discourage individual cops or entire police organizations from doing what they need to do to protect the public from crime.

For instance, in whatever city I go to as an adviser these days, there's always somebody sitting in the gallery seats who starts making noise about how the strategies I advocate contribute to that wrong attitude, how I'm about to import "zero tolerance" tactics that compromise individual rights while aiding and abetting brutality.

I have to confess: There may have been a time—before I became enlightened—when I unwittingly condoned the excesses associated with "zero tolerance" policing.

But that was before I watched one day as several New York City police officers rolled up on a bunch of bare-chested teenagers who were playing basketball in Forest Park in Queens. The cops found an open beer can on the edge of the court, poured out its contents, then ordered the sweating ballplayers to put their shirts back on.

"This has gone too far," I thought.

The year was 1959. I was six years old.

About the only people I've ever had zero tolerance for are bullies—whether they carry knapsacks, badges, or unregistered nines—especially the ones who beat their spouses and abuse their kids.

But applied to any larger demographic, "zero tolerance" is bad policy and a bad strategy. When used as a synonym for "Quality-of-Life Plus," as it often is, it distorts the intent and the reality of how those tactics are carried out in an earnest and well-orchestrated fight against crime. Security forces who wore brown shirts, red armbands, and jackboots practiced zero tolerance, not the guys and gals in blue.

If this all sounds like I'm playing a game with semantics, so be it. The choice of words is important on this issue.

When we first started implementing quality-of-life enforcement in the NYPD as one of our seven central strategies, one enthusiastic borough commander came into a crime meeting all charged up about what he had decided to sell to his subordinates as "in-your-face policing." Quickly, I called a time-out and let him know that though I understood that his intentions were good, his term sounded an awful lot like "fuck-you policing" to me, and that was not at all what we had in mind.

In Philadelphia, some of the holdovers from the Frank Rizzo era talk about "ped stops" in a way that compels John Timoney to remind them again and again that no pedestrian can be stopped without just cause and that the cops and bosses had better be able to articulate why any stop was made. In New Orleans, the cops throw around an old expression about how on this or that investigation, they were "stopping everything that moved." Ronnie Serpas, the chief of operations there, made sure the commanders understood that the rhetoric better be only that there are enough laws on the books for the cops to make stops legally, with no need for a wink and a nod. Besides, the nets the police set for the sharks out on the streets are always supposed to let the dolphins go. To do otherwise lacks a sense of fairness and is a waste of time and resources.

The statistics generated by "Quality-of-Life Plus" can be used by critics to make a department appear overzealous or just petty. Misdemeanor arrests and summons activity rise dramatically, and as serious crime declines, so, often, do felony arrests. Apologies have their place in this business, but there's no reason the cops should be asked to apologize to a city's editorial boards for those numbers: The overwhelming majority of stops are made because citizens have called 911 about crime or quality-of-life problems on their streets and they want the cops to do something about it. Many times the callers even give locations and descriptions. What should the cops do? Stay in their cars? Should the beat officers walk right past a drug dealer as a citizen's description of him comes blaring over their radios?

Of the stops arising solely from police initiative, a significant number result in the arrests on minor charges of offenders suspected of more serious offenses. If you remember, it was a cloned phone charge that locked up the first member of a Queens assassination crew.

It's also happened that as police departments have increased their arrest and summons activity, civilian complaints have initially risen along with them—until training, supervision, and the field experience itself take hold and make the cops better at the job they're asked to do. Even so, the increases in total complaints in both New York and New Orleans came while the ratios of complaints to arrests and summonses were falling. In both cities, it was as if a restaurant that had been serving 100 dinners a night and having 10 sent back to the kitchen increased business overnight to 200 dinners a night, of which 15 were sent back. Complaints at that restaurant have gone up 50 percent, but the rate of complaints has fallen by 25 percent. Even the editors of *The New York Times* would have to expect that if the paper's circulation increased by 100,000, readers' complaints about inaccurate reporting would rise as well.

There are ways we can reduce the tensions that arise as a result of stops, but there are a few sets of numbers that I believe helps keep the concerns about the repercussions of assertive policing in perspective. In 1985, long before Rudy Giuliani, Bill Bratton, and my four crime-fighting principles came along, the NYPD fielded only 26,000 cops but had 7,000 civilian complaints filed against them. In 1998, 40,000 cops engaged in the more assertive style of policing had 5,000 civilian complaints filed against them.

Shooting statistics reveal a similar pattern. In 1990, under a mayor considered to be kinder and gentler than Giuliani, forty people died in the city as a result of police shootings. Don't get me wrong: The vast majority of those shootings were justified, but in 1998, with an additional 14,000 cops on the force, the number of people who died in police shootings was nineteen.

The frequency of police stops became a major issue only recently, after index crime in New York had already fallen by almost 400,000 incidents a year. Stops have never been systematically counted, but anybody who thinks the cops made fewer stops in 1990 is living in a fantasy world. In any city, when the report of a crime goes out over the radio, cops converge on the location given and stop anybody who matches the description of the perp or perps. In 1990, New York City cops were asked to respond to reports of 1,500 more murders, 4,000 more shootings, 25,000 more assaults, 33,000 more drug complaints, 62,000 more robberies, 75,000 more burglaries, and 100,000 more car thefts than in 1998. We weren't winning the war, but due to the higher incidence of serious crime, the NYPD made 6,000 more gun arrests, 605 more arrests for murder, 10,695 more arrests for robbery, 2,722 more arrests for burglary and 11,016 more arrests for car theft—and had to stop many thousands more people to do so. It's simple: Fewer serious crimes mean fewer stops and fewer arrests, which in turn means more kids in the playing fields instead of in potter's field.

The pundits have to give credit where it's due. Police in the United States are more restrained in their use of force than they've ever been. Only a generation ago, you couldn't wait around Night Court in New York for very long before seeing a prisoner come in wearing bandages on his head or a "turban." Judges who reduced charges and sentenced people to "time served" would sometimes note—with approval—that "street justice" had already been administered. When I was a young cop, there were still many people around who'd been raised to believe that anybody who stepped out of line deserved a whack, and we were taught from day one in the academy that we had to be vigilant to prevent other officers from "mussing up" our own prisoners. More than once, I had to hold back a cop or a boss who was looking to do just that.

Not that much longer back, a police commissioner famed as an uncompromising foe of gambling dens, whorehouses, gin mills, and especially the crooked cops who protected them thought himself more than justified in chiding his detectives—while reporters listened in—for letting a particular, elegantly dressed young gangster make it to a lineup with not a hair out of place.

"Men like him should be mussed up," the commissioner announced. "Blood should be smeared on his velvet collar."

To one newspaper reporter, he elaborated.

"We want to be careful not to kill innocent people and we don't want to use brutality on others because of different political faiths," he said, "but with the killers, racketeers, and gangsters, the sky is the limit."

Commissioner Lewis J. "Night Stick" Valentine held the top job in the NYPD for another eleven years without ever having to apologize for those statements, and when he was invited by General Douglas MacArthur in 1946 to reorganize the police, fire, and prison systems of Japan, *The New York Times* bade him farewell with a glowing endorsement. The legendary mayor Fiorello La Guardia subsequently praised his longtime police chief as "a kindly man" who "never caused me to lose a night's sleep."

By the time I joined the force, a commissioner who talked the way Valentine did would be run out of town before the night was over. Even then, however, police beatings were still far more common than they are today.

You could look at training, recruitment, regulations governing the use of force and disciplinary policies to see what internal changes made the most difference in the cops' propensity for unnecessary violence, but we shouldn't forget about external influences—like the Catholic nuns a lot of those older cops grew up with. The Josephites, I remember, especially enjoyed the various implements of torture—the paddle, the ruler with the brass edge, the knuckle of the middle finger applied to the top of the head, the palms clapped against both ears, as if the victim had walked in front of a cymbal player at the wrong moment. Some of them must have watched a lot of pro wrestling on TV, because their best moves were taken straight from Bobo Brazil, Bruno Sammartino, and Killer Kowalski.

Parents back then were just as menacing. If my mother had worn black tights when she used to climb into the top bunk, swinging the bulldog's chain, I would have thought she was Waldo Von Erick scaling the turnbuckles. I can still see her standing at the front door, promising that for once I wouldn't get a beating if I'd just come back inside. That, of course, was always a prelude to a review lesson in why not to trust authorities.

My point is not that many cops of my generation have legitimate grounds for a class-action suit against the nation's parochial schools (though we do), but that the cops' behavior is shaped by a larger culture, then judged against the larger culture's shifting standards.

Civilians forget that a cop is only human. Actors who play cops on TV or in the movies get several takes to get a scene right, but cops have to make decisions in the field about things like reasonable suspicion and probable cause that a panel of judges couldn't figure out if they had a year to mull over the choices. People think of cops the way kids think about their teachers—as if it's weird when the teacher gets caught doing anything a normal person does, like shopping for groceries, standing in line at the movies, or spending a little time at the park with his or her own children.

I once had a prisoner launch a lungee right into my eye as I was putting cuffs on him, and I answered with a quick left hook to the mouth. When the lieutenant at the desk scolded me after I'd told him what happened, I said, "If you spit in my eye, I'd punch you in the mouth too." When the assistant district attorney complained, I said, "If you spit in my eye, I'd punch you in the mouth too. Would you rather I committed perjury? Do you think a jury would believe me if I said that when the prisoner put a goober in my eye, I apologized for letting my face get in his way?"

Maybe nobody else would tell you this anymore, but if you raise your fists against a cop or spit in the cop's eye, expect to get knocked on your ass. That's not the kind of violence we should ever worry about, even though we now want the cop to consider that an eyeful of pepper spray represents a more restrained, and usually more effective, response.

Police stops don't in themselves have to be onerous. In 1997, 1.7 billion U.S. airline passengers were stopped before boarding their planes and there were insufficient grounds to arrest all but 1,000 of them. If cops made only one arrest for every 1.7 million stops, either America would be Mayberry or the crooks would be having a good laugh. Yet very few citizens complain that airport screening infringes on their civil liberties. Their perception is that the danger warrants the inconvenience, but airline passengers are infinitely more likely to be killed or assaulted by an urban terrorist on the ground than by a bomb-totin' maniac in the sky.

Meanwhile, many of the pundits who are shocked—shocked!—by how many stops the police make will shop five days a week in bookstores where they have to check their bags at the door and go home at night to buildings where the doormen stop any visitor who doesn't look "right."

And where did these pundits grow up, anyway? I must have been stopped by the cops 100 times when I was a teenager—in the parks, at Rockaway Beach, sneaking into the movie theaters, or just riding around in a car. There was this one park house where every kid in the neighborhood used to hang out, even though we all knew it was only a matter of time before the cops came by and tossed us. They'd pour out the beer, ripple, or Pineapple Tango and confiscate a few tubes of airplane glue—even though the glue-sniffers always kept a few model planes around to establish plausible deniability. The cops didn't often buy the airplane alibi, so the kids who huffed floor wax didn't even bother trying to argue that they were junior apprentices at janitor school.

If you're young, cops are going to be looking to stop you—often for good reason. In 1997, kids sixteen to twenty-one were only 8.3 percent of the U.S. population, but they accounted for 30 percent of all arrests for serious crimes. Still, I remember it used to be considered better to be stopped by the cops than to have somebody's "old lady" come down to the park house. And I don't mean girlfriends. My mother might have been Waldo Von Erick, but some of those other moms were built like Gorilla Monsoon.

The cops, for their part, have to work hard to get the tone right. I know what a bad stop can be, because not that many years ago, I was pulled over on a Connecticut highway by an off-duty trooper who put his Beretta to the back of my head the moment I rolled down my window. I suspect what set him off was that my only passenger happened to be a friend who's both black and female, but the trooper said only that I had been "traveling too slowly in the left-hand lane."

That cop may have been beyond redemption, but most would benefit from more training on how to make a stop.

Stops can be fatal for a police officer. About 12 cops die in America every year and another 250 are assaulted with a firearm while investigating suspicious individuals or circumstances. During my two-plus years as a deputy commissioner in New York, three names were added to those memorialized in the Hall of Heroes at One Police Plaza: Officer Sean McDonald, who was killed while stopping some thugs who'd just held up a clothing boutique, Officer Kevin Gillespie, who was killed while stopping a car that had been reported highjacked, and Officer Ray Cannon, who was killed while investigating a report of a robbery at a Brooklyn bicycle shop.

The flip side is that the vast majority of stops don't even result in the establishment of probable cause for an arrest, so a cop is obliged to approach every stop with the odds of either eventuality in mind.

The police can improve their batting averages by becoming better informed about current crime patterns, which would also help them articulate the elements that added up to reasonable suspicion that a crime had been, was being, or was about to be committed. Even so, nobody who regularly makes stops is likely to bat .500. In a case that went to trial in New York, two partners who made a gun arrest after pulling over an occupied cab were found justified in making the stop because two out of five times they'd made stops under similar circumstances, they had interrupted cab robberies in progress. That's a great batting average, but it means that three times out of five, the partners' suspicions were unfounded.

That's who the cops need to apologize to: every person stopped for whom no probable cause is established that would lead to an arrest.

True, not every person who is stopped and who clears the legal hurdles is an upstanding citizen, but unless and until the evidence proves otherwise, he or she should be treated with the respect due any pillar of the community.

The apology should always receive a clear explanation of why the stop was made, like: "Sorry, sir, I've never seen a gun-shaped sandwich before, let alone anyone who carried their lunch in their waistband." Or more likely: "We had an alert on the radio about a robbery suspect in this area whose description matched yours. Let me call the dispatcher so you can hear the information we were working from."

Better than an apology, the citizens inconvenienced by a fruitless stop ought to receive a consolation gift, like vouchers to cover their next three parking meter violations or a month's free pass on the city's buses and trains. The policy would be the equivalent of Domino's offer of a free pizza for any customer who has to wait longer than thirty minutes for delivery, and the costs to the city would be more than repaid in goodwill.

In the meantime, the bosses should be mapping all stops, which the cops would memorialized by hand or by entering them into mobile data terminals. Color-coding would distinguish the stops by charge suspected as well as whether each charge was ultimately sustained or determined to be unfounded. The bosses would be able to look at citywide averages or narrow their sights to a single precinct, a single tour, or even an individual cop. Examples of great police work would jump out like the stars over eastern Long Island, and potential disciplinary problems would pop up like pimples on a twelve-year-old.

Police corruption has followed a different trajectory than the use of force.

If police departments have made any progress against corruption over years, it's in the gradual eradication of the systematic graft depicted in the movie *Serpico*. These days, however, corruption usually feeds off the drug trade, and though it only rarely involves anybody above the rank of sergeant, it takes more virulent forms than ever.

Many of the departments I've worked in were just uncovering or emerging from enormous corruption scandals at the time I arrived. In New York, more than a dozen cops in the Three-Oh Precinct were discovered to be taking protection from some drug dealers while beating and robbing others. In Newark, the previous police director had been blowing the department's whole investigations budget on dinner dates with his babes. In New Orleans, the killer cops Len Davis and Antoinette Frank made *Serpico* look like the Disney version of cops gone bad.

Fortunately, the vast majority of cops want the lawbreakers captured. But it's unrealistic to think that by the principle of majority rule, an organization can just wish its way into stopping or arresting these outbreaks. To begin with, the culture that tells the public to mind its own business has to be replaced by a convincing alternative in which loyalty to the badge means something greater than loyalty to everybody who has a badge.

At least half the solution I'm talking about is contained in the previous nine chapters. If the cops see they can win the war on crime, they will be far less likely to seek retreat behind misplaced loyalties and mirrored sunglasses. When cops feel the job's not for real, a few think they're free to rob, beat, and steal.

But every demand I make of the cops presumes the particular organization they belong to is healthy enough to do whatever the fight against crime requires. And since the cops can't think they have any wiggle room, a leader can allow them to think nothing else.

Napoleon, Patton, and George Washington all knew, however, that the troops' state of readiness does demand serious attention. If their heads aren't screwed on straight, they can't go full out against crime and they can even be a danger to themselves or others. A leader has to push them as far as they can go, but with that responsibility comes an obligation to address the root causes of any anger or disillusionment, whether real or imagined.

In most cities where I've worked as a consultant, my partner John Linder runs the diagnostic tests on the departments. Some of the cops call him a "spin doctor," but he's really more of a shrink. Using detailed surveys and informal focus groups, he aims primarily to identify values that are common across rank, gender, race, and ethnicity so that a leader knows what he or she has to build on. But along the way, John finds the old wounds and nagging injuries that can slow the progress of a turnaround or flare up into major distractions.

Cops in any department think the public, the press, and the local prosecutors hate them, but in an unhealthy organization the cops are convinced, justifiably, that the bosses hate them too. The cops invariably rank crime-fighting high on their lists of what the department's priorities should be, but they believe their commanders care more about being embarrassed by them. They believe the only way to move up in the organization is to have a hook, and they believe Internal Affairs investigators couldn't make a case on Hitler for disorderly conduct. Yet they feel that cops who are caught for minor breaches of department rules are treated as if they're war criminals.

The cops also often feel that they're not adequately paid. And they're right. Cops should be able to eat steak and take their families on vacations without having to hold down second jobs. We wouldn't entrust our lives to a heart surgeon who had to be out all night driving a cab, and we should make sure cops have only one job to worry about—catching crooks and keeping us safe. In Birmingham, we promised to award bonuses to every cop in the city if the department met specific goals in three crime categories where the crime declines are particularly hard to fudge—murders, auto thefts, and shootings—but in New York, we let the troops down when we allowed a three-year contract to go through without a dollar's raise in it.

In New Orleans, the cops' anemic paychecks had to get bulked up before we could expect to keep the veterans' minds from turning to dishonest ways of covering their rents or mortgages. And as Vegetius recommended when trying to reverse the decline of the Roman army, it was time in New Orleans to raise the recruitment standards and to once again draw the defenders of the Republic from families of good name.

When bosses in any department have identified the cops' grievances, they must make a sincere effort to address them. That creates the opportunity to recast the posture of the entire organization.

Several chapters back, I said that every newly sworn police officer should be rotated through Narcotics, Patrol, and the Detective Bureau so they can learn early all about how crooks work and how each branch of the force supports the others. To instill in every cop a proper perspective on their interactions with the public, we should have every recruit give six months to "midnight basketball" or some other youth-oriented community service program before the recruit even sets foot in the academy. The cops have to learn that most kids are just kids, not mortal threats.

After six months in the academy itself, the recruits should spend the next six months working as correction officers, which would afford them the opportunity to find out before they're awarded their service revolvers how well they handle some of the real bad boys. If the department serves a city with a mass transit system or public housing, the recruits should spend several months getting to know about life in each of those worlds too.

Beginning in the academy, the message repeated day after day has to be that the cops work for the public, not for a feeling of camaraderie. A police department shouldn't be, as Jimmy Breslin once wrote, "a softball team with guns." Nor can the cops pledge allegiance to any abstract ideals about the law or order if those ideals fail to take into account what the citizens think those ideals should look like.

I don't think only black cops can understand a black neighborhood and only Dominican cops can understand a Dominican neighborhood, but the perception in many minority communities that the police are an occupying army is a serious enough threat to a department's effectiveness that chiefs everywhere should act immediately to reshape their departments to reflect the ethnic and racial composition of the public they serve. I don't care how much has to be spent to recruit substantial numbers of appropriate candidates; the public has to see its own reflection on the faces of its police officers.

The cops shouldn't be told they're subservient to the public. They're not; and even though many cops don't think so, they are professionals, whose skills and experience are called upon the way a doctor is called on by a patient.

What that ideal means on the street is that when a crowd gathers around to find out why poor old Mrs. McGinty is lying in the gutter, the appropriate response is not "Nothing to see here—show's over," or worse, "Move along—mind your own business." If at all possible, the cops should offer a simple explanation: "Apparently, Mrs. McGinty was struck by a bus. I don't know how badly she's injured—it would be great if you could go to the corner to direct the ambulance over when it gets here."

We've all heard the saying "People in glass houses shouldn't throw stones." The cops' thinking should be "People with brass balls live in glass houses." They should take pride in the fact that though they work in a field where their actions can easily be misinterpreted, they have no fear of scrutiny. A police department has to be a transparent organization, with no dark secrets or dark corners hidden from the disinfecting rays of the sun.

Sometimes a cop even has to be willing to look silly. When I was in uniform, I once played ringalevio for about five minutes on 57th Street with a big bruiser of a bag lady who was coming after me, swinging a motorcycle chain. I could have charged her with my night stick raised, but instead I radioed in for some extra hands and kept circling a parked car to stay out of her reach. A cop has to have enough sense not to tackle a woman who looks like Dick Butkus if it's unnecessary—and enough a sense of humor to take a ribbing for it in the locker room.

Aside from imparting lessons on philosophy, the academy must drill the cops relentlessly in actual field tactics.

Lord knows, the instructors already spend enough time teaching recruits the proper ways to fill out forms, but that is the time to warn them against small corruptions of the truth that damage the credibility of all cops and can lead the rookies into grosser transgressions down the line.

If a cop who makes an arrest needs to meet her buddies early the next morning for a deep-sea fishing trip, her partner can process the prisoner without resorting to a false claim that he saw the gun or that he made the tackle. If three cops wind up having to testify in court eighteen months after making two minor drug collars on a street corner, they don't have to meet over breakfast to manufacture a cohesive story; they should review their old notes separately and, if possible, return alone to the scene of the arrests. If the case goes sour because the cops' memories are imperfect, so be it: The courts will have to figure out a way to process cases more quickly.

One of the most common corruption problems a cop can create for himself occurs when the cop, responding to a 911 complaint, tells some crew on a street corner to move along and the crew just sucks their teeth at him.

The untrained cop will then throw somebody against a wall; he may come up with a gun, drugs, and a few stolen credit cards, but he'll perjure himself in the courtroom to keep anybody from finding out that the only offense that preceded the frisk was teeth-sucking.

A smart cop instead would have tipped his hat to the teeth-suckers, retreated to a nearby rooftop, and watched with a monocular until he saw a drug sale, a dice game, or some other legit reason to lock the suckers up. When that cop gets to court, he won't even be tempted to "testi-lie."

The foremost responsibility of the academy, however, is to prepare recruits and veterans for the whole range of street encounters through relentless, realistic training.

In early 1994, a violent criminal named Ernest Sayon died as result of a struggle with six police officers outside a Staten Island housing complex. According to the medical examiner, Sayon had suffocated from pressure applied to his chest and neck while his hands were cuffed behind him. Soon many of his neighbors were marching in the streets.

A task force pulled together by Chief of Personnel Michael Julian looked at how our cops were restraining people and discovered that prisoners of the NYPD were being put at risk of dying of what's called positional asphyxia. The cops hadn't been taught a better way to handle somebody who was resisting arrest, so they'd take a suspect down by the neck and then sit or stand on the prisoner's chest or back. When the prisoner started struggling to get air, the cops would sit even harder.

The accidental death of Ernest Sayon pushed the NYPD to end chest-sitting the way the videotaped beating of Rodney King pushed the LAPD to put away their batons. Both departments learned from those tragedies that pepper spray offered an alternative to the traditional means of restraint that promised far fewer injuries for both the cops and their prisoners.

But in the middle of the Sayon controversy, we were delivered a graphic reminder that academy training in physical combat could never be pared down to a half-hour lesson in recognizing the front side of a spray can. A news station had come up with a video showing a cop in Staten Island clubbing a prisoner over the head with a radio in order to get the prisoner into a patrol car.

I asked, "Do we train the cops on how to put a prisoner into a car when the prisoner doesn't want to go?"

The answer was no. But if the cops don't get realistic training in how to handle the various types of physical confrontations they're likely to encounter, what else can they be expected to do? They improvise.

The proper use of a gun can, of course, cause at least as much damage as swinging it like a mallet, so firearms training has to include many hours of simulated encounters in which officers have to decide whether to fall upon their last resort—pulling the trigger.

With FATS, or the Firearms Training Simulator, a cop is able to interact with characters on a life-sized screen as if he or she were a character in Woody Allen's *The Purple Rose of Cairo*. Several years ago, when I was in for a refresher session on the simulator, I was standing on a street set when a car came roaring past with somebody firing a machine gun from a side window. The training people said they'd never seen anybody else dive behind a desk chair when the car went by, but I said, "That guy had a machine gun—and anyway, I got the license plate."

I always taught the people working under me that the very first thing they should do if they think they're being shot at is look for cover. A cop usually makes the decision to shoot or not to shoot in the midst of tremendous disorder and uncertainty—"the fog of war" is how the Marines describe it. Finding cover can be the best way to buy an extra heartbeat or two to determine if the "pop" that caused the initial panic came from a sniper or from a Snapple bottle dropped on the pavement.

Cops also have to be taught that action is twice as fast as reaction, so the crooks always enjoy an advantage unless the cops have used forethought and sound tactics to avoid being caught in a bad situation—which can end with an unnecessary loss of life. When my crew at Transit was staking out booth robbers, I used to rent an indoor paintball facility, and to teach them about the hazards of relying on quick reactions, I would ask the cop who thought he had the quickest reflexes to press his paintball gun into the small of my back. Even in that vulnerable position, I was easily able to spin around and blast him with my paint gun before he could even get a shot off.

That bit of knowledge should be cause not only for precaution but for courage in seemingly hopeless situations. When two teenagers in Littleton, Colorado, began gunning down their classmates inside Columbine High School, the best hope of the unarmed students was to rush the shooters. The students would only have known that if we taught personal safety management in our schools and workplaces, but the cops who would teach those courses apparently have to be reminded that in similar situations their first obligation is not to stay hidden. Any cop who's not prepared to run toward the danger should drop his or her badge in a mailbox and take up banking.

To increase the effectiveness of simulated encounters on the FATS machine, a department should input dramatizations of the shooting scenarios in which real-life cops screwed up. We can't punish cops for making honest mistakes, but we can do our best to ensure that the same mistake isn't repeated.

When I was deputy commissioner, I responded to the scene of a police shooting in which two armed robbery suspects had been killed and a third wounded by a pair of detectives who had been lying in wait inside the apartment of an elderly Bronx couple. The couple, who made a living by selling phony marriage licenses, had claimed they'd been robbed the night before and that the invaders had threatened to return, so the detectives decided to surprise the suspects when they entered instead of calling for backup and grabbing them somewhere on the other side of the door. The cops fired twenty-eight times before the intruders fired once, but the guys with the badges had left themselves with few other outs.

One of the most dramatic recent examples of an unnecessary police shooting took the life of a New York street vendor named Amadou Diallo as he stood in the doorway of his Bronx apartment building armed with nothing but a wallet and a beeper. Four members of the NYPD's Street Crime Unit fired forty-one bullets at Diallo, and months after the February 1999 shooting, only sparse detail had been provided to explain exactly why any of the officers decided to open fire.

It did come out that the four cops were riding together in a patrol car, looking for a serial rape suspect, when they happened upon Diallo standing inside his door at about half-past midnight. Two of the cops apparently jumped out of the car with no clear plan established, and when Diallo reached into his pocket, the shooting began.

Nobody could have predicted the exact circumstances in which the tragedy unfolded, but if the four officers had been trained to minimize the odds of creating a dangerous situation, they might have seen what Diallo had in his pocket before the first shot was fired. If they had been trained to always seek cover first when they believe they are being fired upon, the bullet count never could have reached forty-one.

The odds against the tragedy would have been further reduced if there was a strong supervisor among the four cops (to prevent the headlong rush into confusion) or if the Street Crime Unit had established fixed roles, based on which seat each of them occupied in the car, for any team of four making a gun stop on the street. In Newark, the cops are trained to yell, "Abort!" to quickly defuse a potentially explosive encounter when any of them discover that the danger is less than was anticipated.

Additional equipment could have helped too. If units like theirs that specialize in gun arrests were given bicycle-style helmets with ballistic visors (the less intimidating the design, the better), maybe the combination of vest and visor would have bought the first shooter just enough time to have made a better decision.

While there may be a long wait before we know all there is to know about the incident, it lends a hollow ring to a sentiment, often repeated among cops, that the first job of any police officer is to get home safe.

That old locker room maxim isn't right. If anything, the cop's job is to make sure everybody gets home safe—especially the civilians, who aren't paid to put their lives on the line. The traditional adage is an encouragement to shoot before seeking cover, to pull the trigger before a suspect's hand comes out of his pocket. When the choice involves the use of deadly force, a cop has to wait until the very last moment to be certain "the fog of war" won't lift to reveal that the threat to his or her life was less than imagined. That way of thinking has to be instilled from the academy on.

Sometimes, unfortunately, the fog doesn't lift in time. One 100-degree day inside the Lexington Avenue subway station, a shotgun was accidentally fired by some hood who then dropped his weapon inside the door of the last car of a subway train. Two cops who happened to be in the station—one off-duty, the other in plainclothes—responded like heroes and ran toward the trouble, but then they made costly tactical mistakes. The first hero to get to the last car, Peter Del Debbio, picked up the shotgun. The second, Desmond Robinson, had his gun drawn and, with no shield in his hand, was still running at Del Debbio when Del Debbio, before shouting, "Police! Don't move!," fired five times. Robinson, fortunately, survived, but almost every year, at least one police officer in America dies from friendly fire. Del Debbio was eventually convicted of assault in the shooting, but I wonder if the jury would have decided differently if they'd spent some time on the FATS simulator themselves. It's hard to convict somebody else when you've hit an innocent victim yourself—even in a glorified video game.

The only thing more horrible than a cop being killed by another cop is when a cop kills an innocent civilian, like Diallo. I've never done anything more difficult than face a family who'd just lost somebody to police gunfire.

The first time the victim was an eighteen-year-old girl who was standing on a subway platform waiting for her train home when a farebeater wielding a carpet knife went after a Transit cop and the officer opened fire. Anthony V. Bouza was the ranking officer who responded to the scene, but he sent Detective Jimmy Armstrong and me to notify the girl's family. Jimmy did the hard part, but I still hear the family's screams like it was yesterday.

The second time John Timoney, as chief of department, had taken it upon himself to attend an evening wake in the Bronx for a man who'd died in a parking garage a few days earlier when he was caught in the crossfire between police and an escaping murder suspect. I agreed to join him, and I'll never forget the pain in the widow's eyes or the tears running down Timoney's Mount Rushmore face as we offered the thin consolation of an apology on behalf of the entire department.

A cop understands, or ought to, that his or her own life may be claimed by the vagaries of the battle. Those victims had never asked for any part of it.

You should know by now that "trust" is not my watchword on matters of police performance. Leaders who make appearances in the field, night and day, can, of course, hope to keep dishonorable tactics or procedures in check, but they should also establish procedures that make it difficult for a cop to do the wrong thing at any time.

Property clerks' offices are swamps of trouble because few of them are governed by operating procedures that would ensure no valuables disappear before the prisoners who came in with them are sprung on bail or before the items are needed as evidence at trial. In Newark, the circus ended only after an undercover walked in a little before closing time and caught a couple cops leaving early with television sets on their backs. While I was working in Boston with Bratton for several weeks in 1993, a gun recovered from the street was found to have been a service revolver that sometime earlier had been taken by the department as evidence in another case. We took a closer look and found that many other guns recovered by the cops had gone missing.

To limit such vanishings and the number of times a crook carrying guns, drugs, or a pocketful of cash "gets a haircut" before he's delivered to the station house, every prisoner should be given a receipt itemizing his or her property, and all the property should be placed in sealed, numbered envelopes. All jewelry and guns should be made identifiable by the attachment of lead jewelers' tags. That way a real Rolex can't be switched with a knockoff by a crooked cop. Conversely, a cop who has been wrongfully accused of stealing can prove his or her innocence.

The use of confidential informants, if not watched carefully, presents further opportunities for corruption. Payments to CIs should be made in the presence of a boss or at least another member of the department so the investigator isn't tempted to take a little off the top. In addition, bosses should interview each CI once every few months to verify that the information they've provided has been followed up on, but also that the detectives haven't been falsifying search warrant applications by invoking the CI as the source of a good tip.

Patrol cops must be well supervised, especially on the midnight tour, when the radio takes its nap. Idleness, as we all know, is the devil's workshop, so it's up to a supervisor to give them specific patrol tasks to perform during the slow hours. A one-to-eight ratio of cops to sergeants has to be maintained in the field, not just on paper, and a commander has to take into account that many of the sergeants are kids who earned their stripes in a testing room with a No. 2 pencil—they're afraid of some of the older cops.

For that reason, every command should have a "sergeant major," who'd be a smart, tough veteran cut from the same cloth as John Dove or Vertel Martin. The sergeant major would be given lieutenant's money, and he or she would be asked to ride herd on the precinct's bad actors and unruly cabals. Because of the nature of the job, the sergeant major should park his or her personal vehicle within sight of a video camera. Some cops don't send their bosses messages on Post-its; they prefer to slash tires. A video would lock them up in a hurry.

Nothing replaces a first-line supervisor, but off-the-shelf technologies can make those supervisors even more effective.

In Brazil, I know, the presence of a television crew wasn't deterrent enough a couple of years ago to keep a couple of Sao Paolo cops from pulling a citizen out of a car and shooting him, but I'd still like to see video cameras mounted in every patrol car in America. Useful for more than just catching bad cops, the cameras would help good cops make better cases, deter imperfect cops from turning wrong, help the bosses identify general training needs, and give the press and public a chance to get a fly's-eye view of policing.

The cars could also be outfitted with a global positioning system to let supervisors track the whereabouts of their people at every moment, which would help not only to monitor the troublemakers but to locate injured cops when they're unable to use their radios or are unfamiliar with the neighborhood they find themselves in.

At the very least, every patrol car should carry a "sergeant in a box," which monitors the vehicle's activities throughout the day—when it was running, when it wasn't, and how fast it was traveling at any given moment. That little black box would discourage "cooping," high-speed chases and a tradition among bullies of stopping under a bridge or on a dead-end street for a few minutes before transporting a prisoner back to their precinct.

Even though I expect cops can buy into the ideal of a police department as a transparent organization, I wouldn't entrust a single wastebasket to the expectation that good cops will one day tear down the infamous "blue wall of silence."

Yes, I do expect cops would be willing to drop a dime on a coward or a thief if the offense in question is serious enough and the department has proven worthy of the informer's trust. But human beings—no matter what the color of their work clothes—don't like to volunteer for the part of rat fink. Most parents would probably rather have Monica Lewinsky for a daughter than Linda Tripp, and Linda only blew the whistle. We are raised to believe that telling on somebody is a form of cowardice, so it takes unusual set of circumstances to knock us off that notion.

How many journalists do you think would turn in a coworker for fudging a source? How many doctors would turn in a colleague for running up an insurance company's bill with a couple of unnecessary tests? How many ambulance chasers would squeal about another lawyer inventing a few crucial details to help a client win a settlement?

That's a good reason for having civilian oversight—in all of these professions. The public shouldn't have to rely entirely on the American Bar Association to police the lawyers or the American Medical Association to police the doctors or the police to police the police. And who looks over the shoulder of an incompetent judge or a Starr-like prosecutor? Civilian oversight of the police should be entrusted to a panel who could mount their own investigations—but only when the chief of police or the mayor agrees that a probe is justified. If the public is unhappy with any of the mayor's decisions, they can choose new leadership at the next election.

Fortunately, bosses aren't restricted by the tattletale code of ethics, so police chiefs need waste no loyalty on the bad boys in blue.

The chiefs' first priority should be putting together an Internal Affairs team that is nothing short of lethal. The bureau's investigators can be widely despised, but even the cops who find themselves shuddering under IAB's hot breath should take some perverse pride in knowing how indomitable the department's internal crook-catchers are. Every cop should be reminded from the first day in the academy of the tremendous resources IAB has at its disposal and of its past exploits in bringing bad cops to justice.

Bratton's predecessor at the NYPD, Ray Kelly, and his IAB chief, Walter Mack, came up with a brilliant way to cultivate and sustain that kind of proficiency—by giving Internal Affairs first pick of every sergeant or lieutenant seeking a supervisory assignment in a detective unit. Since then, the best, brightest, and hungriest crook-catchers in the department have been compelled to complete a two-year tour of duty in Internal Affairs before they get where they want to be.

My only suggestion for improving the policy is that a department should add a guarantee of a pay increase and promotion at the end of the compulsory two years for every cop who dutifully fulfills the obligation. Few cops ever savor Internal Affairs work, but as the pick-of-the-litter policy begins to institutionalize excellence, the two-year detour may come to be widely appreciated as a necessary rite of passage for anybody who wants to be thought of as representing the very best of the organization.

If the police department is responsible for investigating its own civilian and corruption complaints, it should commit a full 5 percent of its personnel to internal oversight tasks—from auditing crime numbers to dispatching an investigative team to every shooting, to running stings at every level. Such a commitment doesn't come cheap, but the integrity of the department is worth it, and so is the speed at which a fully staffed Internal Affairs Bureau can be expected to catch the bad cops and exonerate the good ones.

Like crook-catching of any other kind, the catching of crooked cops is accomplished with accurate, timely intelligence, rapid deployment, effective tactics, and relentless follow-up and assessment. In one way, however, it's easier, because the investigators often start off knowing the names of the primary suspects, their badge numbers, where they live, and where and when they report to work.

IAB's early warning system should include an Integrity Control Officer in every station house who has no other job than to see that the cops are staying inside the lines. Like the precinct commander, the ICO should make surprise visits to watch how a search warrant is executed at four in the morning, to listen to a cop's testimony in court, to watch how prisoners are being debriefed. Among the questions he or she will want to hear being asked in the interrogation of every drug suspect is "Do you know about any corrupt cops?" The precinct's sergeant major would be the ICO's whip.

The ICO would constantly be profiling the cops, looking for the ones who work little or no overtime but are driving new cars, wearing $1,000 watches or $800 suits, and boasting about their forty-foot fishing boats. The ICO would look for teams doing drug raids who seem to always find less cash or contraband than the others. The ICO would make phone calls to IAB to say about the team with the lower numbers, "Maybe I'm just their lucky charm—they seized more cash on the one night I went out with them than they did in all their raids over the previous three weeks. But I think it's time for you to set up a sting."

Civilian complaints—the basic building blocks of any anti-corruption intel system—ought to be recorded and coded according to national standards that would be established by the FBI so that the complaints can be added as a new category in the FBI's annual Uniform Crime Reports. However they're standardized, the complaints should be mapped in every department and precinct by tour and type of allegation, with the hot spots subjected to closer scrutiny. The bosses should be looking at overlays of drug complaints and drug arrests to help them read the civilian complaint patterns, and they should have records kept on the number of times each cop's prisoners are sent to the hospital, resist arrest, or are charged with assault on an officer. A spike in any of those categories can unmask a bully, or reveal a need for additional training.

Every incident in which a cop fires a gun should also be mapped, with coding that allows the bosses to see, among other things, where and when the shootings are occurring, whether the targets fired as well, and how many times the cops were shot at but didn't fire back.

In fairness, the bosses and internal investigators should pay less attention to the raw number of complaints and shooting incidents involving any single officer or unit than to the rate of such incidents in relation to arrests, summonses, and other interactions with the public. When the department watches the rate, a cop who spends only ten days in the field every year but garners two complaints will be flagged. Under normal circumstances, he's overlooked.

IAB, besides assigning its crackerjack detectives to investigations, should be relentlessly running stings—setting up houses or cars with drugs, money, or guns to find out if the cops pocket anything, putting wise-mouthed undercovers at a crime scene to see if the cranky cop being targeted goes to give him a beating. On the highways, cops like the one who held a gun to my head in Connecticut would be tested to see how they treat undercovers of various races or ethnicities as they drive past in various makes of cars. On any police force, the stings should target individual cops who are under suspicion as well as tours and commands that have shown up as hot spots, but the department also must run random stings throughout its jurisdiction to keep the entire force in line.

IAB should hold weekly Comstat meetings of its own, holding all field commanders responsible for the conduct of their subordinates and holding the Internal Affairs investigators accountable for following up all allegations of misconduct with a sense of urgency that reflects the need to act swiftly in chucking the bad cops off the force and exonerating the good ones.

What will IAB do when they arrest a corrupt or brutal cop? Debrief them, of course. Bad cops turn on their homeys just as quickly as any other crooks.

The IAB guys have to be sharp. In a Bronx precinct, IAB once tried to put a sting on a few cops suspected of stealing weapons, but they blew their cover when one of the targets noticed that the same gun had been recovered two times out in the field.

Also, a sting can't become an excuse to let an investigation drag on and on.

During the Thirtieth Precinct investigation, a crooked cop who'd been flipped by the district attorney shot another cop on a Sunday morning right in front of the desk sergeant. Incredibly, the D.A. thought the cop's alibi—that his weapon went off by accident—warranted leaving the shooter out there as an undercover cooperator while his office tried to lock up a few more low-level violators. What the endangered public might not have fully appreciated was that the D.A. was determined to rack up a higher number of arrests than the U.S. Attorney's Office, which had been conducting its own ongoing probe in the Three-Oh.

At only one point, incidentally, did the warring prosecutors share any intel related to the case—but that was when the rat working for one office unwittingly sat down with the rat working for the other and their conversation was picked up by the two hidden wires they were wearing. By and large, both investigative teams came away looking like heroes, but for every minute they let the investigation run, the community lived another minute in danger.

Prosecutors almost always want to squeeze every last charge out of a corruption scandal, despite the obvious risks to the public and the history of police suicides that often accompany major corruption investigations. Police chiefs and commanders—who bear primary responsibility for the safety and welfare of the public—must know in excruciating detail about all investigations involving their subordinates, and they must find ways to take potentially dangerous cops off the streets, no matter what the effect on larger investigations.

At the end of the day, the public's safety is paramount.

Strike that.

At any time of day, the public's safety is paramount.

It is often said that incidents of corruption and brutality tear at that fundamental covenant between the public and the police.

Exactly so. Too often, though, we say those words as if the contract in question assigned all obligations to only one of the two interested parties.

Yet nobody can blame the public if they've come to think the onus is all on the cops. The cops have led them to that way of thinking by withholding information the public would need to remain engaged in an alliance of mutual trust. Both singly and collectively, the cops have bluffed or said "Mind your own business," for too long, and the price they've paid is that they have to be perfect at all times to avoid swift condemnation from the people who send them into harm's way. Yet the public owes it to the cops to withhold judgment about any incident until all the facts come out. In the summer of 1995, the NYPD stayed on a riot alert in Washington Heights for three days after a seventeen-year-old neighborhood kid claimed he'd been pushed off a roof by a cop. At the end of those three days, the kid confessed to his mother that he'd been told by his friends to make up the allegation against the cop.

The public doesn't see what a cop's work is really like, so they lose sight of the fundamental reality that when they are running away from danger, the cops are usually running toward it. The cops treat the public as if they're a breed apart, so the public forgets that cops too come from Planet Earth. There will always be decent cops who make honest mistakes and bad cops who have to be tracked down and hanged. Neither class of offense merits condemnation of the entire profession.

Especially at times when public confidence in them is in crisis, the cops have to fight the tendency to act as if they have something to hide. Which is difficult, because if a public rush to judgment is taking place, it adds to a dispirited cop's feeling that nothing is on the level—that no form of justice ever wins out. The hard and fast rule has to be: If there's a good story to tell about a cop, get it out there fast; if there's a bad story, get it out faster.

The public should be given a wealth of other information as well and made to feel that their police departments are always open for inspection.

The most critical information to share, of course, is information about the crimes taking place in the community. But one particular image springs to mind when I think about the creation of a truly transparent police organization:

It would be a routine day inside the academy, and about a dozen visitors would be jog-walking down a corridor to keep up with the Willy Wonka-like character leading them on a tour. Among the visitors would be a reporter, a pundit, a couple of community leaders, a lawyer, and a protest leader. On other days, full juries could be seen taking in the same sights.

Already, the sightseers would have had a chance to ride for a tour or two in the backseat of a patrol car, and they would now be carrying scorecards indicating how well they performed on the FATS machine when each was handed an imitation Glock and told to shoot only the bad guys.

"The next room I'm going to show you," the tour guide would be saying, "is one we're most proud of."

Some of the visitors might notice overhead a large plaque inscribed with the words of former NYPD Police Commissioner Teddy Roosevelt:

> *It is not the critic who counts, not the man who points out how the strong man stumbled or where the doer of deeds could have done better. The credit belongs to the man who is actually in the arena; whose face is marred by dust and sweat and blood; who, at the worst, if he fails, at*

least fails while doing greatly, so that his place shall never be with those cold and timid souls who know neither victory nor defeat.

"As you know," the guide would be continuing, as he pulled a pair of handcuffs out from under his coat, "today's NYPD is more committed than ever to realistic training.

"But we are not afraid to use ideas that have been employed in this organization for many, many years."

On the door itself would bear stenciled letters spelling out the words RUBBER MAN, and when it opened, it would reveal a stark white room, in the center of which would stand a 250-pound, six-foot-four figure wearing a helmet and a red suit—fabricated, apparently, by the same tailors who suit the Michelin tires mascot. In one hand, he'd be holding the leash of a salivating pit bull of similar build and attire.

"All right, then," the guide would chirp. "Who wants to be first to snap the cuffs on?"

ELEVEN

THE PERFECT WORLD
Everybody's a Louie

In the perfect world, everybody would be Louie Anemone.

I know what you're thinking.

Do we really want to live in a world where everybody works seven days a week, 365 days a year?

Do we really want everybody to dress like George Patton twenty-four hours a day, even when they go to bed?

Do we really want to live in constant anxiety that anybody we have the wrong answer for will scald their temples or curl the wall-paper with the steam that comes out of their ears?

Fair enough. Maybe there are some characteristics we wouldn't want to clone from the NYPD's legendary chief of department, the charm school dropout I referred to at the beginning of Chapter Four as the most valuable player on the nation's largest police force.

But we would want every cop and every citizen to have at least some Louie in them.

We would want them to be equipped with essentially the same pile of information that Louie has in front of him every time he calls a crime meeting to order. We would want them to be at least some-what fluent in interpreting patterns, trends, and chronic conditions from any crime map. We would want, most of all, for them to be as relentless in their demand for neighborhoods and communities free of crime.

Anemone brings to mind another "Lou" who wore a New York uniform—the Yankees' "Iron Horse," Lou Gehrig. More than three years after Bill Bratton, John Timoney and I moved on to other things and about four years after the press began declaring victory over crime in New York City, Louie Anemone was still pushing the cops of the NYPD to be a little better every day, to catch a few more crooks, to save a few more lives. When retirement finally beckoned Louie, in 1999, New York was fortunate that another thoroughbred, Joltin' Joe Dunne, was there to assume Louie's chair.

As we now toe the dugout steps that open onto a new millennium, we finally have a game plan that we know will keep the crooks on their heels. It worked wonders for New York, and cities like New Orleans and Newark that have faithfully followed that example have achieved even greater violent crime declines. (Eat your heart out, Louie.)

To go further—to bring crime rates down to 1960 levels and beyond—citizens everywhere must learn precisely what they should now expect from the police and other law enforcement agencies—and then demand nothing less.

Below is a list of demands that the public can use as a template. Thoughtful additions are welcome, but if these demands were posted on the front door of the White House, the state houses, and every city hall, town hall, village hall in the country, the public would have an agenda worth marching for.

—A CANON FOR CRIME-FREE COMMUNITIES—

1. The city's highest elected official must have the political will to shake up the police department and to stand firm if assertive but honorable police enforcement tactics come under fire.

The mayor also must be self-confident enough to choose a police leader who may, due to talent and the nature of the work, eclipse the mayor in public approval ratings.

2. The leader of the police department must have a vision, must articulate it, and must repeat the message over and over again in both internal communications and through the press.

The message must be direct and concise, communicating that the police department's primary objective is fewer victims of crime, and everything the department does will be directed toward and valued according to its contribution toward achieving that objective. Benchmark goals should be set regularly, such as reducing violent crime rates to 1960 levels within two years.

The leader must anticipate obstacles to achieving the goal and have the intestinal fortitude to overcome them. If there are no obstacles, the vision isn't one worth having, because it is an endorsement of doing business as usual.

The leader also must lead from the front—exposing him or herself to the same dangers and hardships as the cops in the field while monitoring whether the department's tactics and strategies are being carried out and whether or not they're working.

The leader must back the cops when they're right, train them when they make mistakes despite good intentions, and hang them when they betray the public's trust.

3. The leader must choose subordinate commanders who are confident and audacious and who, because they believe in the leader's vision, are able to extend the leader's vision of the entire field.

The subordinate commanders must demonstrate by their presence that the department is an organization open to talent and they too must lead from the front.

Subordinate commanders must be held accountable for the reduction of crime within their commands, and they should be capable of synchronizing the efforts of various operational units so that authority over patrol, narcotics, and detectives can be vested at the precinct or district level.

Compensation for these commanders must be generous enough to attract the best in the department and discourage them from joining the private sector the day they become eligible for their pensions.

4. All cops must be well recruited, well trained, well equipped, well paid, and well supervised.

The training of recruits must be a three- to four-year process that at minimum includes tours of six months each in community service work, in the academy itself, in corrections, in public housing, and in Patrol, Narcotics, and an investigative squad.

All officers who have graduated from the academy must receive four weeks of realistic training each year. Though operational priorities may change, communications with the public must always top the list of topics for review.

5. The police department must be a transparent organization.

Crime maps updated weekly must be made available at kiosks inside each station house, on a World Wide Web site, and also to newspapers, local TV stations, and any other media outlets that can make the information widely available to public.

These information sources must alert the public to crime patterns, crime trends, and chronic conditions and must indicate whether each crime is solved or unsolved. For unsolved crimes, descriptions of the crimes as well as descriptions and sketches of the perpetrators must be made available so that citizens could use that information to avoid dangerous situations or to aid police in solving the crimes.

The press and public must be welcome and encouraged to join officers on patrol for frequent ride-alongs.

If possible, the department should create a "Perp Channel" on cable TV and on the Internet that would broadcast photographs or sketches of wanted perps and photo arrays of everybody arrested each day so that viewers at home could help the cops capture fugitives or link prisoners to other crimes. The hosts of the "Perp Channel" should be free to call commanders or detectives and quiz them about what's being done to solve a crime or crime pattern.

To increase solve rates for property theft, the police must also create and maintain a database that provides buyers of jewelry, electronic equipment, and other valuables a convenient way to register, at the point of purchase, serial numbers or other identifying characteristics of the merchandise.

6. The police must reward the victims of crime same-day service as regards the opportunities to sit with a detective for an interview and the filing of a complaint, to accompany an officer or detective on a area search for the perpetrator, and to view photos of possible suspects.

7. The motto of all detectives and narcotics officers must be: "The initial arrest is not enough." All cases solved and arrests made must be viewed as opportunities to do more debriefings, seize more evidence or contraband, shut down more fences, chop shops, or crack houses, and make more cases.

All investigative squads must constantly strive to raise their solve rates.

Cold case squads must be established to revisit all stalled investigations.

8. Tactics and strategies must be disseminated throughout the department that address, separately or in tandem, all of the following: guns, shootings, murders, drugs, youth crime, gangs, domestic violence and child abuse, missing persons, police corruption and brutality, fugitives, sex crimes, robbery, burglary, auto crime, and quality-of-life concerns.

9. Operations at every level of the organization must be guided by the four steps of Comstat:

- accurate and timely intelligence that is clearly communicated to all
- rapid, concentrated, and synchronized deployment
- effective tactics and strategies
- relentless follow-up and assessment

Performance in relation to the four steps must become the subject of regular crime meetings at four different levels—between the executive corps and field commanders; between field commanders and their lieutenants; between lieutenants and their sergeants; and, most signif-

icantly, between sergeants and their officers at roll call.

10. Five percent of the department's personnel must be dedicated to maintaining the integrity of the organization.

A two-year tour of duty in Internal Affairs should be a rite of passage for the department's most gifted commanders. Every command must have an Integrity Control Officer and a "sergeant major" to keep troublesome cops in line. Internal Affairs must run stings relentlessly.

The department must also maintain one quality-assurance team to ensure the integrity of the department's crime numbers and another to ensure that complaints by civilians are being faithfully recorded and swiftly and fairly adjudicated.

11. "FedStat" meetings must be initiated to team local police with state and federal law enforcement and to focus and synchronize the efforts of the various state and federal law enforcement agencies in combating guns, drugs, murders, and shootings. These meetings should not be just about sharing of information; they should generate concrete plans—driven by a sense of urgency—for synchronized deployment, tactics, and follow-up and assessment.

12. Federal prosecutors and the federal courts must be used to prosecute gangs, drug crews, gun crimes, and in any other circumstances when public safety is better served by federal laws and penalties than by state laws and penalties.

13. The federal government must choose the technology that will be used for the creation of a national ballistics database. Every gun made in or imported to the United States must be entered into the database. Law enforcement agencies in every jurisdiction must have access to the technology so that any guns, bullets, or shell casings recovered in a crime can be immediately linked to previous crimes and traced to each gun's original owner.

14. The states must establish their own "truth-in-sentencing" laws, guaranteeing prisoners serve at least 85 percent of their sentences. All state and federal prisoners should be subject to three years' parole after their release.

Both juveniles and adults released on probation or parole must be ordered, upon release, to report to the precinct or district where they live to be photographed, to be debriefed, and to be reminded of any and all restrictions on their activities. The entire department, but particularly the local command and the commands where each parolee or probationer committed crimes in the past, must arrange for the up-to-date photos to be routinely viewed by crime victims.

Anyone who violates the restrictions of parole or probation must be tracked down and sent back to prison.

All federal and state arrestees must provide DNA samples to be checked against a national database of samples taken as evidence in all open crimes. The samples taken from the arrestees would be stored permanently in a separate national database upon conviction.

If all those demands are met, reducing crime to 1960 levels would be a grounder.

Would the world be perfect?

Of course not. Good policing doesn't feed people who are hungry. It doesn't care for people who are sick. It doesn't give a kid born in the Seven-Five Precinct as much a chance of meeting his or her potential as a kid born in the Silk Stocking District's Seventeenth.

It used to be that my fondest vision of the future was a nation of 300 million tuned in around the clock to their local "Perp Channels"—catching crooks, grilling cops during the call-in segments, and learning about how to keep themselves and their families safe. Now, however, I realize that the programming on the "Perp Channel" wouldn't be quite as riveting as I've always imagined it if all the other demands were taken care of.

So I have another Orwellian vision dancing in my head.

In that not-so-distant future, a crime fighter could take a walk anywhere in America—past schools, hospitals, parks, firehouses, across roads and over bridges—and know that each of the agencies providing those vital services has identified its primary objective and has established a way to measure progress toward that goal, a way to map that information, and a regular forum at which the agency's leaders question their subordinates in excruciating detail about their intelligence-gathering systems, their deployment, their tactics, and their follow-up.

I would really enjoy taking that stroll in my hometown. Maybe what I'd do is start down at the Battery and work my way up Broadway—past City Hall, past Union Square, past Herald Square, and even past the statue of my old pal George M. Cohan—until I could stand at 47th Street in Times Square and look back at the changes our efforts had brought.

At that moment, the murder rate in America would be exactly one fifth what it is in 1999, which would be a sure indication that we hadn't been satisfied when national crime rates were knocked down to levels last seen in 1985—or even 1960.

To remember the kind of murder rates I'm dreaming about, we'd have to be old enough to recall 47th and Broadway when there was no neon, no automobiles, no buildings more than a few stories tall, and no passersby who would have the first clue how to answer if asked directions to Times Square.

Of course, it's true that if we knocked the murder rate down to a level last seen in the year 1900, the world still wouldn't be perfect. There'd still be a scattered few grifters, a handful of second-story men.

But you've got to admit this: It would be a hell of a good reason to catch the next cab to Elaine's for a glass of champagne on ice.

INDEX

Jack Maple began his career as a New York City Transit Patrolman and rose to become Deputy Commissioner of the NYPD. Since leaving the department, he has served as a consultant to police departments worldwide. He lives in New York City.

Chris Mitchell, a writer and reporter, lives in Brooklyn with his wife and daughter.